Praise for *Struck*

"I've known Pierce Hibbs and his work for some years and have greatly appreciated his theological analysis and understanding of human problems. His *Struck Down but Not Destroyed* has been helpful to me. I have had similar problems (though I'd describe them as agoraphobia or introversion rather than anxiety disorder), and I'm grateful to be able to read Pierce's testimony of how Jesus is sufficient to meet such needs. He is right to argue from Scripture than such difficulties can be means of spiritual growth and blessing, as he leads us to respond to them in a godly way. I hope this book gets wide distribution."

> **– JOHN M. FRAME**, author of *Systematic Theology* and the Theology of Lordship series

"It's no secret that most of us live anxious lives in varying degrees. Most people learn how to tolerate this subtle anguish and agitation with less than effective (and godly) coping skills. In other instances, however, anxiety punctuated by panic attacks overwhelms and takes on a life of its own. Pierce Taylor Hibbs brings his life as a person who knows the crippling power of this type of anguish in full view, then takes the reader on the less often walked path that challenges the reader to let God be in charge of their anxiety as he has learned over the years. This approach does not follow the traditional therapeutic model that automatically assumes that the goal of God's work in us is his method of symptom reduction or deliverance. Similar to the anguish Paul describes when discussing his brand of torment, Hibbs points believers in the direction that Paul exclaims as the better path- the powerful presence of Jesus in the midst of anxiety's fire. For a counselor the highest recommendation of a book is buying copies to give to a client. I will be buying this book."

> **– JEFFREY S. BLACK**, Professor & Chair, Department of Counseling & Psychology, Cairn University

"Forged in the crucible of his own long term struggle with severe anxiety, Pierce Taylor Hibbs has written a wise and eminently practical book on living with anxiety. But it is much more. It is an extended meditation on the purpose for which we were created (communion with God), the nature of suffering, and the paradoxical, biblical reality that when we are weak we are strong (2 Corinthians 12:10). Pierce writes winsomely, personally, and passionately, embedding his story of anxiety in the Story of our Triune God's character and redemptive work. Filled with incisive theological insight, honest prayers, reflection questions, and reader resources, he offers a hope-filled path to a deeper relationship with God, not in spite of anxiety, but through anxiety."

> **– MICHAEL R. EMLET**, M.Div., M.D., Dean of Faculty and Counselor, Christian Counseling and Educational Foundation (CCEF) and author of *CrossTalk: Where Life and Scripture Meet* and *Descriptions and Prescriptions: A Biblical Perspective on Psychiatric Diagnoses and Medications*

"It is one of the remarkable oddities of our age that we live at a time where we often enjoy more material comfort and security than ever before and yet where there is also much evidence to indicate that anxiety is a crushing problem for many as never before. In this accessible, personal, and helpful book, Pierce Hibbs uses his own struggles in this area and the teaching of the Bible to offer comfort and advice to those who face their own anxiety problem. An unusually helpful volume."

> **– CARL R. TRUEMAN**, author of *Grace Alone* and *Luther on the Christian Life*

"This is the book I have been waiting for to share with loved ones who suffer with anxiety disorders. *Struck Down but Not Destroyed* is the best I've read on the topic so far, taking a holistic approach that will minister to body, mind, and soul, offering personal testimony, digestible and helpful theology, practical follow-up actions, and beautiful prayers. Anxiety can be incredibly scary and paralyzing. Pierce helps sufferers to know what to do with that fear, truly accomplishing his subtitle to faithfully live with anxiety."

> — **AIMEE BYRD**, author of *No Little Women* and *Why Can't We Be Friends?*

"Accomplished writer and theologian, Pierce Taylor Hibbs, has given those who are afflicted with anxiety a sure-footed, elevating gift. Apart from the author's gripping transparency, the power of his advice comes from the fact that it is wholly and radically biblical and, therefore, counter intuitive — especially so in today's "conquer it ... get over it" culture. The radical biblical truth is that our anxiety/weakness is meant to drive us to Christ and his strength. And, as Hibbs argues, it is meant to endow us with spiritual wings. *Struck Down but Not Destroyed* in no brief fly-over. Each chapter is structured by the triad: Experience – Scripture – Theology, and is rounded- off by penetrating questions for reflection and a carefully wrought prayer. This is a wonderful book!"

> — **R. KENT HUGHES**, author of *Disciplines of a Godly Man* and Senior Pastor Emeritus of College Church in Wheaton Illinois

"I have read scores of books about anxiety. None comes close to this thorough, biblical and most practical study. Most of us, if we are honest, will admit to being captured by worry somewhere in our lives. This book is as good or better than dozens of therapy sessions. I was particularly helped by the emphasis on prayer: most needful, most difficult. And God's grace is woven into the warp and woof. Everyone needs to read it."

> — **WILLIAM EDGAR**, author of *Reasons of the Heart* and *Created and Creating*

"Pierce Taylor Hibbs has given the church a gift with this insightful and compassionate book on anxiety. Placing his own struggle with anxiety in the light, he invites the reader to do the same and to experience the liberty that accompanies such honesty. Hibbs carefully grounds our thinking and experiences in Scripture and offers a wealth of practical counsel. This is a book to read and then read again. I will be commending this wonderful book to all of my fellow strugglers."

> — **TODD PRUITT**, Lead Pastor of Covenant Presbyterian Church in Harrisonburg, VA

"Anxiety often shows up unannounced at the door of the soul, lingering beyond the bounds of our abilities. Through experience and prayer, Pierce Taylor Hibbs describes the battle of living faithfully with this "long-term guest." Rooted firmly in Scripture, this work is filled with theology that is accessible, practical, and personal—with the gospel woven throughout its pages. Hibbs writes with heart, soul, and most of all, biblical truth. Whether you are worried, weary, or whittled down, Hibbs shows how God stewards your anxiety in order to conform you to Christ for His glory and your good."

> — **NATHANIEL SCHILL**, Administrator, Book Store Director, and Elder at Calvary Chapel Quakertown

STRUCK DOWN BUT NOT DESTROYED

Other Books by the Author

- *The Trinity, Language, and Human Behavior: A Reformed Exposition of the Language Theory of Kenneth L. Pike*

- *In Divine Company: Growing Closer to the God Who Speaks*

- *Theological English: An Advanced ESL Text for Students of Theology*

- *Finding God in the Ordinary*

- *The Speaking Trinity & His Worded World: Why Language Is at the Center of Everything*

To receive free downloads and connect with the author, visit piercetaylorhibbs.com.

Connect and Learn More!

Want access to more resources for dealing with your anxiety? Check out the reader resource page for this book. Go to http://piercetaylorhibbs.com/struck-down-but-not-destroyed/. Then join the Facebook group "Christians Battling Anxiety" to engage in more discussions and immerse yourself in a prayerful community. You can also follow the author on Twitter (@ HibbsPierce), Instagram (@pthibbs), and Facebook (@wordsfromPTH).

STRUCK DOWN BUT NOT DESTROYED

Living Faithfully with Anxiety

by

PIERCE TAYLOR HIBBS

STRUCK DOWN BUT NOT DESTROYED
Living Faithfully with Anxiety

ISBN: 9781706119753

Cover art by Jessica Shapiro

For Christina. Thank you for kneeling beside me when I'm struck down.

CONTENTS

Introduction

I f you're holding this book right now, I'm assuming you're clawing your way through hell, or you have in the past, or you know someone who is. I don't know *where* you are—buried under blankets in a dark room, sitting on a bus with your body stiff as steel, gripping a steering wheel like your life depended on it—but I don't judge. I've been in the worst of places with my anxiety. I also don't know *how* you are—whether this is a "good" day or a "bad" day, whether your anxiety seems distant like a memory or coiled around your neck like seventy-pound boa constrictor—but I promise I have something you need to hear in this book. When it's all boiled down, the message is plain and simple: your anxiety is *not* accidental. It's doing something in you; it's *working*. And once you find out how, you'll never see it the same way again.

There are scads of books out there on anxiety and panic—some by doctors, some by psychologists, some by counselors, and a whole slew of them by overly excited lay people who believe they've found the golden ticket to paradise. I've read many of them. And for me all of them have the same basic flaw: they assume that anxiety is first and foremost something to be gotten rid of.

I don't see it that way. I'm convinced that Scripture teaches something quite different. For starters, note that the world says certain things when it hears trigger words. The world hears "problem," and it says, "solution." The world hears "disease," and it says, "cure." The world hears "pain," and it says, "relief." That sounds well and good, but remember this: when the world heard "Christ," it said, "crucify." The voice of the world is not your true North. In fact, the world is confused about the most elementary truths of Christianity. Our faith is foolish to their eyes and ears (1 Cor. 1:18). Why would the world be right when it comes to your anxiety? As a follower of Christ, your ear should be bent toward the good book. That's what I'm aiming to do in these pages. And the good book reveals that the triune God can use anxiety—even an anxiety disorder—to shape your soul in ways you never thought possible, as long as you're committed to speaking with him and hearing him speak back to you in his word.

So, here's my promise: if you listen to the voice of Scripture amidst your anxiety, God will change you in ways you couldn't even dream of; he'll build the muscle of your soul, increase your mustard-seed faith, and give you compassion that runs deeper than the Atlantic. That's a big promise, I know. But I'm making it because I've seen it come true in my own life and in the lives of others.

I've gone from lying in the fetal position, convinced I couldn't leave my room without dying to taking a train into Philadelphia by myself for jury duty. I've gone from being paralyzed by fear because of a thirty-minute commute to watching God work through my nerves in a six-hour traffic jam. I've gone from refusing to attend events with large groups of people to praying intensely for those surrounding me in public places. Don't get me wrong—I still struggle. Many things still draw out my anxiety, but I've seen God do so much through it that I can say without hesitation: "God, I'm okay if you keep using this." With God at the helm of our ship, it always finds its true North, because it always finds *him*, no matter what anxious gale whips through our sails.

As you're clawing your way through hell (or coming alongside of someone who is) and looking for hope and healing around every corner, I'm asking you to stop and listen—*really* listen—to these words: "You're going to be okay because of Christ." I say that not because your anxiety is going to dissolve as you delve into these pages, or because I think that, logically, your anxiety has to go away at some point, or because I've found the optimal blend of antidepressants and self-help methods. I say that because you're going to be conformed to the image of Christ through your anxiety, and that's ultimately what it means to be "okay." To be okay is not to be free *from* all pain and suffering; it's to be free *in* all pain and suffering because you're indwelt by Christ. In fact, you're indwelt by the Father, Son, and Spirit (John 14:23; Rom. 8:11). God, my dear reader, lives in you and is going to use your anxiety to do great things—not good things, *great* things. Don't ever loosen your grip on those words. Clench them with white-knuckled fists. In the torrents and hurricanes, in the swells and the storms, hold fast.

Now, these great things I'm talking about are going to emerge from a one-syllable word: *trust*. The popular self-help books use words like "defeat," "overcome," "cure," and "conquer"—but my approach is different. So, to start, I'm going to ask you to trust *me*. I've been battling an anxiety disorder for over twelve years now. I've been through counseling. I've consulted with doctors for years about balancing medications. I've been thirty pounds lighter in two weeks because I couldn't eat. I've been reclusive and withdrawn. I've crawled through the caverns of hell more than once. But I've also come out the other side and done some things I thought were impossible with my anxiety. And God has shaped and pressed himself into me in ways that now seem impossible apart from it. If I can do anything that we could call "great" in the Christian sense, it's because of that little word: *trust*—trust that I wasn't going to end the day with my throat closing up or strapped to a hospital bed, trust that my extreme discomfort and frustration were purposeful, trust that there is a spiritual war going on for my soul, and I know who wins. There is nothing so powerful as God-given trust, for it frames our perception of what's happening and gives us a course to follow.

In the pages ahead, I'm going to walk you through what God has been teaching me about anxiety, and I'm going to reinforce a message that may sound counterintuitive in our world: *anxiety is a spiritual tool in the hands of a mighty God.* In that sense, it's not something to flee from; it's something to be learned from, something to use in order to draw nearer to God. I want you to work with me on changing your perception of anxiety so that you can open yourself to God's sovereign use of it in your life. I can promise you that by the end you won't view the absence of anxiety as supremely important. Instead, your focus will fall on the status of your soul before an all-powerful, soft-voiced shepherd, leading you moment by moment, calling you to trust, pulling your neck gently with his shepherd's crook, bringing you back into the fold, fixing your ears on his voice.

Now, here's how I've organized the book. Because I believe that we need a context to interpret anything in life, I'll be giving you pieces of our biblical or theological context in each chapter. We'll explore who God is, who we are, and what the world is like. I've tried to make these contexts bite-sized chunks. I'll also add my experience and the biblical counsel God has been applying to that experience. So, in each chapter you'll be able to see the following elements overlapping.

I also walk progressively from darkness to light, from intense and acute periods of anxiety to less intense periods. This reflects my own experience, but since anxiety comes in waves, you should be able to benefit from earlier parts of the book as well as the later parts, depending on which period you find yourself in right now.

Lastly, you'll see that each chapter ends with reflection questions and a prayer. There are also special "Reader Resources" at the end of most chapters. That's because I don't want you to just read this book; I want you to *use* it. I want you to take it with you into you daily routine and put it to work.

I encourage you to answer the questions in a group setting, to pray the prayers, and perhaps to even write some of your own prayers in light of what you're learning. Writing out prayers helps us articulate what we feel, what's beneath our feelings, and what we're asking for from the God who gives the greatest gifts.

If you're blessed by this book in any way, then I ask of you one thing as a writer: tell someone about it and leave a review on Amazon. These little things go a long way in spreading the word about a biblical message that other souls need to hear.

Now, brace yourself. We're about to enter the dark country of anxiety. We'll have a light that can't go out (Scripture), but the darkness is real and unsettling. Let's step slowly.

CHAPTER 1

We Are Crushed To Be Called

KEY IDEA: God may crush us in order to call us.

I have heard it said that when God wants to do something impossible, he takes an impossible man and crushes him. In other words, God crushes those whom he calls. He breaks the ones he beckons. The Apostle Paul is a perfect example. With his vision, zeal, and bravado, Paul could do nothing for the kingdom of God. He could only cause harm (Acts 8:11–3). But once he was blinded and brought low (Acts 9:3–9), once he learned how to be led around by someone else's hand, *then* he could do "all things" (Phil. 4:13). The impossible is made possible through crushing.

As I write this, I serve at a seminary where I teach international students what we call "theological English."[1] I also work with native-English speaking students, guiding them in how to write various types of theology. My passion and calling, however, is to write theology myself.[2] In 2006, if you would've told me that *this* would be my occupation and passion, I would've said, "Impossible." I had no interest

---

1   See Pierce Taylor Hibbs, *Theological English: An Advanced ESL Text for Students of Theology* (Phillipsburg, NJ: P&R, 2018).

2   My ThM thesis at Westminster Theological Seminary has been published as *The Trinity, Language, and Human Behavior: A Reformed Exposition of the Language Theory of Kenneth L. Pike*, Reformed Academic Dissertations (Phillipsburg, NJ: P&R, 2018). I've also written two more popular works: *Finding God in the Ordinary* (Eugene, OR: Wipf & Stock, 2018) and *The Speaking Trinity & His Worded World: Why Language Is at the Center of Everything* (Eugene, OR: Wipf & Stock, 2018).

in attending seminary and learning theology. I loved to write, but I didn't know where my place would be in the writing world. That was before God crushed me. So much for impossibilities.

Let me start where my life took a darker turn. My father battled a brain tumor for about twelve years, and I was naive about what that really meant until the age of seventeen. That's when I began to digest the fact that his death would come early, that it was a miracle he hadn't died already. After his third and final major brain surgery, the cancer took the reins of life and steered him away into silence. Due to the pressure the tumor was putting on his brain stem, he'd lost his ability to speak. Quiet and subdued, he came home on hospice care like a bird with broken wings. He spent the final three weeks of his life on a railed bed, getting all of his nutrients from a little plastic tube. He was slowly detaching from the world of the living. His flights were finished.

His final night came on June 3rd, 2004. I was eighteen and had just finished my first year of college. That night, his respiratory system moaned to a halt for two hours. Then the hospice nurse told us he had about three breaths left. (I've never counted to three like that since.) With the final breath, there came a noticeable absence of *him* from the room. There had been nine of us just a moment before. Now there was eight.

"To be crushed is to be reduced, to be emptied of all the false hopes of self-sufficiency."

There aren't many words I've found since then to describe what I went through on that night and for the months that followed. But I think *crushed* is the best one—not destroyed, but *crushed*. There's a great difference between the two. To be destroyed is to be dissolved without hope of recovery or resolution. To be destroyed is to be no more. But to be crushed is to be reduced, to be emptied of all the false hopes of self-sufficiency. To be crushed is to realize that you're thoroughly *dependent*.

But my crushing went to new depths about two years after his death. I was back at college, waiting on the curb outside one of the dormitories for my girlfriend at the time, Christina, who is now my wife (another impossibility made possible). I remember the comfortable evening air hanging over the campus. As I took in the smell of fresh-cut grass and a hint of smoke from a nearby cigarette, a wave of heat crept down from my head and rushed through my back and legs. My breath grew shallow; my throat closed up, and I couldn't swallow.

As she walked towards me, I struggled to stand up in a world that now felt like a great spinning ball. "Um, I'm having a panic attack." I didn't even know what that meant; I just knew I needed help—fast. I begged her to drive me to the hospital, thinking there would be some consolation in that, but every step I took towards the car added tension in my chest and shoulders. Within a matter of seconds, the whole world looked black and foreign and terrifying. I knew it as soon as we started driving: I was going to die, right here in this car on the way to a hospital in Hershey, Pennsylvania. This was it.

I'd love to tell you that I met that moment with resolve, but that would be a lie. I wasn't brave. I was paralyzed with panic. Something very bad seemed to grip my whole mind and body and *squeeze*. The next twenty minutes were hell on wheels. A few miles into the car ride I started yelling and calling out for help, moaning and gasping for air. An eighteen-wheeler churned down the dark country road ahead of us.

"Can you go around him!?"

"It's a double line!"

Christina was crying, but I couldn't think about calming down for her sake. Panic makes you blind and deaf to anything except your own preservation. With the little air I had in my lungs, I yelled, "Please, just GO AROUND HIM!" She pushed the petal to the floor, both of us hoping that no one was around the bend in the opposite lane.

I took out my phone and dialed 911. I'll never forget that conversation with the operator.

"911. What's your emergency?"

"Yea, I'm having a panic attack, and I can't breathe."

"Okay, sir. Can you tell me where you are?"

"I'm in the car, on my way to the hospital . . . in Hershey."

"So, you're already on your way to the hospital?"

"Yes."

"Alright, well we can't do anything if you're already driving to the hospital."

My heart dropped. I paused for a long second. I was dying. This was really it. I gave up all reservations. No pride. No pretending to be okay. Complete vulnerability.

"Okay, well, can you at least pray for me?!"

"Sir, if you're already on your way to the hospital, there's nothing I can do from here."

"But can you *pray* for me?!"

CLICK.

She hung up the phone on a "dying" twenty-year-old!

That was the first time in my life I really asked for prayer. It wasn't the sort of asking that I'd done before: the kind where you don't really care that much if the person prays or not. It wasn't prayer as a formality. This was real, earnest pleading. It was lifeline begging. It was all I had: a voice and a question. And even in that moment of raw panic, I was thrown by someone's *refusal* to pray. Maybe she didn't believe in prayer, or in God. Maybe she was just embarrassed or indecisive. I'll never know. But it brought my crushing that night to a new low.

A few minutes later, I was thanking God out loud for getting us to the hospital safely. "It's okay," I said with shivering vocal chords as we hobbled across the parking lot under the fluorescent lights. "It's okay—people are praying for me." Christina nodded sympathetically—she must have been just as amazed as I was that we were still alive after that nightmarish drive.

I checked into the hospital and sat on a bed in the hallway for about an hour, sipping ice water and breathing with ten cinderblocks on my chest. My friends came to make sure I was alright. Doctors told me that I had a reaction to a type of Tylenol cold medicine and that my symptoms would disappear over the next few hours. I was relieved, even though I still felt the same way: like an alien in my own skin, struggling to perform the basic bodily functions of breathing and speaking.

But the symptoms didn't go away. Back at my dormitory, I wandered up and down the hallway all through the night. I couldn't keep my shoulders down; they crunched whenever I squeezed them (one of the body's ways of reacting to stress). My throat felt like a pinhole. Just a few hours before, I was carefree and casual. I was a stone comfortably set in my routines, happy to find solace and solidity each day. I was stable. But now . . . I wasn't a stone. I'd been pressed too thin. I was a piece of paper ready to blow away in the wind. I was *so* fragile. I was so . . . *crushed*.

The next morning, I walked around the campus, trying to shake off the feelings. But they wouldn't leave. So, I went to the nurse's office. What should've taken thirty seconds to explain took ten minutes. I had to take deep breaths in between sentences just to tell her what had happened the night before. She handed me a brown paper bag. "Breathe into this," she said. "You're really fighting? Do you want me to call an ambulance to take you back to the hospital?" I nodded my head and took another deep, brown bag breath. My chest ached from heaving. "Yea . . ." Another brown bag breath. "Yea . . . I think so."

A few minutes later I took my first ambulance ride. Laying on a gurney, holding an oxygen mask to my face while two teenagers wearing EMS shirts made awkward conversation—not exactly the stuff of Hollywood. They called my mom and Christina, who met me at the hospital. The doctors drew blood and ran tests, but they didn't find anything. "There's nothing wrong with you physically," said one of the doctors. "You're free to go." Free to go? *Free* to go? My own skin was a prison. I was an alien among humans. I could blow away any second: I wasn't *free* to go anywhere.

I never seek out controversy, but I looked straight into his eyes and said, "I'm not leaving here until you give me something." He came back a few minutes later holding a pill bottle filled with Ativan—a drug that essentially slows down your brain. Clutching the pill case in my hand, I walked out of the hospital feeling delirious, confused, and frustrated. But more than anything, I felt helpless and low. I felt *crushed*. Everything in the world was the same, but I was drastically different. I was now a foreigner in the familiar.

"My mind flapped wildly in the wind of the ordinary."

I decided to go home to rest and figure out what was happening to me. For the next few weeks, I felt like fractured glass, ready to shatter at the softest touch. *Everything* required effort, even eating. I lost 30 lbs. in about two weeks. It was difficult enough to breathe and swallow, let alone eat. I was also extremely sensitive and hyper-vigilant. I've since heard others who struggle with anxiety disorders say that they "couldn't feel comfortable in their own skin." That's a good way of putting it. It's like being scared by someone who jumps out from behind a door, but then that mix of horror and surprise never really goes away. It just lives in your blood.

My mind flapped wildly in the wind of the ordinary. All of the normalcy and automaticity of routine had vanished. I was too aware of myself, looking at my fingers as I ate and my feet as I walked. Every few seconds I would feel the backs and edges of my teeth with my tongue. I tried not to look at myself in the mirror. It felt too bizarre.

I couldn't find peace. I couldn't find stillness. I couldn't find rest. I couldn't find contentment or joy or even distraction. All I could do was feel terrible and terrified *for no reason*. That was the most disturbing part.

After several days, I remember saying to myself, "Nobody can live like this. I'm not even a real person." This was my rock bottom: weak, joyless, hopeless, and spread thin. I couldn't function. I even shut out Christina, the most important person in the world to me. I shut her out not because I wanted to or even because I chose to; I simply couldn't process anything outside of myself. I was paralyzed by panic and hyper-vigilance. What was happening to me? And why?

I had no answers. But I learned one thing very, very quickly. My reader, please hear this: *when you hit rock bottom, your ears and eyes begin opening.* You hear and see more than you ever have before: too much. I imagine this sort of thing happened to the Apostle Paul. It's hard to describe—sort of like a lifting fog that once protected you, that once kept you from being overwhelmed by your surroundings. Fear and panic rush in like open air and light. They surround you. And even though you have to shield your eyes with your hands just to walk around, you start getting used to it. The loudness of all the sounds and the sharpness of the light become more familiar.

Time churned painfully forward like an old rusted train, but as the gears grinded and clicked, as I dealt with the shock and isolation of anxiety, I started to see and hear *more* of the world around me—more than I ever had before. The landscape began to clear. Shapes appeared . . . and the sound of birds. And in this clearing landscape, my ears and eyes were on high alert for signs of help and hope. I didn't hear and see much, which was disconcerting, but I was still listening and looking. I was so desperate that I turned to an old hope long neglected: the voice of God. Could God—who had really only ever been a sweet-sounding *idea* in my childhood—be real? Could he help? My crushing turned me toward him.

I had no pride or illusions of independence at this point, so I rummaged around for my father's old Bible and found it on my brother's bookshelf: tattered leather edges and well-worn pages—fields where fingers had lived. The black leather cover was soft and flimsy from use. I opened to Genesis and began reading. And I didn't stop.

I can't say why, exactly. It wasn't as if I could hear an audible voice telling me that everything would be okay, that one day I wouldn't feel like my own skin was a prison, or that I could have peace if I only believed—none of that. I just had a sense that this was the only way out, if there *was* a way out. That sense kept me focused on every creased, highlighted, pen-marked line of prose in that little black Bible. It never left my sight or side, and seldom left my hands.

I might not have heard the voice of God yet (in the way I wanted to), but I was listening more intently than I ever had before. Everything else—places, food, people—became quiet, as if the volume were turned down on life—and yet the base of Scripture kept thudding. In between waking and sleeping, that Bible might as well have been sewed to my palms. I was always clinging to it, staring at my strange fingertips running over the tiny letters. My life was becoming linear. My days were oriented around sequences of sentences, chapters, and books. The printed page gave crystal clear directions to my crushed soul: move from left to right, top to bottom. Then turn the page and repeat. My mind did not flap as wildly in the wind when I was reading those words.

The mental anguish I experienced for those first weeks and months was enough to halt everything else: relationships, aspirations, passions. Things became very simple: survive. Breathe, and bring that little black Bible with you everywhere. These are the goals of someone who's been crushed.

We Are Crushed To Be Called

I didn't know it then, but my crushing was the beginning of my calling. I may not have been hearing an audible voice from God, but I was *reading* his voice in Scripture. I was listening. I was learning and moving in a direction marked only by words. I was being called. And if I hadn't been crushed, I wouldn't have followed. I wouldn't have started chasing after a divine voice etched onto the pages of my father's Bible. I was crushed, in other words, so that I could hear the call and start walking down a different path. I had no idea where that path was leading, but I knew *who* was leading me. And I knew I would follow this path and no other.

My point in this first chapter is a simple one: God has a purpose for allowing us to be crushed by anxiety, and that purpose is helping us to hear his call. It's nothing novel, really. I didn't understand back then, but now I know that God is constantly calling us to himself. He's *always* asking us to be part of his kingdom (Matt. 6:33), to put that kingdom first and follow the voice of the Good Shepherd (John

10:11). But we don't hear the call. We're lost in distant pastures. And in our lostness, rather than seeking the soft voice of a sovereign shepherd, we deafen ourselves in a thousand ways with a million distractions. We fill our ear canals with noises. God is always calling; we're just not listening.

My reader, we are crushed so that we can *listen*. We are crushed to be called; we are brought low so that we can hear the high things of God.

But why? Why is this the way it has to be? That's where the theology comes into play.

Theology: What You Need To Know Right Now

I told you in the introduction that each chapter will have a bit of theology for you: bite-sized chunks that you need to store in your mind's pocket as we keep walking together through these pages. Here's the first bit: in order to understand your being crushed and the purpose it serves, you have to know who God is and who you are.

Let's start with the greatest question we could ever ask: Who is God? You have to know the answer to this question if you want to understand your anxiety and the role it's playing in your life. Why is God allowing you to be crushed by anxiety? The short answer: because he wants to communicate with you. He's calling you. That makes perfect sense if you know who God is. God is what we would call a *communicative Spirit*. He is a being who speaks with himself in three persons (Father, Son, and Spirit) and speaks to his creation by way of revelation—in the world around you (Ps. 19:1–4; Rom. 1:20) and in Scripture. Why is that so critical? Well, if you want to have a relationship with this God, if you want to understand why and how he is using your anxiety, then you have to communicate with him. You have to listen (hearing his call) and speak. Language (speech), in other words, is at the core of who God is, and it's how we come to know him.[3]

Second, let's ask the follow-up question: Who are *you*? That question has an answer that parallels that of the former question because we're made in God's image. The simple answer to the question of who we are is "creatures made for communion." But we need to spell out what that means.

If language (speech) is central to who God is, it's also central to who we are. When God made us, he created us in his image (Gen. 1:27). But what does that mean? I love the definition for image-bearers that Geerhardus Vos (1862–1949) gives, and

---

3   See *The Speaking Trinity & His Worded World: Why Language Is at the Center of Everything* (Eugene, OR: Wipf & Stock, 2018).

I'll be repeating it throughout the book: "That man bears God's image means much more than that he is spirit and possesses understanding, will, etc. It means above all that he is disposed for communion with God, that all the capacities of his soul can act in a way that corresponds to their destiny only if they rest in God."[4] "Disposed for communion"—we are creatures made for interpersonal communion with the Trinity: that's what it means to be made in God's image. With everything in us, we long for communion with the Father, Son, and Spirit. We need it. We're not whole without it. The yearning for communion with God is buried in our blood. It's what makes us human.

"The yearning for communion with God is buried in our blood. It's what makes us human."

Okay—that's enough theology for now. We'll draw these things out in more detail later. Remember to keep these truths with you as we move ahead: God is a communicative Spirit, and we were made to commune with him.[5] These twin truths are going to have everything to do with how we see God using our anxiety to do great things.

Putting this theology in terms of what we've developed in this chapter, we might say that we're crushed to be called because of *communion*. Communion with God is our lifeblood. It sets vigor in our veins. It gives us purpose, meaning, and consolation. We can't do without it. Why might God be crushing us with anxiety? He's calling us to communion. Anxiety will help you drop any illusions that fulness of life resides anywhere except in the God who communes with himself (John 10:10), the God who has called *you* into communion with him. We are crushed to be called for communion.

---

4   Geerhardus Vos, *Anthropology*, vol. 2 of *Reformed Dogmatics*, ed. and trans. Richard B. Gaffin Jr. (Bellingham, WA: Lexham, 2014), 13.

5   I develop my view of language as *communion behavior* in *The Speaking Trinity & His Worded World: Why Language Is at the Center of Everything* (Eugene, OR: Wipf & Stock, 2018). You can also reference "Closing the Gaps: Perichoresis and the Nature of Language," *Westminster Theological Journal* 78, no. 2 (Fall 2016): 299–322; and "Words for Communion," *Modern Reformation* 25, no. 4 (August 2016): 5–8.

Reflection Questions and Prayer

1. When did you first encounter anxiety in your own life? How did it crush you?

2. How is being crushed both a good and a bad thing?

3. Discuss with someone else the effects of being crushed. What happened to you as a result of being crushed?

4. I said that I felt anxious and hyper-vigilant *for no reason*. How does our reasoning play a role in our anxiety? (We'll discuss this in a later chapter.) What sorts of reasons do you give for your anxiety? Are any of those reasons spiritual?

5. I defined God as a *communicative Spirit*. How does that definition help you relate to God? What things keep you from having a deeper relationship with him?

6. As an image bearer, you are made for communion with God. What sorts of things interrupt or prevent your daily communion with him? Are there concrete steps you can take to address those issues tomorrow? There's no point in waiting!

7. Discuss what implications there might be if you *don't* consistently commune with God through prayer, worship, and through the body of Christ. What happens when communion is absent? Draw on your own experiences.

Prayer

God, I am crushed.
I am low. I am listening.
You make me breathe and think and talk.
You uphold me at every moment.
You are *all* to me.

Build me in my smallness. Please.
Build me minute by minute, brick by brick,
Into that temple of your Spirit.
Oh my God, help my smallness
To find strength in your greatness,

One moment at a time.

And as my anxiety rushes towards me,
Help me to prioritize communion with you,
Through your word,
Through prayer,
Through your people.
Make *communion* the keyword for my life.

Reader Resource: Anxiety Self-Reflection

Making progress in your battle with anxiety has a lot to do with *self-awareness*. Where are you with your anxiety? Take the following self-reflection seriously and be candid. You're the only one looking. Use the "Explanation" column to record the specifics of your experience: how exactly does your anxiety feel? When does it crop up? When does it go away? You can jot down words and phrases to help you remember particulars. I've answered the first question as an example.

Question	Yes/No/ Sometimes	Explanation
My anxiety often prevents me from doing things I'd like to do.	*Sometimes*	*I've learned a lot over the last 12 years, but I still get freaked out by things like flying, traveling without my family, or speaking in public. I have ups and downs, but I haven't crashed in a while. I'm limited, but not paralyzed.*
My anxiety makes it difficult for me to perform basic daily functions.		
I have triggers for anxiety in certain situations.		
I have developed habits or tools that I use to deal with my anxiety.		
I feel that I'm understood by my family and friends when it comes to my anxiety.		
My goal is to eliminate my anxiety as soon as possible.		
I think a lot about why God might have put anxiety in my life.		
I agree that God sometimes crushes us to call us to himself.		

CHAPTER 2

Living Life on a Leash

KEY IDEA: Our anxiety leads us to develop patterns that either imprison us or free us.

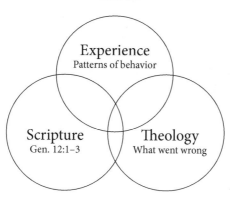

I put the hard truth up front: God may crush us to call us; he may break us down in order to build us up to commune with him. It's a long building project—with daily disruptions scattered throughout, unseen costs around each corner, and plenty of panic-inducing surprises. We don't have access to the grand plans. We can't see who we will be, only who we are in the moment. And in each moment, we have the choice to *trust* the builder or to distrust him, to see everything that's happening to us as purposeful, as working to shape us for a relationship with the almighty God, or to scramble and scrape together our own short-sighted blueprints.

I wasn't prone to trust as early as I'd like to have been. In the beginning of my battle with anxiety, I blindly trusted in my own embarrassing blueprints. I clutched orange bottles of medication wherever I went. My hope came in tiny white cylinders and powder-packed capsules, marked with black numbers and letters. I measured hope in milligrams, not in the mighty promises of a personal God, even though I was now hearing those promises every day. I focused all of my attention on feelings.

At the beginning of a class on the history of rhetoric and media, I sauntered up to my professor and told her that I was dealing with a lot of anxiety and would stay in class as long as I could that day. As class began, I followed the discourse, trying to focus, looking for a stone to tie my mind to. I found one for a while. We were talking about Plato's *Gorgias* and the true nature of rhetoric. I was genuinely interested (I'm a nerd that way), but then I felt a heat flash run down my spine. It nudged me too close to panic. I got up, pushed in my chair, and nodded to the professor as I pointed towards the door. The feeling said, "Flee!" So, I fled. The doctor said, "Start with half a Xanax," so I did. I walked out of that little classroom, swallowed a pill and prayed for change. Not such an impressive blueprint for personal growth, is it? My only goal was to eliminate the feelings, to get back to "normal," to stop struggling. If *this* is what it meant to be crushed and shaped, then in my heart of hearts, I wanted neither. I just wanted my old self back, a strong self. The weakness made me sick.

For me, constant weakness was the real pain in being crushed. The rapid heart rate, the heat swells, the sense of removal from reality (de-realization or disassociation), the hypervigilance, the pinhole throat, the tingling limbs—each is a fifty-pound weight that pulls you lower and lower and lower. The symptoms of anxiety shrink us and suck out our life. They make us feel anemic and brittle. And the world says, "Run the other way! Get away from this! Address the symptoms and get back to living your best life. Take pills. Get counseling. Do *anything*—just cut out the weakness and fill the void with strength!" That's a shortsighted blueprint for change.

Do you want to know the blueprint for the long haul? Brace yourself. It's a blueprint God himself showed to the Apostle Paul: "my power is made perfect in weakness" (2 Cor. 12:9). "In weakness"?! What's your heart's response to those words? Be candid. Here's mine sometimes: "God, *please*—anything but weakness! In *humility*, in *kindness*, in *love*—even *self-sacrifice*, but not *weakness*!"

"What our hearts often hope for is not what our souls always need."

My dear reader, what our hearts often hope for is not what our souls always need. "In weakness"—that's the phrase our souls need to embrace. I know these words are not welcome in the soul's house. We have to work hard to show them hospitality. We have to find a way to welcome them. We have to turn them from unwanted guests to long-term residents. So, chant them. Ruminate over them. Emboss them on your mind every morning. In *weakness* we find the power of God. With anxiety, you may feel like a fractured glass of water, ready to split and spill out at any moment. I know—I've dealt with it for twelve years and counting. I'm begging you sincerely: don't run from the weakness. Weakness is not a threat to avoid at all costs. As J. I. Packer once put it, *weakness is the way*.[1] God is going to use that weakness to do great things in your soul. That's the thesis of this book. What sorts of things? We'll unpack that question in the chapters ahead.

In this chapter, let's focus on how we develop *patterns* of behavior to cope with anxiety, to cope with the weakness, and how God can use those patterns to shape us and lead us to freedom in relationship with him. We'll also see the other side of the coin: how prone we are to use our patterns to avoid the weakness. Those sorts of patterns imprison us.

Let me get back to my story. I learned a whole lot in those initial months. For instance, I learned that paralysis attacks the mind as well as the body. I was ashamed by feeling utterly unable to do things that everyone else did thoughtlessly. I remember being asked if I wanted to drive ten minutes into town to go to the grocery store with one of my brothers. That sounded more like, "Would you care to scale a 100-foot precipice without any harness, all by yourself, in the middle of the night?" No, thank you. I'll just stay here.

I mumbled that little sentence so often: "I'll just stay here." I became a hermit, hardly ever leaving the house. I would take our golden retriever, Hunter, for a walk sometimes, about a hundred yards down the street, but halfway through the walk, I would already feel anxious about how far away from home I was. What would I do if I stopped breathing? If my throat closed up? If my limbs started to tingle and go numb because they weren't getting enough oxygen? Hunter would put the leash in his mouth and pull me towards the stop sign. *He* was leading *me*. He had a collar and a leash, but I was the one restrained and restricted.

Anxiety pushes you to live life on a leash. And that leash is strong, threaded with fibers of fear. You can't move about freely in the world because the physical symptoms are so constricting. And when you do move, you can't go very far because fear keeps you close to your safe zones.

Around this time, more family and friends learned of what I was dealing with, and so advice began pouring in from anyone and everyone. People just want

---

1   J. I. Packer, *Weakness Is the Way: Life with Christ Our Strength* (Wheaton, IL: Crossway, 2013).

to help—I know. But nothing they said was very helpful because all of them took the same approach. The approach is what I'll call *pure rationality* or *bare reason*. I say "bare reason" because there's a kind of biblical reason, which we'll get into soon, that sheds much light on our anxiety and how God can use it to shape us. Bare reason, in contrast, is reason used without any conscious attention to God, his word, and our spiritual development.

"What are you anxious about?" "Why do you feel so nervous?" "Do you know of anything that's causing you to panic?" These aren't bad questions. In fact, we often need to ask them. But what many people simply don't understand about anxiety is that you *can't* always reason your way out of it. Make no mistake, the mind is potent—God made it that way—and we can use it to combat symptoms of anxiety, but it's still limited. There's not always a rational explanation or a direct cause for anxiety that we know of. More importantly, God is doing things with it that we're not aware of. So, my answer to most of the questions people asked me in those first few weeks was often, "I don't know." This always made me feel worse because the anxiety seemed chaotic and uncontrollable. It's one thing to feel terrible; it's quite another thing to feel terrible for no apparent reason! That's why people who struggle with anxiety feel crazy: it's the chaos of not knowing why.

My lack of answers and paralyzing symptoms combined to drive me into deeper helplessness. My brain was broken. Everything that I used to do—driving back and forth to college, going to classes, watching a movie, eating breakfast—was now an obstacle. Life was essentially problematic. I didn't enjoy my days; I survived them.

Anxiety, in its most severe form, leads you around on a leash. It puts you in the back seat of your own life. And if you're in the back seat long enough, you start to come up with coping mechanisms—patterns of behavior—that appear to ease your distress. Patterned behavior is our attempt to deal with perceived chaos.

Patterns That Free and Patterns That Imprison

When you think about it, life is all about patterns: the pattern of night and day, of eating and sleeping, of speech and silence. We're people looking for patterns. My favorite linguist once said that beyond all abstractions and ideas "lies person in commitment to the sheer joy of the pattern chase."[2] *Pattern-chasers*—that's who we

---

2   Kenneth L. Pike, *Linguistic Concepts: An Introduction to Tagmemics* (Lincoln, NE: University of Nebraska Press, 1982), 127.

are, made in the image of a patterning God. The trouble is that we're prone to seek out and adopt patterns that imprison us rather than protect us or free us. We grasp for patterns that bring comfort, control, and pleasure; we shun the ones that offer shaping, surrender, and discipline.

Let me get into some of my patterns. As I already mentioned, for weeks I had developed the pattern of reading my father's Bible multiple times a day, living my linear life, seeking sentence after sentence. I was finding a growing sense of consolation from it. This didn't really affect my symptoms all that much, but it did make me feel as if my toes were touching down on a rock in the middle of an ocean (Ps. 18:2). I could stand on this book. I could stand on the shoulders of the one who wrote it. Though I still felt crushed, oppressed, and hyper-vigilant most of the day, I carried around in my hands a whisper of hope, a candle in a cavern.

The hope and consolation I was beginning to notice came from both the *content* and *medium* of what I held in my hands.

In terms of *content*, I was continually addressed by a voice that was not my own. And because I had been crushed, I was no longer deaf. When you're full of your*self* and believe the *self*-told lie that you're *self*-sufficient, your ears get blocked up (Isa. 6:9–10; Mark 4:12; Matt. 13:14).[3] The only voice you hear is the one inside your head (and it's not all that brilliant). So, in terms of the content of Scripture, I was now fully receptive to the truth of what I was reading. This really was God: the Lord of all things who condescended to commune with his little rebellious creatures and who continued to guide them with his speech—a speech that not only created the world but governs it and upholds it at every moment (Heb. 1:3; Col. 1:17).[4] This was the speaking God of *persons* whom he knew by name: Abraham, Isaac, Jacob, Moses, David, Elijah, John, Paul. These were *real* people in *real* relationships with the *real* God. Farmers and fisherman, tribesmen and tax collectors—no divine invitation to relationship was withheld. This was a God who was more patient, more kind, more just, and more loving than I could understand. I read the words on every page of Scripture with awe, as if I were learning a new language that had unlocked a door to something I desperately needed. There is a personal God who knows my name,

---

3   I reference these biblical texts because the deafness, the inability to understand what was spoken by God, was actually an act of judgement upon God's people. In my own life, I saw a similar phenomenon. I was raised in the church and was always hearing the word of God, but I had a habit of not understanding it, not truly hearing it. When I actually began understanding what I was hearing in Scripture, I realized that I had been spiritually deaf for years.

4   See chapter 3 in *The Speaking Trinity & His Worded World: Why Language Is at the Center of Everything* (Eugene, OR: Wipf & Stock, 2018).

and he is gracious . . . overwhelmingly gracious. There was hope here, and only here. This was all the more strange to me since I'd read the Bible before. I grew up in the church, but I had never really read Scripture for what it is: the voice of God.

In terms of the *medium*, I found consolation in the printed page. My life became linear. There was a very real sense in which the structure and stability I found came right from the printed pages of my father's old Bible: two-column text with footnotes and cross references. I lived on those pages. I ran my fingers across them, but, in another sense, I put my feet down on them, and I stood. The chaos of my feelings seemed to submit (though never without a fight) to the words on the page. The gift of print gave my mind the structure it needed amidst swells of panic. So, I clung to that book as if it were part of my body.

And I was beginning to be changed by it. The greatest change was that I was *listening*. I listened as I read. I listened more intently than I had ever listened to anyone. That, after all, is a fitting behavior for someone whom God has crushed. God had my undivided attention. Though I didn't know it at the time, this was a pattern that was going to lead to spiritual *freedom*—not the sort of freedom that others might long for, but the best kind of freedom we can have in this world, a freedom within the borders of God's speech. Understand, however, that this did *not* mean the absence of anxiety. Patterns that free us don't remove hardship from our lives; sometimes they even push us towards it. But they always ground us in the true, life-giving promise of God—that he will always be *with* us (Matt. 28:20).

But while there are patterns that free us, the most important of which is reading and submitting to the speech of God in Scripture, there are also patterns that *imprison* us. I still clung to self-given solutions for anxiety, and it's a temptation to do that even now, more than twelve years later. We're not so enthusiastic about walking by faith. We rush toward the concept but sprint from the practice because it's painful and terrifying. So, I returned over and over again to that little sentence, "I'll just stay here." "Here" would be whatever place I felt comfortable in: home, my dorm room, the college campus: *safe zones*. It was during this time, within a few weeks of my hospital trips, that I was diagnosed with and began being treated for an anxiety disorder, which meant that my doctor prescribed medication (the topic of a later chapter). That medication began to be part of my patterns, for better or worse.

I developed other patterns that imprison, patterns that I believed would keep me comfortable. "I'll just stay here" was only one of them. Doing the same things every day, in the same order, at the same time, was another one. Routine is the riches of an anxiety-ridden person.

Now, there's nothing inherently wrong with routine and patterns of behavior. We all have them, and the God of Scripture is a patterning God, one who reveals himself in regularities and consistencies. Yet, while patterns of behavior can bring us solace in a world that is unpredictable, they can quickly crowd out the place of faith in our lives. That's when patterns become problematic. That's when patterns imprison, when they lock us behind bars of predictability and comfort. It's at these points that faith is perceived not as a divine gift but as a troubling threat. It's at these points that we shudder most at the phrase "in weakness."

"Faith, in one sense, is pattern-breaking. It's a walking away from familiarity and comfort."

Faith, in one sense, is pattern-breaking. It's a walking away from familiarity and comfort. When Abram was living in Haran, amidst his family and countrymen and all that he knew, he was living a patterned life, just as we do today. It was in the context of this patterned life that God spoke to him and delivered a call to faith.

> [1] Now the LORD said to Abram, "Go from your country and your kindred and your father's house to the land that I will show you. [2] And I will make of you a great nation, and I will bless you and make your name great, so that you will be a blessing. [3] I will bless those who bless you, and him who dishonors you I will curse, and in you all the families of the earth shall be blessed." (Gen. 12:1–3)

We often focus on the blessing in this passage, which is a good thing. But look at what Abram is leaving behind: country, kindred, and his father's house. In other words, he is leaving *everything* that is familiar to him. And where is he called to go? Not to a neighboring city or country, but to "the land that I will show you." God asked Abram to break away from his patterned life and trust the divine voice—not a vision or a plan or a destination, but a *voice*.

Reading that story as someone who struggles with anxiety, I can tell you how ludicrous that sounds. Why would you leave all familiarity? Why would you leave your safe zone? I had read about the calling of Abram dozens of times in my life, but I had never seen it as I did now. My jaw dropped at what Abram did. How did you . . . why would you . . . what's the point of . . . ?

For someone like me on the tight leash of anxiety, Abram looked like a superhero. It was God, of course, who called Abram and gave him the faith he needed, leading him through the countryside, protecting him from his enemies, and bringing him to his destination. God is the real hero. But from the human side of things, I couldn't sympathize with Abram's actions. I could marvel at them, but I couldn't sympathize. Why?

The short answer is that I was deeply entrenched in a patterned life that had imprisoned me. I was governed by fear, not by faith. There is a sort of fear that's spiritually healthy, and we'll talk about that later, but this was not it. This was imprisoning fear. My patterns were custom-made not to *guide* me but to *govern* me. And because of how I continued to feel physically—hyper-vigilant, overly self-aware, like an alien in my own skin—I was happy to let my imprisoning patterns rule. Given the choice between fear and faith, I took the former almost every time. "Better to be safely imprisoned than out wandering the wilds of faith." That was the unspoken conviction of my heart.

On occasions, I would fight against the fear and get into a car at night or go somewhere I didn't want to go, and there always came a moment in those experiences where I felt liberated and empowered by God. But that feeling came after severe anxiety had peaked. It took so much effort to do this that I usually avoided it.

Living a patterned life—something we all do by nature—can easily turn into living an imprisoned life, a life surrounded by walls that seem too large to scale and too thick to break through. There was only one thing that started to make doorways in my walls. And I wish—I really wish—that I could give you a different response here. But the only thing that will help you get outside the prison of anxiety is to do what Abram did: follow the voice and start breaking the patterns that imprison. God will not leave you pattern-less; he will give you the pattern of listening to his own voice in the words of Scripture. And your anxiety can actually become the thing that opens your ears and turns you toward the one who is speaking. In the chapters ahead, we're going to learn what it's like to live by the freeing pattern of adherence to God's voice.

The Benefit of Pattern-Breaking: Sympathy

Before we look at the theology for this chapter, I'd like to end by noting one of the most precious benefits of pattern-breaking: *sympathy*.

Hard things happen to everyone. It doesn't matter that you can't see many of the hard things others are dealing with—especially in light of our Instagram culture. The hard things are there, in the daily struggles all around you: snarky put-downs, sexual harassment, broken promises, failed parenting, ailing bodies, frustrated ambitions, financial stress. It's a long but quiet list of largely unnoticed things. We can sympathize with others on many of these troubles, but not all of them. And sometimes we forget that other people are struggling, even if they're struggling in the same way that we are. Pattern-breaking, however, can lead you to sympathize with others in ways you hadn't imagined. That sympathy leads to deeper awareness and understanding of the tired souls surrounding you.

I recently watched a CNN interview with comedian Stephen Colbert.[5] He was talking about the grief he had worked through in coming to grips with losing his father and two brothers as a child. The interviewer, Anderson Cooper, asked him about something he had said elsewhere about the tragic event: "I learned to love the thing that I wished most had not happened. . . . What punishments of God are not gifts?" Amazed at this statement, Cooper said, "You really believe that?" Colbert's answer was deep and beautiful, betraying years of maturity in coming to grips with grief: "What do you get from loss? You get awareness of other people's loss, which allows you to connect with that other person, which allows you to love more deeply and to understand what it's like to be a human being." I think most of us would say that having crippling battles with anxiety is something "we wish most had not happened." We don't like it; we don't want it cracking the glass of comfort enveloping our little lives. But because we have it, because we suffer with anxiety, with can connect with others and love them more deeply. Anxiety makes us *feel* less human, but it has the potential to make us *be* more human.

I remember talking to a friend whom I had classes with at seminary. On the top floor of the library, I mentioned casually that I was dealing with a lot of anxiety. "Do you mean, like, in general or because of something in particular?" he asked. "In general," I said. "I've been battling an anxiety disorder for several years." He paused for a moment, nodding his head. "I actually deal with that a lot too." As soon

---

5   You can see a piece of the interview here: https://www.vanityfair.com/hollywood/2019/08/colbert-ander-son-cooper-father-grief-tears.

as the words left his mouth, I felt immediately closer to him. Why? Because I could sympathize. Our experiences aligned to make us feel more like brothers and less like strangers. Brothers share a heritage with each other. I share a world of memories with my three brothers. But fellow sufferers share a similar heritage. The sympathy we can feel with others because of our anxiety—because of our constant attempts to break the patterns that imprison us and just exist in the world each day—is truly a gift. It's the gift of humanity, of communing with others, of relating to them and feeling pain and pressure *together*.

Our sympathy for others who are suffering from anxiety is no small thing. Finding ways to break your imprisoning patterns is never going to be easy, but it's going to make you more human because it's going to lead you to sympathize with others. In other words, it's going to lead you to communion. And that draw to communion is precisely what makes us human.

Theology: What's Wrong?

In the previous chapter, we looked at who God is and who we are, and we saw that *communion* is central to both questions. But we don't have that communion very often, do we? Our communion with God often seems lost. It comes back into our lives now and then, flippant and fleeting, like a butterfly wandering on the wind. This is especially true in the context of anxiety. When we're anxious, communion with the God of peace is like a hand that's just out of reach. We know it's there, and that it must be possible to grab onto it, but we can't figure out how to stretch far enough. To make matters worse, every time we reach for it, anxiety seems to jab us in the ribs and makes us recoil into our feelings. Why is this the way things are?

"When we're anxious, communion with the God of peace is like a hand that's just out of reach."

We need to spend some words examining this because the breaking of our communion with God has everything to do with our forging patterns that imprison us. Again, I'm keeping these sections on theology brief so that we can take what we need as a biblical context for interpreting our anxiety, and leave the rest for another time.[6]

---

6   See my little ebook *In Divine Company: Growing Closer to the God Who Speaks.*

So, let's stare at a simple question for a few moments: what went wrong? The Great Story of Scripture has a concise but crushing answer to that question: *sin*. That answer fits well with what we explored in the first chapter: God crushes us to help us hear him; he crushes us to call us. In a different sense, we're crushed to know that sin is the reason behind our broken and intermittent communion with the God of peace. Why? Well, when you think about it, that answer is very personal. The problem with the world is not social misunderstanding, a lack of education and scientific advancement, or the spread of harmful ideologies. *The problem is something inside of you.* That's crushing. It crushes your ego. It crushes your confidence. It requires that you accept something that very few people can: something inside of *you* is responsible for the horrors in the world, for the decay and destitution, for the hate. Something inside of *you* . . . And do you know what that little something is? *Distrust.* I bet you didn't think *that* was behind the Holocaust, or every domestic disturbance call, or drug addiction, did you?

But it's all there in Genesis 1–3. At the start of the Great Story, we read that the God of communion, the God who speaks to himself in three persons, created a world with his words. His speech set the world in motion. That speech created and controlled not only what we see but also how it functions (Gen. 1:11). The centrality of speech in creation is absolutely vital, for it points to the very nature of reality as something spoken, something that requires the *trust* and engagement of those who receive or partake in that speech.[7]

Speech, you see, requires trust. It assumes trust. And in the very beginning, that trust was there, between the speaking God and his speaking creatures. And that trust wasn't groundless. The very first humans had every reason to trust in the goodness of God, for he had provided them with purpose and with all they needed for food. Their purpose was to multiply and govern the earth for God's glory (Gen. 1:28), in addition to tending the garden that God had spoken (Gen. 2:15). The very first humans were gardeners, after God's own heart. God's goodness is also revealed in his providing food for them (Gen. 1:29–30).

And yet, perhaps the crux of the story in Genesis are the words that God spoke to protect his creatures from death: the ultimate prison. He spoke words that offered them an opportunity to show their trust in his goodness. In Genesis 2:16–17, God's puts trust in the foreground. He tells his creatures what *not* to do, and he tells

---

7   For more on this, see *The Speaking Trinity & His Worded World: Why Language Is at the Center of Everything* (Eugene, OR: Wipf & Stock, 2018).

them what will happen if they violate his words. In this little episode at the beginning of our existence, God spoke a foundation of trust. Adam and Eve would have the opportunity to stand upon that foundation, to live and move and breathe in light of the words of God (Acts 17:28), or to distrust those words and choose another foundation.

And we know how the story goes. They chose a different foundation. They chose to trust the words of a slithering serpent rather than those of the speaking God. The serpent spoke a message that was antithetical to God's. God told his creatures all that they *could* have, and only after that did he tell them what they *couldn't* have. The serpent reverses that message and also distorts it. First, he puts a question to Eve: "Did God actually say, 'You shall not eat of *any* tree in the garden?'" (Gen. 3:1). Do you see how that's basically the opposite of what God said? God had originally told them, "You may surely eat of *every* tree of the garden" (Gen. 2:16). The serpent gives Eve an inverted message. He distorts the original. He exaggerates. And look at what that does in Eve's response: "And the woman said to the serpent, 'We may eat of the fruit of the trees in the garden, but God said, "You shall not eat of the fruit of the tree that is in the midst of the garden, neither shall you touch it, lest you die"'" (Gen. 3:2–3). First, Eve leaves out the bounty of God's gift. God had said "every," but Eve left that little word behind. That's not insignificant. Eve is beginning to forget or ignore the greatness and plenitude of God's good gift. Second, Eve adds a little clause: "neither shall you touch it." Where did that come from? God didn't mention anything about touching. The most probable explanation is that Eve has fallen into the path of exaggeration set out by the serpent.

In this little encounter between a snake and a human, a seed of distrust was sown in Eve's heart. We can imagine the thoughts that may have begun tumbling through her mind: "Maybe God *doesn't* have our best interests at heart. Maybe he *is* hiding something from us. It's just *one* piece of fruit. Could it be that potent? What would be the harm in just trying a small bite?" The seed of distrust sprouted roots.

And here's the thing: once those roots sprout and grip the soil of the heart, communion with God grinds to a halt. You can't have communion with distrust. They're like oil and water; no amount of shaking will get them to mix. If you want communion, you need trust. More specifically, if you want communion, given who God is and who we are, you need trust in divine *speech*, in God's words. Trust in God's speech fosters communion. Distrust in that speech causes disunion. Union is the effect of faith in speech; disunion is the effect of skepticism in speech.

What does this have to do with our patterns of behavior? Every pattern of behavior is built on *trust* in someone or something. My pattern of just staying in my safe zones, for example, is built on trust in my own ability to control my experience. "If I stay where I'm comfortable, I won't have to deal with the feelings of anxiety." Or, on the other side, "If I get into a car at night, I'm going to have a panic attack." Do you see the element of trust in my own self-control? There's no room for faith, no room for Abram's footsteps in a foreign country, no room for trust in God's words. I have no place in my heart and mind for the words of David: "Even though I walk through the valley of the shadow of death, I will fear no evil, for you are with me; your rod and your staff, they comfort me" (Ps. 23:4). With my imprisoning pattern, I'm not even willing to walk through the shadow of the night without fearing evil, let alone the shadow of death!

"Every pattern of behavior is built on trust in someone or something."

But hope is not lost. We can forge new patterns of behavior by the power of God's Spirit. We can ask God to give us the faith we need to walk into our foreign country on any given day, whatever that country might be: a social engagement, a commute to work, an airplane, a broken relationship. We can ask for faith in God's speech and find corresponding words from Scripture to meditate on as we walk. This is the pattern that frees us, for it is the only pattern that puts our trust in God's speech at the center of our decision-making.

I'll end with a recent example. Many times on my commute home I've butted heads with the snake of anxiety, fighting to push his coils off of my neck. I've felt the symptoms early in the afternoon when I'm still at work, the same run-of-the-mill lineup: difficulty swallowing, hyper-vigilance, overt awareness of breathing. By the time I get on the highway, I'm having real trouble focusing on anything other than anxiety. So often I think, *Why am I anxious?* That question can be quite revealing, since it brings our attention to situational and heart-related factors that may be influencing us. So, we need to ask it sometimes and be transparent when we answer. However, I have now made a habit of asking another question that helps me focus on trust in God's speech: *What are you teaching me, Lord?* On one drive home, I could feel the Spirit pushing me to meditate on Psalm 9:9–10. I had been reading this psalm the day before.

> The Lord is a stronghold for the oppressed,
>
> a stronghold in times of trouble.
>
> And those who know your name put their trust in you,
>
> for you, O Lord, have not forsaken those who seek you.

Remember that there is great power in the word of God (Heb. 4:12). And Paul reminds us in Ephesians 6:17 that God's word is not simply a soft consolation; it is a searing *sword*. It attacks whatever is attacking us. I spoke the words of the psalm out loud, over and over again. I went from reciting them to putting my faith in them, praying them, *wielding* them. Everything else became secondary as God's words filled the car. The promise of God's protection and presence grew heavier, outweighing the bodily symptoms I was experiencing. Within a few minutes, I was calm and began praying about many other things that God was laying on my heart.

Notice here, that if I would have asked the other question, "Why am I anxious?" I might never have found an answer, or I may have found an answer that short-circuited my spiritual formation. But I quickly was given one when I changed my question. That's precisely because I was making an effort not to *eliminate* anxiety but to *learn* from it in my relationship with God. Recall the thesis of the book again: *Anxiety can be a great spiritual tool in the hands of God.* On that afternoon, I tried my hardest to treat the anxiety as a tool God might be using to show me something, and through that to conform me to Christ. And he did show me something: Nothing can touch you when you're in the stronghold of God himself, the stronghold of God's speech. It requires trust to stay there, but God himself will give you that trust if you ask him.

The real paradox of anxiety, my reader, echoes the paradox that Paul voiced in 2 Corinthians 12:10. *Weakness through anxiety is strength in the Lord.* While anxiety seems to cripple us, it has the potential to give us spiritual wings, allowing us to rise above what's around us and helping us to see the spiritual purposes that God has for the hardships at our fingertips. When anxiety makes you weak, ask God questions that can make you strong. "What are you teaching me, Lord?" He always answers. And he'll always give you the faith you need to wait for his reply. That's how we combat the distrust that leads to our broken communion with God in a sin-stained world.

Don't flee from your weakness. Lean into it. When you do, you're leaning into Christ. And Christ will walk with you, holding your clammy fingers until you get where you need to go in that moment.

Reflection Questions and Prayer

1. In what ways has your own anxiety given you a short leash? Talk with a friend about what opportunities you think you're missing out on because of this.

2. What are your "safe zones," places that you don't want to leave? Talk with someone about how you feel when you leave them? What are your greatest fears hiding behind the experiences you avoid? What is a passage of Scripture you could memorize that applies to that fear? You might even start with Ps. 9:9–10.

3. In what ways do you think the leash of anxiety might be (or could be) conforming you to Christ's image? In what ways is it keeping you from being conformed, keeping you stuck in distrust?

4. We'll touch on this in a later chapter, but what do you think Satan's hope is for our anxiety?

5. In what ways has sin lead you to distrust in your own life?

6. What are other sources of authority in your own life that you seem to trust? List them. Why do you trust them, and how do those sources compare with the God who knows your name?

7. If you're struggling with an anxiety disorder, you probably "trust" your bodily sensations without question (those "fight or flight" instincts): heat flashes, rapid heartrate, tightening chest, shortness of breath. Will you commit this week to making *one* attempt to trust God's speech *more than* those bodily sensations? Start by memorizing Psalm 9:9–10. Say those words out loud when you begin experiencing these sensations.

8. Why do you think we choose patterns that imprison us over patterns that free us? (Go deeper than just saying "sin.")

9. What are some of your own imprisoning patterns?

10. In addition to reading Scripture, what are some patterns that free us, patterns that you might implement in your own routine?

Prayer

My God, I am being led around
By a cruel master.
But he is not mine.
You hold the reins of my life.
Help me to take one step at a time
Knowing that you are always behind me,
Before me, beneath me, and beside me.

I know that you are the Lord of patterns.
You have spoken a world with borders and layers,
Seasons and days, governed by laws you have uttered.
But my own patterns hem me in and bind me up.
I am imprisoned by myself.
Please help me to find a patterned life
That is free and open to your direction.
Let me know and trust that the openness of faith
Is the greatest pattern you have called us to,
And there is freedom in your voice.

God, if I'm honest . . .
There are dozens of things that I trust
More than your word.
I trust my feelings. I trust my doctors
And the medical community.
I trust my parents. I trust my friends.
But you have always given me words of life (John 6:68).
In Genesis, your words *made* life.
In Jesus, through the power of the Spirit, you *give* life.
And you know everything.
Everything. Everything. Everything.
Your words are the *most* trustworthy.
But my heart is sick. My head is diseased with doubt.
I long for words from another, and I listen to ignorance.

Please . . . help me to trust your words

Above all else,

Above my feelings and fears,

Above my own wishes and the whims of the world.

I know that your words are life.

Help me to choose life over death

In every concrete moment.

Reader Resource: Pattern Tracking

It's helpful to track your patterns of behavior. If you don't know what they are and how they're affecting you, there's a good chance you'll never change them. Use the diagrams below to identify a pattern, its effect on you, and the problems it might be causing. You can then start a new pattern, how you think it may affect you, and the freedom it may bring.[8] See the next pages for an example.

What is the pattern?
Why do you have it?

What are the effects (positive and negative)?

What are the problems?

What is a new pattern you could implement?

---

8   I was inspired to put this together after reading Drey Dyck's book, *Your Future Self with Thank You: Secrets to Self-Control from the Bible and Brain Science* (Chicago: Moody, 2019).

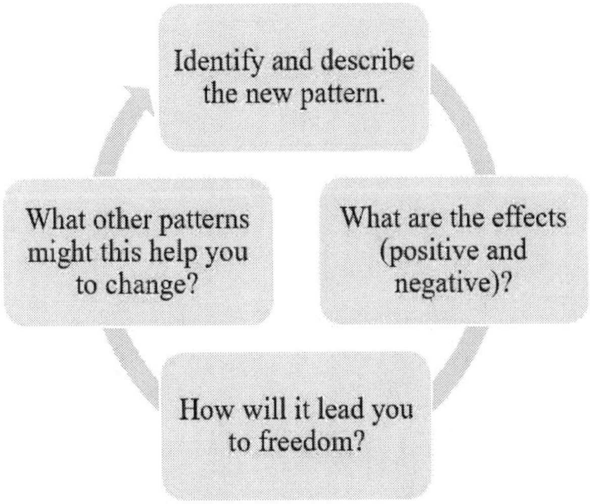

Top diagram (cycle)

Identify and describe the new pattern.

What are the effects (positive and negative)?

How will it lead you to freedom?

What other patterns might this help you to change?

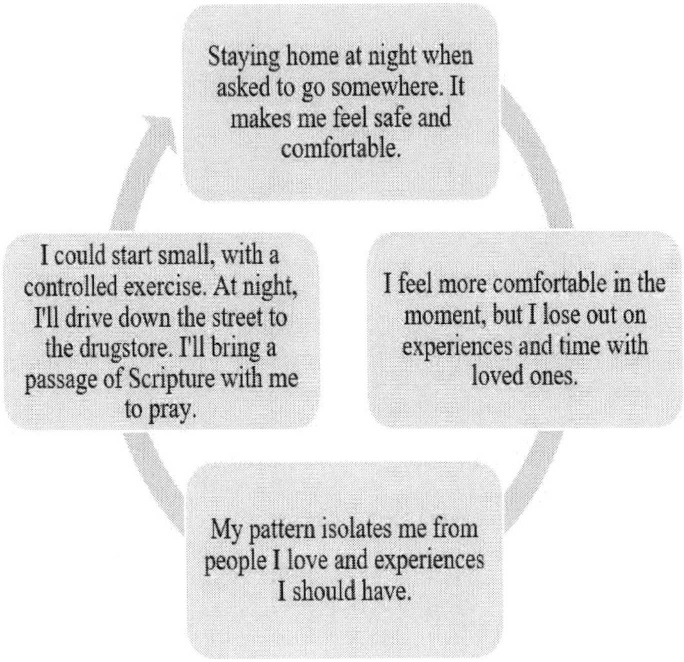

Bottom diagram (cycle)

Staying home at night when asked to go somewhere. It makes me feel safe and comfortable.

I feel more comfortable in the moment, but I lose out on experiences and time with loved ones.

My pattern isolates me from people I love and experiences I should have.

I could start small, with a controlled exercise. At night, I'll drive down the street to the drugstore. I'll bring a passage of Scripture with me to pray.

CHAPTER 3

Baby Steps of Faith

KEY IDEA: Small steps of faith will draw you into reliance on God.

We have covered a lot of ground so far, and it's only the third chapter! We've seen that God can use our anxiety to crush us so that we're open to his calling—whatever that might be. In the previous chapter, we noted how anxiety leads us to develop patterns that imprison us or free us. In this chapter, we look more specifically at the sorts of steps we take in faith to combat anxiety, watching how God will use it to shape us to Christ's image. Keep in mind the truth that we ended the last chapter with: *weakness through anxiety is strength in the Lord*. We're all in a life-long ceramic process (2 Cor. 4:7–9). Our weakness is the water that softens us so that God's potter hands can push and bend us to the shape of Christ. That pushing and bending is going to happen one step at a time.

Now, I know—I *really* know—the last thing someone with anxiety wants to hear is that you have to break your patterns, leave your safe zones, and take steps to follow a divine voice that hasn't confirmed where you're going or when you'll arrive. I get it. My heart still wishes for another way. But what I began to learn early on in my struggle with anxiety is that things aren't going to change just because I want them to. Doctors may encourage you to treat the symptoms of anxiety, and the fact that we can treat these symptoms is a gift of God's grace. But purely symptomatic treatment will never develop lasting change. In this book, we're focusing on how God uses our anxiety in shaping our relationship with him. The key is the word *relationship*. A relationship requires trust. And trust requires risk in small, concrete steps. Those sentences are painful for you to read if you have anxiety. (They're painful for me to write!) But they're true. To develop lasting change, to grow in our anxiety and be shaped to the image of Christ, we have to put our foot down in a foreign country, just as Abraham did. And we have to do it again and again and again and again. As I tell my students who are working on improving their writing, the only thing that breaks an old pattern is a new pattern.

"We have to put our foot down in a foreign country, just as Abraham did."

To be candid with you, I had no interest in doing this for several months, even though I had a sneaking suspicion that I would have to. And I wasn't too keen on it for the following years. Even now, more than twelve years later, I'm not enthusiastic about breaking patterns and doing the unexpected. When I do something out of the norm, when I break a pattern, when I take a tiny step of faith, it's a big deal. I know that sounds silly to some people, but anxiety radically alters your perception of what's possible.

Let me rehash an example from the introduction. I used to feel I could never travel anywhere alone. If I did, I would be exposed to death-dealing peril. I would be lost, helpless, and isolated from those who knew me and cared most about me. In fact, if I went anywhere alone, I would probably stop breathing, get dizzy, seize up in the fetal position, and die. Sound ridiculous? That's what anxiety does to your mind. It replaces a thought with a nightmare and convinces you that the nightmare's more likely. So, it was a mammoth-sized challenge for me to take a train into Philadelphia for jury duty several years ago. I had to leave every safe zone and go somewhere without my wife, somewhere other than the seminary where I work, and I couldn't be in control as I went there; I had to trust the train. Fetal position, here I come.

I stepped onto the train with my Bible in hand, sat down next to a window, and began reading. Eventually, I picked up my head and watched the urban landscape go by as we clicked down the tracks toward the city. Every few moments I had to return to Scripture and remind myself of God's presence—not just with me on the train, but right outside the train in the poor neighborhoods and the abandoned factory buildings, behind the brick and soot-stained apartments, in the streets littered with cigarettes, in the faces of a thousand strangers. God was *here*, and God was *there*. I was surrounded by him. I fixated on that truth, and when I had trouble trusting it, I turned my eyes back to the pages of Scripture. Scared sheep shouldn't stray far from their shepherd's voice. After about an hour, the train arrived at Market Street Station in the city. I stepped off into the subway and took a breath. I did it, with a lot of prayer, with my Bible, and with continuous attention to my nerves throughout the trip. But I did it. I set my foot in a foreign county, and I was still alive!

A lot of books would have told me to rejoice in that moment: to rejoice in the building of my own strength. "*You* did it!" But I know that isn't true. *God* had done it, and I was just along for the ride. *He* had given me trust in him every moment of the commute, as I stared out the window and looked into the faces of strangers. *He* had shepherded my wild thoughts. *He* had used the crook of his word to pull me back to his voice. God was the reason I was still alive. God was the reason I wasn't in the fetal position. The baby steps of faith in taking that train led to trust in and reliance on God. The result—please hear this—was *not* the absence of anxiety. That's not what you get from taking a baby step of faith—though self-help books try to build your confidence that way. The result was further reliance on God, a clearer sense that God's presence and shepherding got me where I needed to go. It was strength *in the Lord* that emerged out of my weakness. My steps of faith led to a deepening, a strengthening of my *relationship* with God, a relationship built on trust in his speech, trust in his words.

Now, that's one little success story in a pile of failures. Just to balance things out, here's an example of the latter. Years earlier, during our engagement, my wife wanted to take a quick trip to Target at night, about twenty minutes away. She asked me if I would go with her. For most people, that's a run-of-the-mill request. They would make that decision in a matter of seconds. But I wrestled with it for an hour. I wanted to go, but I hated driving at night. I was angry that fear was governing me, but I didn't know what else to do. I put faith and trust in my safe zones, in my imprisoning patterns. And after a lot of conversation (and no small amount of patience on her part), I decided I would stay home. An errand to Target—that's what broke my spirit. I didn't follow Abram into a foreign country of faith that night. I kept my feet in the land of familiarity. And there was no growth in my relationship with the

Lord; there was only self-doubt, distrust, and discouragement.

I'm sure you have your own failure and success stories. What I learned back then, and what I hope you'll learn soon enough, is that someone with anxiety is frequently confronted by the terror of change. For those of us who battle anxiety on a regular basis, there will probably always be steps before us that we don't want to take. There will always be imprisoning patterns to which we cling, habits we hold onto, fears that follow us everywhere. We will always hate the foreign country. But the most important thing I can tell you in this book is that the terror of change, the breaking of imprisoning patterns and habits, is a faith-opportunity, a chance for trust, a moment of potential deepening for your relationship with the God of peace. In fact, you may even come to the point where you see a kind of spiritual *need* for anxiety.

I've already told you that I've dealt with severe anxiety for over twelve years. I've had plenty of time to do self-studies in the presence of God, by the light of his word. Along the way, I've noticed something very disturbing in one sense, but reassuring in another: *anxiety seems necessary to cultivate and strengthen my relationship with God.* Faith, for me, tends to come only after fear. We'll explore the biblical roots of this phenomenon in another chapter. For now, I'll just say that when I feel relatively relaxed, I almost instantly start drifting toward sinful behaviors from my past or idols I raise up in the present. I hated anxiety; I still hate it; I'll always hate it. But I know that it never fails to present an opportunity for me to check my heart and remember that I've been crushed, called, and asked to take steps of faith before an ever-present God. In other words, God has faithfully used anxiety to turn my head away from everything else, to close my mouth, to open my ears, and to fix my gaze on him. Anxiety has a purifying effect: it simplifies life to a single *relationship*. What Ernest Hemmingway said of war we can say of anxiety: It burns the fat off our souls.

Let me put this in the context of another example. I love poetry. I used to read a lot of Rainer Maria Rilke. He was raw and honest, even if that was unsettling at times, and I felt as if he wasn't trying to win anyone over with his verse. He was simply opening his heart and mind and letting words fall onto the page that expressed his inner questions and turmoil. One of his poems has resonated with me at different times in my life, from his *Book of Hours*. It has always touched me when I'm in a place of spiritual numbness, that is, when I'm not feeling particularly anxious. At one point in the poem, he writes, "The wall between us is very thin. Why couldn't a cry from one of us break it down?"[1]

Now, setting aside the theology behind the poem for a moment (which has significant problems), this is a vivid portrayal of how many of us feel in seasons of spiritual numbness. We feel like there's a distance, a wall, between us and God. We want it to fall, but we can't seem to do anything to knock it down.

Now, here's the encouraging part: I've *never* felt like this when I'm battling a swell of anxiety. Do you know why? Because I can't stop talking to God! My life-blood pulses through prayer. When the faceless master of anxiety grips the reins of my life and puts me on a short leash, I have no reservations about going to God's word and speaking to him in response. In fact, it's at those very moments that I'm utterly convinced that God is the only one who can help me—not just because the Father is all-powerful but because Christ has suffered in every way just as I have (Heb. 4:15), and because the Holy Spirit is my divine comforter (John 14:16). The one who conquered all has all-encompassing peace, and he's given that peace to *us* (John 14:27). We just have to ask God to help us rummage around for it amidst the mess of distractions and idols in our own lives.

"Prayer is personal communion with God for conformity to his Son by the power of his Spirit."

Don't get me wrong: It's not a mathematical equation. It's not ANXIETY + PRAYER = PEACE. If you want to think of it as an equation, it's ANXIETY + PRAYER = CONTINUAL RELIANCE ON GOD. That reliance, that trust, eventually will bring peace, but the thing that it gives you immediately is the thing you want most and the thing God has designed us for: *relationship*. Remember: God is always calling us to *trust* as he builds our relationship with him. When we pray, we act on that trust. We trust that God is listening to us and that we're communing with him through speech, drawing nearer as we utter words. It's not that God leaves us when we stop praying, but prayer is an intentional way of handing over our questions, our

---

1   Rainer Maria Rilke, *Rilke's Book of Hours: Love Poems to God*, trans. Anita Barrows and Joanna Macy, 100th Anniversary ed. (New York: Riverhead, 2005), 53.

fears, and our doubts to the God who sees and knows *all*. And as we hand those things over, as we trust him, there is a personal, relational nearness that blossoms. This is no mere conversation with a nebulous divine force. This is the God who knows your name! This is the God who knows my name! He knows exactly how we fit into all that he sees and knows, and he wants to comfort us as we start to look more and more like his own Son. Prayer, in other words, is personal communion with God for conformity to his Son by the power of his Spirit. And that willingness to pray in moments of anxiety is a baby step of faith. Don't write it off as well-wishing. It's a step of faith, and it draws us into reliance on the God who speaks.

But what if we feel that God is silent, and we can't even focus enough to pray? That happens sometimes (a lot of times). God might seem absent or distant, and anxiety is linked to panic attacks for many of us, so we need some way to settle our minds and bodies enough to pray. In those moments of panic and shortness of breath, the only solution I've found is to begin reading the Bible. Close out everything else, and just follow the words on the page. Live your linear life. This is more than an exercise in distraction—an attempt to push your mind onto something else. It brings you back to the word-by-word, peace-giving power of divine speech.

I remember feeling on the edge of panic one weeknight. I went outside to take some deep breaths. It didn't help. (Of course, I could've spent more than two minutes.) I went back inside and sat down on our couch with my Bible. I resolved to keep reading even when heat swells and surges of panic crept up my spine. I set my heart to keep breathing and keep reading. The passage I was working through at the time was John 8, and as my finger followed the words below, my heartbeat began to slow.

> [31] So Jesus said to the Jews who had believed him, "If you abide in my word, you are truly my disciples, [32] and you will know the truth, and the truth will set you free." [33] They answered him, "We are offspring of Abraham and have never been enslaved to anyone. How is it that you say, 'You will become free'?" [34] Jesus answered them, "Truly, truly, I say to you, everyone who practices sin is a slave to sin. [35] The slave does not remain in the house forever; the son remains forever. [36] So if the Son sets you free, you will be free indeed. (John 8:31–36)

Freedom—I wanted that so badly! That's exactly the opposite of how we feel under panic, isn't it? In panic, we feel restricted, trapped, and bound. And here was the Son of God himself telling me, right now, in my living room, that the truth *will*—not can or should or may, but *will*—set me free. It was a promise worth pouring all of my faith into. I began praying fervently in my heart, "Yes, please, God—give me that freedom! I'm in your word right now. I'm in your truth. Please give it to me!" That was my baby step on a weeknight. And God met me right then and there as I relied on him and trusted in his speech. I felt something lift off of my chest, my breathing became more natural, and my heart began to slow down. I knew I was going to *be* okay even if I didn't *feel* okay. And that's a huge truth to digest!

You see, there's a great chasm between *being* and *feeling*, and we can't ever confuse the two. The way things are and the way things will be aren't always reflected by your *feelings*. In fact, most of the time, your feelings are fickle and false. They tell you what God says in his word isn't true. I had to learn through hundreds (maybe even thousands) of encounters with panic that just because I *felt* a certain way didn't mean I *was* a certain way. There's a gap between feelings and finality. God's word gives you the latter to govern the former.

If you still feel as if you can't do this, if you're too panicked to even sit down and read Scripture, that's okay. We all get knocked to our knees sometimes. God's not going to leave you on the ground. His presence isn't affected by you. He's with you whether you feel him or not. Though you may feel completely alone when you're panicking, as if the devil's foot were on your throat, you're not alone. God never leaves us simply because our strength fails or panic wins a battle. He's got the war, remember? He's already won our freedom. The greatest prison is death, and Christ cut a key for us with his resurrection.

You see, because Christ has defeated death, there's no dark apparition waiting for us at the end of a panic attack. There's no threat of utter isolation; there's no dreaded shadow. And because that's true, God can use every other instance of suffering (including anxiety and panic) for his *good* purposes. The final threats that anxiety makes inside your head *must* come to nothing. They can't come to death, because that's been destroyed by the Word of life! In light of Christ's defeat of death, God uses your panic to draw you closer to him. Like every other form of suffering, anxiety is a path to relational depth. *Your* brokenness is going to lead to *his* blessing. And the greatest blessing God can give us is his presence. When your spirit's broken by panic, take heart. As the psalmist says, "The sacrifices of God are a broken spirit; a broken and contrite heart, O God, you will not despise" (Ps. 51:17). When you're broken by anxiety, God is right there with you. He knows you're in a perfect place to rely on him. He knows that your hope for comfort is in his Son. As you continue to have dialogue with him through Scripture reading and prayer, you may sense his nearness.

"Like every other form of suffering, anxiety is a path to relational depth."

This is a good time to mention what many of us neglect or feel shy about: asking others to pray for us. Remember how I asked the 911 operator for prayer? If she would've prayed for me, I would've hung on her every word. I would've fallen upon her speech as a railing for my crippled soul, fully trusting that God would hear and act in his faithfulness. Don't be shy about asking people to pray for you. We should be asking for prayer all the time with boldness, not embarrassment. And if your brothers and sisters in Christ don't pray for you (if they agree to but walk away and never end up following through), shame on them, for prayer—speech with God—is the thudding heart of Christ's body. As it beats, it pushes hope and healing through the veins of the church. Prayer isn't well wishing or positive thinking; it's something that God commands of us (James 5:16). You shouldn't feel guilty or awkward asking for prayer. You should feel aligned with the very word of God. Leave the guilt with those who don't pray for you.

Now, before we move on to the theology for this chapter, I want to make one thing abundantly clear: while anxiety has the potential to do great harm to us and those we love (which is why we're warned about it by Jesus himself in Matt. 6:25–34), it also has the potential, a very powerful potential, to work redemptively. Satan would love for anxiety to send us into a self-made prison. But God has shown me how he really does use all things for the good of those who love him—anxiety included (Rom. 8:28).

I want to make a personal request of you. As you continue turning these pages, will you join me in taking steps that we don't want to take? I know you'll feel uncomfortable and scared (I'm right there with you), but I promise that once you take some steps forward, God will lead you to places you can't even imagine. Your relationship with him will deepen, your habits will change, and your trust will build with every concrete act of faith. In the following chapters, I want to help you start taking these steps with me by sharing more of what God has taught me through anxiety. But we have to start by resolving to take baby steps. That, after all, has always been the pattern of God's people.

Theology: The Baby Steps of God's People

God's people have a history of taking small steps forward in faith and twice as many backwards in doubt. In the previous chapter, we looked at how distrust in divine speech led to the brokenness that characterizes human history. The centrality of divine speech never leaves the center of Scripture. It's always the thing at stake. God's people are always confronted with the choice to trust or distrust that speech.

It started in Genesis 3, when the promise of salvation was whispered through the wind of judgment. God tells Eve that her seed will bruise the wicked serpent's head (Gen. 3:15). That slithering seducer, who *planted* a seed of distrust in the hearts and minds of the first humans, would himself *be crushed* by a seed. That little promise was set like a star in the sky for God's people—distant, but always burning, always giving off light. It would be their true North. And it would also set the template for God's people throughout history. As time passed, one thing remained constant: the call to trust in God's voice. With that constant call, however, came the common result: *God's people struggled to trust in his speech and commune with him because sin lead them to distrust and disobedience.*

By the time Noah left the womb and entered the world, life on this little planet was growing darker by the day. Distrust and deceit started off as black marks on the white page of God's good creation. But as time went on, more marks were made. And then more. And more. Eventually, the whole inkwell of sin tipped over. "The LORD saw that the wickedness of man was great in the earth, and that every intention of the thoughts of his heart was only evil continually" (Gen. 6:5). Yet, Noah stood out in his generation as a man who "found favor in the eyes of the LORD" (Gen. 6:8). Do you know why he found favor in the Lord's eyes? Because he developed the habit of trusting in the speech of God. After God gave him a warning of the flood and instructions for building the ark: "Noah did this; he did all that God commanded him" (Gen. 6:22). After God told him how many animals to take with him and his family on the ark: "Noah did all that the LORD commanded him" (Gen. 7:5). When God told Noah to leave the ark because it was now safe and life was again being sustained on the earth: "Noah went out, and his sons and his wife and his sons' wives with him" (Gen. 8:18). By the grace of God, Noah developed a habit of hearing and heeding the words of his maker. He kept communion with God because he trusted and obeyed God's speech.

But it didn't last. In the time of the patriarchs, Abraham is a classic example of someone with a checkered history of faith in God's speech. He sometimes exemplifies incredible faith; but at other times he falls back into the ditch of distrust. We've already looked at Genesis 12:1–3 and the incredible faith it draws out. God puts out a call to leave everything Abram knew—his country, his kindred, and his father's house—to go to a land that remains unnamed and un-located. (That would cause most of the people reading this book to have a panic attack, including the author!) God doesn't tell Abram to go to another country that he's heard of. It's not as if God was telling someone in Pennsylvania to go up to Canada. God simply tells him to go to "the land that I will show you" (12:1). Submitting to that call takes no small amount of faith! And Abram has it!! "So Abram went, as the Lord had told him." Notice the same pattern of godliness, in line with Noah's habit: Abram begins his journey of faith by trusting in the speech of his God. He also speaks back to God in prayer and worship, by building an altar and calling on the name of the Lord (12:8).

But as with Noah, Abram's faith was short-lived. As he went to sojourn in Egypt, he feared he'd be killed because his wife was so beautiful. So, rather than trusting in God's protection, which was expressed in God's promise to give Abram land and uncountable offspring, he took a page from the serpent's book and lied: "Say you are my sister, that it may go well with me because of you, and that my life may be spared for your sake" (12:13). His lie led to affliction and plagues for the Egyptians (v. 17). Distrust in divine speech never has a happy ending. And we'd be wrong to think Abram learned his lesson here, since he does the exact same thing when he comes across another threat (Gen. 20:2)! Though he's often viewed as the father of faith, Abraham was never consistent in his decision to trust in God's speech. Like Noah before him, he wandered off the beaten path of faith and fell into distrust and disobedience.

Many years later, after God's people had grown from a family to a formidable nation, we find the pattern of distrust in God's speech on a national scale. But let's start with Moses. Though Moses is, in many ways, an example of one who trusted in God's words and even communed with him "face to face" (Exod. 33:11), he also had a spotty record of faith. His distrust in his own God-given calling to lead Israel is almost humorous (Exod. 3:10–4:17), and he eventually pleads with God to choose someone else to lead the people out of Egypt. When he finally takes up the call, he has a respectable pattern of following God's words to the letter, but he does have a moment of disobedience that ends up taking from him what he wanted most (Num. 20).

The people of Israel, however, were far worse. Their story is a narrative of complaint. From the moment they left the land of their oppressors, they quibbled and bickered and doubted and groaned. All throughout the books of Exodus, Numbers, and Deuteronomy, they lifted up their voices in distrust and set their hands to disobedience. Even when they vowed to take God at his word, Moses saw right through them (Deut. 30:18). Before the conquest of Canaan, Moses reminded the people of the one thing they always needed to do: love their God and *obey his voice* (Deut. 30:20). Trusting in the speech of God—that was to be the watermark of their lives. But it never really showed up on the page. They distrusted and disobeyed God's word with laughable predictability, even in the midst of God's guidance throughout the conquest of Canaan. And then they entered a cycle of sin, oppression, and deliverance in the time of the Judges.

We could go on. The book of Judges presents a patchwork of leaders who fall into this pattern of distrusting and disobeying. Though there are times of hope and prosperity in the reigns of the kings, most of the time we find a lamentable example of distrust and disobedience. Even the highest king in Israel's history, King David, fell into adultery and murder—not the sort of qualities you look for in a king. And the prophets are woven through the history of the monarchies as little echoes of God's voice. Oftentimes they began their communication with "Thus says the LORD." In every instance, they are bringing God's voice back into the drama of Israel's history. Through them, the speech of God goes ringing in the ears of kings and in the hearts of the people, but they distrust and disobey—just as Adam and Eve did, just as Noah did, just as Abraham did, just as the judges did. The children's song "Trust and Obey" has far deeper theology than we realize. It strikes at the core of God's people.

By the end of the Old Testament, we find that no matter how hard they try, *God's people struggle to trust in his speech and commune with him because sin leads them to distrust and disobedience.* If something is going to change this, it's going to have to be something that God himself does. God, in other words, is going to have to restore trust and communion with his people. For there to be any hope, God will have to utter a Word that shatters all of our distrust, a Word that eternally establishes a path to communion with him by faith. And that, my friends, is exactly what God does. We'll get to that in the next chapter.

Reflection Questions and Prayer

1. What are some steps in your own life right now that anxiety is keeping you from taking? How do you feel when you think about taking those steps? Make a list and write down your thoughts.

2. Describe a time in which you stepped into a foreign country, like Abraham, and God was faithful to you in the midst of your anxiety. How might you use this experience to take another step in the near future? (Just think of one step, even a small one.)

3. Now describe a time when you lost control and gave in to panic. How did you feel and what ended up happening? How might you use even that failed step to try again? Remember that you will probably *feel* very anxious taking that step, but God is present with you regardless of your feelings. Recite his promise in Matt. 28:20 as you encounter the feelings.

4. Why do you think people throughout Scripture struggled to trust in God's word?

5. In Scripture, there's a clear relationship between *distrust* and *disobedience*. How has this truth been realized in your own life?

6. Do you get frustrated with your lack of trust in God's word? If so, how do you respond? What do you think is the biblical way to respond?

7. Often, we distrust God's words because we have a sinful desire to trust words that promise us something we want. What is something that you want right now? Will you get it by trusting God's words?

8. If you're struggling with a rough patch of anxiety, you might be tempted to trust the words of your doctor, in the form of medical advice, which is perfectly normal and acceptable. But how does that advice align with God's words in Proverbs 16:24? (Note: There may not be disagreement here, but have you factored in the grace-giving effect of God's words in the treatment of your body?)

Prayer

God, I am not enthusiastic about change.

I do not look for opportunities to grow.

But I want to trust you.

I want relationship.

When I see something that brings me anxiety,

When the feelings rise up in me,

Call me to trust.

Call me to relationship.

Call me to yourself

So that I might grow in faith

And do with boldness the things

That I do not want to do.

Help me to put every ounce of my faith

Into your words

And step out upon the waves

That you govern with your speech.

I know, Lord, I am part of a people

Slow to trust the only words worth trusting.

And that's lead to disobedience in a host of ways.

Our sin brings us to a foreign country of greed,

Where the speech of love and grace is a strange dialect.

But the only true speech *is* of love and grace,

Given by you, our Father, through the Son, in the power of the Spirit.

Give us the ears to hear it.

Today, break through the icy shell of our disregard.

Grip our souls with holy language.

Draw us out of our caves,

Into light that first burns,

Then warms, and then illumines.

Bring us to the feet of your Word incarnate

And help us to listen . . . just listen.

We want to grow closer and closer to you.

May your Spirit work in us like a magnet,

Pulling us to the weight for the whole world:

You.

Reader Resource: Planning Your Steps

If you don't have a plan, you won't make progress. It's just that simple. In the last chapter, we talked about taking baby steps. I want you to write down three baby steps that you're going to work towards. The first one should be simple and achievable, an easy step. The second should be more difficult, a challenging step. But with the third one, I want you to dream—write down something you can't imagine yourself doing. I'm doing this with you, so you can see my answers below. As we move through the book, think about what you can do to move closer toward taking one of these steps. I'll be thinking with you.

Planning Steps	Easy Step	*Doing something unplanned on a family outing*
	Challenging Step	*Giving a presentation in front of a large group of people*
	Dream Step	*Flying on a plane*

CHAPTER 4

Clinging to Christ

KEY IDEA: We can use the CHRIST acronym to take steps of faith.

I n the last chapter, we approached baby steps of faith in the midst of anxiety. These are steps we are often afraid to take—terrified, if we're honest—but God calls us out of the comfortable and familiar to trust in his voice. The current chapter offers you a powerful tool that you can pull out as you take those steps of faith. I'm really excited to put this tool in your hands, since it's taken me years to develop with God's help! In some ways, this chapter is the heart of the book; it offers a bridge you can cross continually—monthly, weekly, daily, even *hourly*—in the midst of anxiety so that you can watch God use that anxiety to do great things in your soul, shaping you to the image of his suffering Son who was raised in glory. So, read slowly. Meditate on the Scripture. Ask questions in the margins. Camp out here as long as you need to. It's taken me years to learn these things, and I'm still learning them. Let's get to it.

I've talked a lot about how anxiety was for me. I was crushed to be called (as you are). God brought me down to the dust through anxiety. I lost almost everything: self-confidence, pride, distractions, aspirations, body weight. I was lying low when I first was hit with anxiety. And from there, from my knees, I developed patterns of behavior that imprisoned me: a constant reliance on safe zones and medication, areas of comfort. Once I developed those imprisoning patterns, it was very hard to break free of them. But the Spirit of the living God can break our imprisoning patterns with a word—and always *through* the words of Scripture. The Bible gave me a linear life, a rope to clutch as I began taking baby steps of faith out into a foreign and terrifying world. With each step, with every grasp of the rope, God was building the muscles of my faith. They had atrophied so very much because I wasn't using them. I was stagnant, settled into a life that didn't challenge me or ask me to take any Abram-steps of faith. As God built these muscles one concrete step at a time, he called me to trust in his speech, and to trust in his Son. This would take years (and it's still happening as I type these words), but over time, moment by moment, God was granting me the trust that I needed in his Son, handed to my heart by God's own Spirit. Over the years, I developed an acronym that guided my soul through a lot of dark times. That's the acronym we're going to unpack in this chapter. And it should be easy for you to remember: CHRIST.

This is something I think you might use for the rest of your life, since anxiety comes and goes. For me, sometimes the anxiety-wracked recluse who got walked by his own dog is buried deep in the past. Other times he's my shadow, almost back in the present. This is especially the case whenever I'm asked to do something outside of my comfort zone, something that I have no experience with. But since I've had to do that countless times, I've grown accustomed to keeping this acronym in my back pocket, pulling it out whenever I feel threatened and spread thin by the feelings of anxiety. The more you use it, the more you'll learn about the strength of your faith, your trust in God's speech. In that sense, it's like a litmus test for trust.

CHRIST

Here's the whole thing up front. I'll spend some words unwrapping each step, exploring the biblical roots and offering some examples to help you implement them. As we work through the rest of the book, we'll draw on what we've found here and apply it to other stages and dimensions of anxiety.

Consider the feelings.

He knows.

Remember the promise.

Identify a focus.

Stay engaged.

Talk.

These steps are meant to be followed in order, but I've found that I don't always have to start at the beginning. I might start in the middle or keep repeating the same step until I feel more settled.

Now, before jumping into the explanation and biblical backing for each step, remember what the point of our anxiety is. Our anxiety is a tool in the hands of a grand physician who knows our name, who knows where we are right now. God has all of our experiences in mind all the time. So, we can be sure he will use our experiences with anxiety to whittle away at our soul and shape us to the image of his Son. Using this acronym, in other words, helps us fixate on the divine *purpose* for anxiety. Our goal, remember, is not to get rid of anxiety; it's to *use* it and learn how God is shaping us through it. Whenever you experience a swell of anxiety, ask the following question prayerfully of your heavenly Father: *What are you teaching me?* In my experience, God is always faithful in answering that question—maybe not right at the moment, but if you ask it and seek out the answer, especially in reliance upon Scripture, you'll find it. And just asking the question will build your relationship with him! Now, let's get to the first letter.

C - Consider the Feelings

You know the feelings I'm talking about: dry mouth, pinhole throat, difficulty swallowing, surges of heat, rapid heartbeat, shallow breath, tingling limbs and fingers, a sense of feeling removed from reality (de-realization or disassociation). These feelings, which seem like death-threats to our sensory system, are not actually death threats. As many others have noted, these feelings are your body's response to *potential* threats, fight-or-flight instincts. But I don't want you to think of them as merely physical. When we do that, we ignore the spiritual purposes God has for our anxiety. So, when I say, "Consider the feelings," I really mean *consider the feelings as spiritual medicine*. The feelings, in other words, have to be interpreted in a context, just like everything else we experience. At the end of each chapter, we've been unfolding the Great Story of Scripture to get a sense of that context. We've looked at who God is, who we are, what went wrong, and what remains central in our redemption (trust in the speech of God). Later in this chapter, we'll look at what happened when the eternal speech of God, the Word, became incarnate. But for now, can you see how all of these things are helping us construct a context to interpret our experience, especially the experience of anxiety? We are building a framework, and the cornerstone of that framework is a simple truth: *God's primary purpose is calling us into a trusting relationship with himself, and he can use our anxiety to do that.* Bolt that truth to the floor of your mind. All of our suffering—anxiety included—has a spiritual purpose: to draw us into the sufferings of Christ so that we can experience his resurrection power. Sound strange? It won't in a few paragraphs.

> ## "God's primary purpose is calling us into a trusting relationship with himself, and he can use our anxiety to do that."

Let me make this first step—*consider the feelings as spiritual medicine*—more vivid for you. You know that nasty, tar-tasting red gel we call "cough medicine"? The stuff you drink while blocking your nostrils so the taste gets dulled? It's horrible. No one likes it. But everyone likes the *effect* that it has on their cough. Think of your anxious feelings that way; they're *spiritual medicine*. You don't like them. I don't like them. We'd rather pinch our nose, swallow them, and move on to comfort. But they have a purpose. They are going to affect us in powerful ways if we let them—more accurately, if we let *God* use them and work through them rather than seeking the most immediate means of eliminating them.

What's the effect these feelings are going to have? Remember Hemming-way's quote about war that I mentioned earlier? "War burns the fat off our souls." It's similar with anxiety. After all, anxiety is like a war in its own sense, isn't it? Don't you get tired from constantly being in the trenches—the raised shoulders and never-ending hypervigilance, the over-played scenarios of panic, the way all of life can seem like something to survive rather than enjoy? It's exhausting. *War* is exhausting. In the war with anxiety, we are crushed and reduced. But, analogous to physical war, our war with anxiety burns the fat off our souls. It burns away the dross of sin, in all of its ugly manifestations: self-centeredness, pride, materialism, envy, lust, discontentment. These things start to burn away as the flame of anxiety grows. Our widespread vision during times of comfort becomes tunnel vision during times of anxiety. We focus on what matters most: a constant and thriving relationship with the God of peace. In this sense, the feelings of anxiety have a purifying effect.

It's true, they also make us feel extremely weak. But that, also, is part of our spiritual medicine. The Apostle Paul famously pleaded with God to remove his "thorn in the flesh"—some form of suffering in his life. What was God's response? Slow down and chew on these words: "My grace is sufficient for you, for my power is made perfect in weakness" (2 Cor. 12:9). *Power* through weakness. God's power—*the greatest power there is*—comes to perfection in our *weakness*.

Now, how does Paul respond to God? He responds with what seems paradoxical to everyone who doesn't know the Great Story of Scripture: "Therefore I will boast all the more gladly of my weaknesses, so that the power of Christ may rest upon me. For the sake of Christ, then, I am content with weaknesses, insults, hardships, persecutions, and calamities. For when I am weak, then I am strong" (2 Cor. 12:9–10). *When I am weak, then I am strong.* Get some rope from your memory right now and bind those words to the truth you bolted down earlier. Tie the knot so tight that you won't ever be able to untie it. This little truth is so counterintuitive and yet so massively important that we simply can't afford to let go of it! Your weakness, my weakness, that is our *strength*. While the rest of the world loses hope, while their joy wanes at suffering and pain, our hope and joy *grows*. It grows because we know the effect. The divine strength and power of the God who raises from the dead is expanding. It's expanding so much that it's covering our weakness and pointing everyone who's watching to the God who triumphed over every evil by going *through* weakness *to* strength, *through* the cross *to* the throne, *through* suffering *to* sovereignty.

My dear reader, our feelings of anxiety are painful and distressing. They draw us down to weakness. But that is precisely what is *supposed* to happen to people following the path of their crucified and risen Savior. We go down into weakness so that God's strength and life can be manifested in us. That's Paul's message.

The point of spiritual medicine, then, is to shape us through weakness. As I said in the previous chapter, the point of our weakness is to soften us with water so that God's hands can shape us to the image of his Son—but that Son went *through* weakness to get to glory, *through* weakness to get to strength. We follow him.

In other words, spiritual medicine (which can come in the form of our anxious feelings) goes down bitter and draws us into weakness, but it raises up God's power in that weakness. Our weakness is the arena for God's strength. You and I have to fight, tooth and nail, to take feelings that seem overwhelmingly negative and interpret them as positive. That's the paradox we hold: to stare our harrowing feelings in the face and say, "Yes. Welcome. Come in and weaken me. Reduce me. . . . because you can only make me *stronger* in Christ."

That's where we start: *consider the feelings as spiritual medicine.* Welcome the weakness, for in doing this you are welcoming strength, which comes at the end of the path of Christ. But even before the end, God gives us little tastes of it, moments of strength amidst swells of anxiety.

H - He Knows

Considering the feelings as spiritual medicine is a great first step. It grounds us in the spiritual truth of what we're experiencing. Our feelings are not mere physical manifestations of a broken body. Remember, it's not a matter of getting rid of symptoms; it's a matter of using them to get closer to God, of being shaped by him. The shaping can hurt. We'll squirm and turn away. We'll look for an exit. But we need to *stay*, just as our savior stayed on the path of suffering, just as he stayed among crowds that slung insults at him, just as he stayed when spit upon by strangers, just as he stayed when a crown of thorns was crushed into his skin, just as he stayed on a splintered cross. He stayed. We stay.

But staying can be lonely and terrifying. Feelings don't disappear just because we decide to stay. We need power from God to stay. We need power in communion with him. And we have that communion and power through Christ, by the Spirit. That's where the second directive comes into play: *He knows.*

One of the most relieving moments I had in my early dealings with anxiety was reading a vivid description from an anxiety workbook. It described exactly how it felt to battle panic—the heat swells, the shallow breath, the rising heart rate, the hyper-vigilance, the sense that I was somehow slightly removed from my body and seemed to be looking at myself from a few inches above. (I've since learned that the latter phenomenon is referred to as *de-realization* or *disassociation*, the sense of being withdrawn or removed from reality). Reading that description was such a relief to me because for the first time I felt as if I wasn't crazy. I wasn't an isolated head-case. I wasn't *alone*.

Feeling alone and isolated is one of the most disconcerting experiences we can have as humans. Why? Because we were made for *communion*. We were made as *with-creatures*. Adam was made to be *with* God and *with* Eve. You and I are made to be *with* God and *with* others. Buried in our blood is not a desire for communion, but a *need* for it. Without communion, our souls shrivel up and lie still like fish out of water.

This is precisely why Hebrews 4:15–16 is such an important passage for anxiety-ridden humans. "For we do not have a high priest who is unable to sympathize with our weaknesses, but one who in every respect has been tempted as we are, yet without sin. Let us then with confidence draw near to the throne of grace, that we may receive mercy and find grace to help in time of need." We gloss over the word *sympathize*, but it has epic implications. The Son of God *sympathizes* with us in our weakness. He knows our suffering. He knows how it feels. He knows what we long for. He knows what we need. *He knows.*

> ## "Feeling alone and isolated is one of the most disconcerting experiences we can have as humans. Why? Because we were made for communion."

Often it's at this point that our faith fails. "Does he *really* know? Does a dead and raised Nazarene from a two-thousand-year-old Mediterranean world really know how anxious I feel when I'm driving down the Pennsylvania Turnpike each morning?" Yes, dear reader. He really does. Christ is God, and God is all-knowing. He doesn't just know facts and math equations and the climate patterns of Africa. He knows how your neighbor feels as she's caring for her mother with Alzheimer's. He knows how tired your garbage man is when he picks up your weekly trash. He knows why that girl that's always waiting for a bus on the outskirts of town has a scar over her left eye. He knows your every thought, your every movement, your every fear. He knows.

Why is that such an encouragement? Because it's a direct answer to the most powerful question we ask in our suffering: *Am I alone?* Because of what God has done through Christ in the power of the Spirit, the answer to that question is *always* "No!" A friend and teacher once wrote, "Hardships give us good reasons to be anxious, so God gives better reasons to trust him."[1] The greatest reason God has given us to trust him is not a proposition; it's a *person*. It's Christ. Christ knows what you're feeling, what you're thinking, what you're doubting and dreaming and lamenting. He's been there. He's lived a suffering life. And lest you think that Jesus hasn't experienced your particular difficulties, Jesus Christ was crystal clear about *both* his humanity *and* divinity, Son of man *and* Son of God. Because he's God, his

---

1   David Powlison, *God's Grace in Your Suffering* (Wheaton, IL: Crossway, 2018), 49.

knowledge has no boundaries. He knows the past, present, and future. He knows every word your mother ever spoke, or thought about speaking. He knows how many hairs are on your father's head. He knows the one-thousandth thought of your great, great grandfather. He knows the temperature of the ocean just off the coast of New Jersey and just off the coast of California. He knows *all*. You and I are always in the company of the God who knows.[2] This is the God who's reached out to us in the person of Christ, "who in every respect has been tempted as we are, yet without sin."

And it's not just that Christ is with you or next to you. Christ is *in* you, in your heart of hearts. In fact, the entire Godhead is *in* you. Jesus told his disciples in John 14:23, "If anyone loves me, he will keep my word, and my Father will love him, and we will come to him and make our home with him." And when Paul is writing to the Corinthians, he asks them a wonderful question: "Do you not know that you are God's temple and that God's Spirit dwells in you?" The Father, Son, and Holy Spirit are not simply *with* us; they are *in* us. God is that close, even when we can't feel God's presence. Feelings are no match for the finality of God's promise.

You and I can take great comfort in that! When the waves of anxiety are crashing over us, when the white-water seems to be choking out our life and breath, we are not alone. We are *with* the God who knows. We suffer *with* Christ, not apart from him, because he knows.

We can take great comfort in this . . . *unless* we don't believe it. If you don't believe it, then I want you to stop reading right now. There's something far more important that you need to do: pray. Pray that your heart would truly fall into the promise of God's presence. Pray that God would help your unbelief (Mark 9:24). Pray that your feelings would flee and that your heart would grasp the dense and heavy truth: God. Is. With. You.

We need reminders of this all the time, especially when we struggle. So, don't be ashamed to pray the Mark 9:24 prayer over and over again. We never outgrow our need for God's presence, or, sadly, our proclivity to ignore it.

R - Remember the Promise

After we've considered our feelings as spiritual medicine and meditated on the fact that Christ knows exactly what we're going through, we move on to remember a promise. Which promise? God has made many promises in Scripture, and he holds true on all of them. For every promise in Scripture, the Father says, "I will," the

---

2   For more on this, see my ebook, *In Divine Company: Growing Closer to the God Who Speaks* (2018).

Son says, "Yes and amen," and the Spirit says, "Open your hands." But perhaps the greatest promise is the one that we haven't seen fulfilled yet. It's the one we won't see fulfilled until the moment after our death. It's God's promise that we will be *with* him in paradise. In other words, it's the promise that God will take us safely where we most long to be.

Think of Jesus at the end of his life and ministry—skin torn, ligaments stretched, blood flowing, hands pierced. Sore, exhausted, and spent, he turned to a criminal one cross down who mumbled a request swollen with hope and desperation: "Jesus, remember me when you come into your kingdom" (Luke 23:42). Jesus answered with the greatest promise we could hope to have fulfilled: "Truly, I say to you, today you will be with me in paradise" (v. 43).

Jesus makes the same promise to all those who believe in him (John 3:15; 5:24). He makes that promise to *you*. He makes it to *me*. One day we *will* be with him in paradise. We *will*.

That great promise has a ripple effect on all of the other little promises and hopes we have each day. Those of us who struggle with anxiety are *what if* experts. What if I stop breathing on my way to work? What if the plane runs into a thermal and nose dives? What if I open my mouth to give a presentation and become paralyzed with fear? What if I have a panic attack while I'm on the highway and swerve my car into the concrete barrier? What if my throat closes up? What if my anxiety gets so bad that I can't get out of bed in the morning? What if . . .

Do you know what I've realized? All of these little *what ifs* are under the sway of the ultimate *what if*. What if I die? And that, my friends, is a *what if* with a clear answer. You *will*. And so will I. But Christ has already given us an answer to that *what if*. It's the same answer he gave to the thief on the cross next to him: "Today, you will be with me in paradise." God, you see, has already decided to take you where you most want to go: in his presence.

I used to carry around a little piece of computer paper with a tiny list of things to remember when I was dealing with a rough patch of anxiety. It was laminated with Scotch tape and fit nicely into a mini Bible I carried around in my pocket. One of the items on that list was this: "God has already decided to take you safely where you need to go." When you're dealing with anxiety, you feel out-of-control and helpless. You're utterly convinced that someone else is driving your life. And you're right! God is the one who is in control of everything. You're not in the driver's seat. You never were. But the wonderful thing about not being in control of your own life is that the one who has the greatest love for you and has made the greatest promises to you—that one *is* in control. And he's already decided to bring you safely to his side for eternity. That's your destination. That's my destination. It's fixed and final. It's written. Take a deep breath. Smile. Your ultimate *what if* goes silent before the divine company you're promised.

"All of the little what ifs we ask eventually hit the wall of God's final promise."

All of the little *what ifs* we ask eventually hit the wall of God's final promise. Our fears flail their arms and run crazily towards the darkness of abandoned hope. But they hit a wall, a hard wall. They eventually smack right into the brick barricade of God's great promise. And so they lose their power. They fall away—not without a fight, I know. But they *do* fall away. No matter how loudly your anxiety screams, God's voice will thunder it into silence. And in that painful process, he'll draw you closer to his sound, the beautiful chords of his enduring presence.

So, remember the promise. Always. Rehearse it. Restate it. Recite it. God has already promised to take you where you most want to go.

I - Identify a Focus

Now, we still live in this world, so while meditating on the great promise is a necessity, we also need to find a way to cope with the immediate. Anxiety, I've learned, requires our *attention*. That may not sound very profound, but hear me out. If you divert your attention to something else, anxiety begins to lose its power. It's like a parasite that requires oxygen to sustain itself. The oxygen is our attention, our focus. Take away the oxygen, and you take away the power source of anxiety.

I recently read an article about how doctors are experimenting with distraction as a means of pain management for patients with serious wounds—burn victims and amputees. The study showed how patients that were given a painful medical treatment (such as a skin graft) while playing a simple video game were less aware of and affected by the pain of the treatment. Why? Because their minds where directed elsewhere.

Your mind can't be everywhere at once. It can't be on your anxiety *and* on another task with the same degree of attention. If you divert your focus from anxiety to a concrete task in front of you, it begins to subside, or at least loses some of its potency.

But before we establish a concrete focus, we need to remember what our broader, background focus needs to be throughout every hardship we encounter, anxiety included. That focus is God himself. Throughout Scripture, God calls people in affliction to focus on him. Psalm 46 is a brilliant reminder of this. When trouble comes, we gaze at God, our refuge and our conquering King.

> [1] God is our refuge and strength,
>> a very present help in trouble.
> [2] Therefore we will not fear though the earth gives way,
>> though the mountains be moved into the heart of the sea,
> [3] though its waters roar and foam,
>> though the mountains tremble at its swelling. Selah
>
> [4] There is a river whose streams make glad the city of God,
>> the holy habitation of the Most High.
> [5] God is in the midst of her; she shall not be moved;
>> God will help her when morning dawns.
> [6] The nations rage, the kingdoms totter;
>> he utters his voice, the earth melts.
> [7] The Lord of hosts is with us;
>> the God of Jacob is our fortress. Selah
>
> [8] Come, behold the works of the Lord,
>> how he has brought desolations on the earth.
> [9] He makes wars cease to the end of the earth;
>> he breaks the bow and shatters the spear;
>> he burns the chariots with fire.
> [10] "Be still, and know that I am God.
>> I will be exalted among the nations,
>> I will be exalted in the earth!"
> [11] The Lord of hosts is with us;

the God of Jacob is our fortress.

God controls all. We start there. Notice how the psalmist moves from a focus on God as the all-controlling refuge for his people (v. 1), and then stands on that truth as the ground for security when everything else seems chaotic (vv. 2–3). *Therefore* and *though* are like signposts marking failed threats to our security. A crumbling world, sea-sunken mountains, waters roaring like a thousand lions—these cannot assault our refuge.

Verses 4–5 glorify the God who dwells in the city of his people. But this is a foreshadowing of what Christ brings in the New Testament. We noted earlier that God will inhabit not just cities, but selves. He inhabits persons, through Christ and by the power of his own life-giving Spirit. Every Christian can utter verse 5 with the utmost confidence: "God is in the midst of *me*; I shall not be moved. God will help *me* when morning dawns."

Verses 6–7 draw us to the voice of the speaking God—its power over the peoples of the earth, and the surety we have of protection *because of God's presence*.

Verses 8–9 keep our focus on God and his work in the world—ending wars, breaking bows, shattering spears, charring chariots. This is God the great warrior.

And then we hit verse 10. This is where God breaches the page with an infinitive. He comes right out to us and speaks squarely to the soul: "Be still, and know that I am God." How hard those words are to follow in a swell of anxiety! "Still?! How can we be still when adrenaline courses through our veins, when our feet tap wildly, when our shoulders rise up, when it takes effort just to breathe?" God gives us the answer in a repeated promise: "I will be exalted among the nations, I will be exalted in the earth!" This is a reminder for us in our weariness and weakness, in our desperation and despair: *The King of the universe, who knows everything we're experiencing, is still on his throne.* He's never left it. He's never going to leave it. Every measure and moment of trouble we have is fodder for the glory of God, who *will* be exalted. And you and I will be at endless peace as we exalt him . . . one day. When anxiety churns within us, stirring up feelings of chaos, we remember this—God's promise of exaltation and rule. And then we go back to verse 11, where the psalm began: "The Lord of hosts is with us; the God of Jacob is our fortress." We begin with a focus on God as our refuge. We end with a focus on God as our refuge. Our primary focus throughout every earthly trauma and travesty is God himself, the God who is with us.

That's our background focus. Yet, when we're in the midst of anxiety, don't we need something a bit more concrete to focus on—something to touch or hear or taste? It's true in my own experience that we need something tangible to focus on during a swell of anxiety. We need to identify a focus in our immediate environment. But there has to be a greater background focus for us when our mind begins to pull us away from that focus (and it will; trust me). That greater focus is God himself, and it will take hours, months, and years of practice for that to become our default (that may be tough to hear, but it's the truth). So, don't feel discouraged if you find it very hard to keep your attention on God in the midst of your anxiety. This is a lifelong effort for us. But we have to keep striving for it, and the Spirit of God himself will do all that we need to complete this work in us as we prayerfully ask him to (Phil. 1:6).

Now, having said that, God has given us the gift of a concrete world, a world that everywhere reveals him.[3] And the broader focus of God frees us up to focus on this world. Remember, the point of this focus on something concrete is to divert our attention—to evaporate the life source of anxiety. There's no shortage of examples here, so I'll offer just a few to give you a sense of your options.

Example one: license plate scrabble. When I'm confronted with anxiety while driving, I often revert to looking at license plates. This is efficient, since they're right in front of me. I start by trying to form as many words as I can with the letters. And if no words can be formed, then I start getting creative with possible acronyms I could make. This can be (and usually is) humorous. And humor is a great distraction from anxiety. HBX? Healing by Xylophones. GBH? Gathering of Blue Herrings. TSC? Total Subjection to Coffee. The possibilities are endless.

Example two: staring at an object or landscape. If you're driving, you can focus all of your attention on the landscape around you—no thinking, no analyzing, just staring. Be an immersed observer. Take it all in. The longer you keep your mouth closed and your eyes fixed, the easier it will become to get lost in your surroundings, and that's a good thing. Sometimes I focus on the dotted lines in the middle of the road. You can even start counting them, or counting the potholes that could give your car a flat tire. If you're not driving, pick an object in the environment and start studying it. Right now, I'm looking at one of our deck boards. I can see the grain of the wood flowing out from a knot like ripples of water. I count the layers of the grain until the next knot: 11. I count how many can fit on the 6-inch width: 13. I look at how the board sits in relation to the other boards: it's slightly shorter, and doesn't curve up at the end as the other boards, which are warped by the sun and the rain. Gather

---

3   For examples, see my book *Finding God in the Ordinary* (Eugene, OR: Wipf & Stock, 2018).

as many details as you can. When you run out, move to another object. Remember, the goal is to pour your attention into something *other* than the feelings of anxiety that are troubling you. God has instilled a ridiculous amount of detail in his world. That detail is one of his countless gifts to you. Open each one . . . slowly. Enjoy the concrete gift of creation right in front of you.

"Enjoy the concrete gift of creation right in front of you."

Example three: a rubbing stone. Someone once gave me a smooth stone that fits perfectly into the impression of your thumb. During anxiety, you can rub your thumb up and down on the stone, letting the texture distract you. If you need more distraction, start counting how many times you can rub the stone in one sitting, or how many times you can rub the stone on your walk to the car.

Again, there's no shortage of examples. We live in a concrete world, and God will help you use that to divert your attention. As a bonus, you'll come to a deeper appreciation of the world around you because you'll be more engaged with it. This is especially helpful for dealing with the sensation referred to as *derealization*, the sense that you're a few inches removed from your body and are hyper-aware of every little action your sensory system is taking.

With practice, you can begin to learn about the nature of God from your surroundings. My book *Finding God in the Ordinary* is largely an exercise in this. Because God reveals himself everywhere in the world around us (Rom. 1:20; Ps. 19:1–4), we can train our minds with Scripture to see his reflection wherever we look. Note this latter point: you can't go drawing conclusions about the nature of God without listening first to what he's said about himself in Scripture. The Great Story of Scripture gives us the interpretation for the little stories of our lives.

In sum, within the broader focus of God himself (his final exaltation, his complete control over your present circumstances), we can focus on something particular in our environment to draw our attention away from anxiety.

We've now gone through four letters: C, H, R, and I. Two more.

S - Stay Engaged

With anxiety, you quickly find that your attention span is much shorter than you thought. Your mind flits and flutters like a crazed bird in barn rafters, never wanting to set its feet down for more than a moment. It's one thing to identify a focus; it's something else entirely to *stay engaged* with that focus.

I experienced this in epic proportions when I first dealt with anxiety. And I turned to something that tied my mind down and made me walk on a linear path: reading. I mentioned this in an earlier chapter. Reading is a linear activity. It trains your mind to move in a fixed course and helps you stay engaged by requiring you to deduce meaning from words without interruption. The same principle, of course, applies to anything that you read, but I recommend Scripture first because those words are the very words of God himself. Commit to following the words where they lead you: left to right, top to bottom. Let the voice of God be your constant light in the threatening darkness of anxiety. Don't take your eyes off it.

Another engaging activity is exercise, which we'll talk more about in another chapter. Running is my preference. Again, it's the linear, repeated process that helps us stay engaged—foot after foot, arm swing after arm swing, breath after breath. As the heart rate increases naturally, your focus is drawn to your body and movement—in a good way. The regularity and physical exertion help your mind to stay focused on the present, the immediate. That's what you need, since one of the strongest moves of anxiety is to remove you (mentally) from your surroundings. Anxiety can easily make you feel isolated and lost, but gripping something tangible in the world around you helps you to feel integrated and found again.

At the very least, staying engaged can keep your mind distracted. One person I spoke with recalled how he dealt with a lot of anxiety when his wife and kids were traveling without him. He was struck by the anxiety that came along with the simple truth of knowing he was not with them to protect them and keep them safe. What did he do? He kept himself busy. He focused on the work he could do at home. He tied his attention to the present. And after a while, the knots on those ropes continued to hold. Staying engaged with something else meant that he couldn't stay engaged with his anxious thoughts. Our attention can't be everywhere at once.

If you're not reading or exercising or keeping yourself busy with housework, then you'll have to resolve to keep going back to your focus in some other way. And make no mistake: it's *exhausting*. There's no way around it: dealing with anxiety all the time makes you fatigued. I'm always amazed at how tired I am after I've dealt with a swell of anxiety on a given day. It taxes your mind and your body. That's why rest is also critical. Again, we'll talk more about that in another chapter.

T - Talk

The last letter in our acronym goes back to the nature of God and to our identity in the Great Story of Scripture. God is a self-communing being who speaks with himself in three persons. We are image-bearing creatures who speak to him and to others. Language is not merely part of our identity; it's the heart of it.[4] That's why my last directive is simply to *talk*.

There's something about vibrating your vocal cords that brings a steady calm. Even humming can have this effect. I believe the ultimate reason for this is that speech is what we were made to do. We start with God (prayer), and then move to others.

The priority of prayer deserves an entire chapter in its own right. For now, I'll just say that talking to God isn't an option for anxiety-ridden image-bearers; it's a necessity. Remember that anxiety is something that God has used to *crush* you. But that crushing isn't meant for your destruction. It's meant for your development. Anxiety is a strong testament to what God is doing throughout your entire life: Son-shaping. As David Powlison put it, "Your entire life is a holy experiment as God's hands shape you into the image of his Son."[5] That shaping can be painful. But just as it was for the thief on the cross next to Jesus, it's preparing you for paradise, for the fulfillment of God's greatest promise: his eternal presence.

"God isn't a concept there to make you feel comfortable. He's the all-controlling speaker who's in charge of where your life is going."

God permits anxiety to crush us, but he also provides prayer to pick us up. Talk to God. And don't say what you think you *should* say. Pray as the psalmists; pour

---

4   I unpack this more fully in *The Speaking Trinity & His Worded World: Why Language Is at the Center of Everything* (Eugene, OR: Wipf & Stock, 2018).

5   Powlison, *God's Grace in Your Suffering*, 83.

out your terrors at his footstool. "O Lord, how many are my foes!" (Ps. 3:1). "Answer me when I call, O God of my righteousness!" (Ps. 4:1). "Give ear to my words, O Lord; consider my groaning" (Ps. 5:1). Groan before God. Be honest *and* humble. Speak your fears and feelings into the open air. Doing this is one of the most powerful ways to stop treating God as an idea and to start treating him as a divine, communicating *person*. God isn't a concept there to make you feel comfortable. He's the all-controlling speaker who's in charge of where your life is going. And he loves to commune with you. So, speak.

Prayer is certainly our priority when it comes to talking, but then we can transition to talking with others. This does a lot to remove the focus we have on ourselves. I'll give you an example.

Since I've dealt with anxiety, I've never been too keen on driving at night. I always have to get over a sense that the darkness is somehow threatening or isolating. But one evening we were making the drive with our kids up to the family lake house. There was no getting around the nighttime driving. And as we settled into the long haul up the Pennsylvania Turnpike, I started to feel my shoulders rise. I became more conscious of my breathing and swallowing, and the rest of my little quirky anxiety symptoms started showing up. It was nothing surprising. But I knew about CHRIST by this point, and I decided to jump right to the "T." I turned to my wife and asked with genuine interest, "How have things been going for your website?[6] And then as she answered, I focused on her. I listened to her words closely. I asked follow-up questions. I offered encouragement and showed my enthusiasm for the great things that God was doing through her work. I wasn't waiting for my turn to speak. I was listening—pure and simple.

In all of this, there was a wonderful side-effect. Not only was I learning more about the woman I love and showing sincere interest in her daily life; I was also removing the focus from myself: how I was feeling, what I was thinking, where I would feel more comfortable at the moment. Talking to Christina was a blessing to *her* and an impediment to *my* anxiety! And the more I did this, the more I realized that speech is our God-given ability to shift self-focus to others-focus. The gift of *talk* is the gift of *otherness*. And when you're dealing with anxiety, you're extremely *self-focused*. You need that otherness to pull you away from yourself, to bring your attention to another.

---

6   My wife has a DIY website that she pours her heart and soul into. You can check out her work here: https://christinamariablog.com/.

So, now you know the acronym that's helped me through countless anxiety swells. I'll reflect more on it in the chapters ahead, but feel free to start using it. Make it personal and practical. Bring it to life in the context of your own circumstances. And watch God work! You can also share your experiences on the Facebook group I've created for this book.[7] Connect with other strugglers and share your insights.

Theology: The Word in the World

In the previous chapter, we ended by noting that if something was going to change for God's people, who were constantly distrusting and disobeying his words (just as we do today), that change would have to come from God himself. And it did—in fact, it *was* God himself.

If distrust in and disobedience of God's speech is what broke the world and brought us to ruin, then trust and obedience would seem to be the solution. But if we had a problem with hearing and following God's words, what could God possibly do to deliver us? Speak again?

Well, yes, but in a profoundly different way—in a way no one could have imagined. On a starry night, in a sleepy stable, God did speak again. But he spoke *himself.* The eternal Son of God, whom the Apostle John later tells us is *the Word* of the Father (John 1:1), was uttered into flesh. The Word of eternity was spoken in time. God spoke himself on our behalf. Jesus Christ, the greatest Word the world has ever heard, trusted in the speech of his heavenly Father, from his inception to his crucifixion, from the cradle to the cross. It's hard for us to wrap our minds around this, but we need to try.

Jesus, even before he was born, came into the world according to God's speech. There are many texts in the Old Testament that prophecy about the coming of Christ, but perhaps one of the most well-known is Isaiah 53. There we read that the stable-born king would have "no form or majesty that we should look at him, and no beauty that we should desire him" (53:2). His treatment at the hands of the religious leaders would confirm that "he was despised and rejected by men" (53:3). And his healing ministry and passion would make it abundantly clear that this was "a man of sorrows and acquainted with grief" (53:3). Yet, the greatest mark of this man, this eternal Word of the Father come in the power of the Holy Spirit, would be his sacrifice. Isaiah wrote, "Surely he has borne our griefs and carried ours sorrows; yet we esteemed him stricken, smitten by God, and afflicted. But he was pierced for

---

7   The Facebook group is called "Christians Battling Anxiety."

our transgressions; he was crushed for our iniquities; upon him was the chastisement that brought us peace, and with his wounds we are healed" (53:4–5). God laid on his own Word "the iniquity of us all" (53:6). And in what is likely the greatest irony of history, Christ did not defend himself. "He opened not his mouth" (53:7). The speech of God himself remained silent so that we would be able to speak in the glory of God's salvation, that we would be able to worship before the throne of God forever. He was silent so that we might sing.

In his youth, Jesus showed that trusting in the speech of God was always at the forefront of his mind. When he stayed behind in the temple during the Feast of Passover (Luke 2), he sat at the feet of the religious teachers, listening to them and asking them questions about the recorded speech of his Father (the Old Testament). Everyone was amazed at his understanding (Luke 2:47). And why shouldn't they be? This was the very speech of God incarnate, opening their ears to what God had said and was saying! Nothing could be more glorious, or more natural. Jesus's response to his parents' scolding was plain: "Did you not know that I must be in my Father's house?" (Luke 2:49). It's as if he were saying, "I am the speech of God, and this is where the speech of God is proclaimed. This is where I belong."

Jesus's public ministry was also marked by his trust in God's speech. We see this in his excessive quotations of God's words from the Old Testament. The New Testament records Jesus actually quoting from the Old Testament over 70 times, but that doesn't count allusions or implied references, and the New Testament certainly doesn't record everything that Jesus ever said. When pressed by questioners, Jesus said that he came to fulfill the law, every letter, every vowel point (Matt. 5:18). He came to do everything that his Father willed, everything that his Father uttered (John 6:38). There was a history of distrust in God's speech that traced all the way back to Adam, but Christ was the great reversal, the one who trusted fully in his Father's speech, through whom the grace of God would abound for many (Rom. 5:12–17).

Even Jesus's death was marked by his trust in God's speech. As he hung on the cross, the scoffers remarked, "He trusts in God; let God deliver him now, if he desires him" (Matt. 27:43). Even at this insult, while he was on death's door, he quoted the speech of God in Psalm 22:1, "'Eli, Eli, lema sabachthani?' that is, 'My God, my God, why have you forsaken me?'" (Matt. 27:46). He lamented only through the words that God had given. And later in Psalm 22 we find hope, for the psalmist writes, "he has not despised or abhorred the affliction of the afflicted, and he has not hidden his face from him, but has heard, when he cried to him" (Ps. 22:24). The

Father *always* hears the speech of his children, of those who put their trust in his speech. Always. For no one was this truer than for the Son of God himself at his greatest hour of need.

And Jesus's resurrection proves it. God did not abandon his Son. He did not cast aside his eternal speech. Instead, through Jesus's bodily death, God spoke louder. Jesus rose from the dead, just as he *said* he would (Matt. 28:6; Luke 24:6). The speech of God cannot be silenced, not even by death (Acts 2:24). The eternal Word of the Father came, lived, died, and was raised according to his trust in holy language. His perfect trust in God's speech lead to perfect obedience, and thus to perfect communion with God (John 17:21, 23).

It's only through faith in this great Word that we receive the gift of perfect obedience, of a righteousness more blinding than the sun after fresh snow. None of us can perfectly trust in the speech of God (the Great Story makes that obvious), but through the work of Christ, we're considered righteous and perfect for his sake. As the Apostle Paul put it, the free gift of God's grace in Christ brought "justification," God's own declaration that we are righteous *in* Christ (Rom. 5:16–17).

There's a poetic circularity in the Great Story. By his Word, the Father spoke the world into motion. By his Word he sustains it and governs it (Col. 1:17; Heb. 1:3). With his words, he tested his image bearers. Distrusting his words, they fell. Restoring his people, God spoke words again. But they were continually met with distrust and disobedience. By the Word that began it all, God put a definitive end to evil and rebellion. And by that eternal Word, God will renew all things (Rev. 21:5). We might put it this way:

> By the Word, God made.
> By the Word, he held.
> Against it, we disobeyed.
> Against it, we fell.
> Through it, he redeemed.
> Through it, he called.
> Against it, we dreamed.
> Against it, we brawled.
> In it, he came.
> In it, he spoke.
> In it—a name—

Our distrust broke.

In it, hope lives.

In it: communion.

In it, God gives

The gift of union.

In the next chapter, we'll look at how this Word in the world gives us incredible *hope* in our suffering. And that hope is essential if we're going to keep taking steps of faith with the CHRIST acronym.

Reflection Questions and Prayer

1. What parts of the CHRIST acronym seem most helpful to you? Why?

2. What parts of the acronym seem most challenging? Why?

3. Where do you anticipate having to use the acronym in your daily life? Consider writing down some ideas for each letter in the acronym so that you can apply it to a concrete situation.

4. What other things help you to deal with your anxiety? Do you see a biblical reason for why a particular thing helps?

5. Think of someone else you know who struggles with anxiety. What parts of the acronym might be most encouraging to them? How might you help them (directly or indirectly) to use it? How might you pray for them? Write your prayer out and give it to them.

6. Think of a moment of anxiety that you've experienced lately. Then utter the words, "He knows." You might even say them a few times, just to let them sink in. How does an awareness of Christ's sympathy affect your perception of that experience? Do you find yourself doubting the sympathy of Christ? If so, ask for prayer. God always hears the words of his people when they're asking to put their faith in the Word that he's given.

7. Christianity can seem like a set of ideas that people must agree with in order to be considered "in the group." But real Christian faith is *particular*. It manifests itself in your concrete situations each day. What is one thing that you're currently facing that will provide an opportunity for particular faith in the Word of your heavenly Father? Ask the Spirit to strengthen your faith as you approach it. Then ask for prayer from others. He'll answer; I

promise.

Prayer

Christ, you are my shape.
But I'm not fitted to you yet.
I curve in on myself.
I try to stay the same.
Change is painful.
But I know I need it;
I know that your Father and Spirit
Are doing what's best for me.
As I'm shaped to you,
Draw me closer.
Let our relationship blossom
Like a head-heavy peony,
Full of hands that bend and touch
The open air of your grace.
In my anxiety, help me consider my feelings,
To know that you know,
To remember your promise,
To identify something concrete in your world,
To learn more about you from it,
To persevere with the pain,
And to talk.
In my anxiety,
Let me be art in your hands.

Oh Lord,
My speaking God,
Who could have imagined that you would speak yourself
On our behalf?
You have always spoken to us.
But we have a humiliating history of distrust and doubt.
So you became trust and faith for us.

You gave grace to gain what rightfully belonged to you.

And now, here we are—still broken and bleeding.

But you have been broken and bled for us.

You know.

You know our struggles . . . even better than we do.

Spirit, plant a strong seed of faith in us,

Deep in the soil, where no one can see.

And make it strong.

Work around it with the water of your word.

And when it breaches the surface,

May we find that it is mighty,

Knowing that our great gardener has been tending it.

All we want, all we need, is *faith* in your Son.

Grant us that much.

The rest is detail.

Reader Resource: Self-Study with the CHRIST Acronym

Try to apply the CHRIST acronym in a concrete situation from your own life. Implementing the acronym is the only way to benefit from it. Write down your thoughts and experiences below. Which element of the acronym was most helpful? Which was easiest to implement? Which was most difficult to implement? Consider this an exercise in soul-study.

Christ

Consider the feelings as spiritual medicine.

He knows.

Remember the promise.

Identify a focus.

Stay engaged.

Talk.

CHAPTER 5

Living with a Long-Term Guest

KEY IDEA: Treating anxiety as a long-term guest can help us focus on its spiritual purpose.

S o far, we've learned that anxiety can crush us so that God can call us. In that crushing, we develop patterns of behavior that may lead us to take steps of faith or to avoid them. We can use the CHRIST acronym to take those steps, as God uses our weakness to display his strength. At the end of each chapter, I've laid out some theology that helps to give us a context for interpreting our anxiety. And along the way, I've given you windows into my own experiences with anxiety. We'll now delve more deeply into what it's actually like to live *with* anxiety in daily life. I assume that you're doing this right now, or someone you love is doing it. Living with anxiety is sort of like living with a long-term guest that you'd rather not have around. But the thesis of this book is that God can use that guest to mold and shape you in ways you can't even imagine. In this chapter, let's explore what it might mean to think of anxiety as a long-term guest.

When we talk about anxiety as a long-term guest, we're really focusing on the *duration* of anxiety. When I first tasted how bitter anxiety was and how paralyzing it could be, I hoped with all my heart that it would be a phase, an era in my life. I would look back one day and say, "Man, those were rough years." But twelve years later, it's alive and well, always finding new outlets. That sounds like terrible news, but it's not; it's *really* not, especially given the way that God has used anxiety in my life. One thing that I've learned over the last decade is that when anxiety lingers, God continually uses it to shape and form us. *When anxiety stubbornly stays, God sovereignly shapes.*

I'm going to give you two images for this chapter. First, imagine anxiety as a long-term guest—someone who shows up to your house uninvited, leaving his bags and belongings scattered on your floor. He's ragged and rude, and your impulse is to grab him by the arm and escort him back out the front door. How dare this creep interrupt your routines and plans for self-fulfillment. You have enough to deal with as it is without some hobo waltzing through your front door and demanding you put him up in a room!

Now, pause that. Switch frames and imagine anxiety as a criminal who's broken a lock to your front door, crept around stealing electronics and jewelry, and then made a quiet exit. You wake up and look around your house, measuring the damage. You feel violated, frustrated, and angry. But you're also relieved that he's gone. You'll install a better security system. You'll call your insurance company and file claims. You'll get your life back soon enough. You say to yourself, "What a jerk! I hope he never comes back." And you're fairly convinced that he won't. This was an unwelcome interruption in your life, but it's gone now.

Which image best captures how your anxiety has been? Which image best captures how you *want* your anxiety to be?

> ## *"We'll learn a few things from living with the house guest over time, but that won't really be the case for the criminal."*

You see, anxiety *the criminal* is very different from anxiety *the house guest*. For the criminal, our goal is to get him out as fast as possible. He's a threat; he's a thief; he's a nuisance to the life we want to live. He takes away what we treasure, but we can replace what he's stolen easily enough. However, it's different with the house guest. For the house guest, our goal is to find a way to keep living in his presence, changing our routines and expectations to accommodate him. We'll *learn* a few things from living with the house guest over time, but that won't really be the case for the criminal. We want the criminal out so that we can get back to life as normal. But with the house guest, we're forced to create a new normal. We're shaped by the house guest. Ultimately, we're shaped by the one who has control over the house guest, including when he arrives and when he leaves—and that shaper is God himself.

The way I see it, anxiety's not always a criminal who picks the lock of your soul and takes you hostage until you give something up, whatever that "something" is. Anxiety can be like that for some people. But for others, it's different. Though it does feel as if anxiety breaks into our souls like a thief, he doesn't seem to want to take something and go. He stays. He lingers; he doesn't want to leave. Now, that doesn't mean we shouldn't *ask* him to leave (as Paul asked God to remove his "thorn in the flesh," 2 Cor. 12:8–9), and that God won't usher anxiety out of our lives in shackles, all in his own timing. That may very well happen. In fact, my reader, I hope and pray that happens for you. But for many of us, anxiety is the long-term guest. He's renting a room in our soul. And with God's help, despite all the unpleasantries and disruptions that anxiety brings along, we can learn to live *with* and *from* this house guest.

Now, I know, to some people that sounds horrible. If you're struggling with a swell of anxiety at this moment, you want to hear about an end, about hope and healing, about being able to breathe without feeling as if the air around you is disappearing. I get it. Remember, I'm a twelve-year veteran. And I can tell you with certainty that there *is* hope and healing—found in an ever-deepening relationship with the Father, Son, and Holy Spirit. But the sort of hope and healing we *want* immediately is very different from the sort of hope and healing we *need* eternally.

The hope and healing we need eternally comes in a special way, a way that God has ordained in eternity and governs daily. As creatures of God in a fallen world, we find hope and healing through *process* and *relationship*. This is very clear throughout Scripture but very repulsive to twenty-first century problem solving, and to common medical treatments of anxiety today. We've noted already how the common approach to anxiety is to treat it as something to be gotten rid of, something to remove. In other words, it's most common to treat anxiety as a criminal, rather than a house guest. The goal of modern medicine is not first and foremost to *learn* about what God is teaching us through anxiety. Its goal is to eliminate it, or at least to dull our awareness of it. We can't fault modern medicine too much for that approach, since we're responsible for asking for it. I don't remember waltzing into my doctor's office and saying, "How can I learn from my hyper-vigilance?" Or, "Do you have any resources for personal growth in light of my panic attacks?" No—I marched my rigid body into the closest examination room and begged for something, *anything*, that would stop the symptoms. In the early months, I couldn't eat; I lost 30 lbs. in two weeks. I couldn't sleep; I had only skeletal relationships with everyone in my life. I didn't want to *learn*; I wanted to *live* the way I used to live. I wanted my life back. I wanted the uninvited house guest out! He had interrupted *my* normalcy, *my* routines, *my* ambitions.

Do you hear the possessiveness in those last two sentences? Possessiveness is a clear mark of someone who has no awareness of or concern for God's purposes. In other words, it's a mark of someone who doesn't want to be crushed by God or called by him. And I really didn't want to be crushed or called. I didn't have an awareness of God's purposes for me twelve years ago, even though I'd grown up in the church, even though my father had been a pastor, even though I professed my faith and talked about God on a regular basis. I had no deep awareness of the basic truth that the all-powerful, ever-present God of the universe had specific purposes for *me*. Neither did I know that those purposes would require that I be shaped to the image of his Son (Rom. 8:28), and that this shaping might hurt—might even require that I be *crushed*. To be honest, I really didn't know much of anything back then. The Great Story of Scripture that I've referenced throughout the book was all around me, but its words hadn't penetrated my heart. They fell like drops of rain on an old metal barn roof, a roof that kept me dry but also held me in the dark. Until I walked out of the barn and let the rain hit my skin, until I saw uninterrupted light, I could *hear* the words of God, but I didn't *listen* to them. I didn't start listening until I was crushed, until I had to learn how to live with a long-term guest.

Once I realized that anxiety might be with me for a long time, I began studying my own reactions to it. Do you know what I learned almost instantly? How we approach the physical problems and hardships we encounter reflects much of what we think or know spiritually. Remember: we always need a context to interpret our behavior. If we don't have the context of the Great Story, then we have some other context, perhaps the context of modern medicine and psychology. With those sorts of contexts, we might approach anxiety as something to be eliminated, something to be held at bay so that we can get back to our normalcy (a state in which we might be *unaware* of God's presence and purposes). But in the context of the Great Story of Scripture, we can approach anxiety as a teaching tool in the hands of the great physician. Treating anxiety as a long-term guest can help us do that. How, exactly? One of the ways it does this is by reforming our understanding of *weakness and suffering*. We want to treat weakness and suffering as criminals. We want them out of our lives as fast as possible. But, like anxiety, weakness and suffering can be long-term guests from whom we learn, not because they're intrinsically good, but because they will *always* be used by an intrinsically good God. In fact, this is almost always how Scripture treats weakness and suffering.

Let's look at a biblical example of how weakness and suffering can be long-term guests that God uses to teach us so that we can trust him in our relationship. Our case study is the Apostle Paul. Paul is undoubtedly one of the heroes of Scripture. God used him to spread the nascent Christian faith throughout the Mediterranean world, and the Holy Spirit spoke through him to develop much of the New Testament. By any standard, Paul was a man of God. But Paul is not a hero of our faith because of his *strength*; he's a hero because of his *weakness* (2 Cor. 12:9–11) and his Spirit-given ability to be content in all circumstances (Phil. 4:11–13). Paul submitted his experiences of weakness and suffering to the sovereign purposes of God in Christ Jesus. In other words, he interpreted the events of his life in the context of the Great Story, just as we're trying to do in this book. And he found that God has much to teach us through these unwanted, long-term guests.

First, let's note how God worked in Paul's life through process and relationship, since this is part and parcel of the Christian life. Then we can explore how Paul viewed his hardships as opportunities for Christ-conformity. Both of these things will help us understand what it means to live with anxiety as a long-term guest.

Process and Relationship in Paul's Life

When we think about it from the perspective of God's providence, the road to Paul's conversion and ministry is a strange one. If Paul would one day be such an influential preacher and missionary, why would God have him go through years of rebellion, torturing the church and throwing God's people into prison (Acts 8:1–3)? Why not just convert Paul early in his life and use him to do even more good for the sake of Christ?

Answering these questions would involve too much speculation. We don't know the secrets of God's providence. However, we can at least say that God *intended* to work this way. God governs all things according to his divine purposes. So, anything that comes to pass is fully in his willful control. God has ordained not only *what* comes to be but *how* it comes to be. He intended that Paul would embrace the truth of the gospel *after* tormenting followers of Christ, *after* persecuting Christ himself (Acts 9:5). Why?

"God has a history of working through process and relationship to redeem his people."

I believe we can do more than simply admit that God's ways are mysterious. God has a history of working through *process* and *relationship* to redeem his people. We don't find in Scripture many examples of instantaneous redemption (though that would align better with 21st century problem solving). Instead, we find God patiently enduring the shortcomings of his servants as they grow slowly in their relationship with him. Abraham is a prime example. At times in his life, Abraham had childlike faith in God's word (Gen. 12:4). At other times, he used deceit to protect his own skin, rather than trusting in God's promised protection (Gen. 12:11–13; 20:2). God could have snapped his providential fingers and brought a doubting man to full faith in an instant. But he didn't. He willed to work through process and relationship, allowing Abraham time to grow and learn from his missteps. Over the course of his life, Abraham would mature in his relationship with God, just as all Christians do today.

God, you see, is ultimately concerned with *relationships*. In fact, God in himself *is* relationship: the Father loving and glorifying the Son, the Son loving and glorifying the Father, the Spirit loving and glorifying the Father and the Son. As my friend and teacher reminds us, "The New Testament indicates that the persons of the Trinity speak to one another and enjoy profound personal relations with one another. These relationships within God show us the ultimate foundation for thinking about human personal relationships."[1] We value our personal relationships because we are made in the image of a God who has eternal relationship in himself. So, it makes perfect sense for the Trinity to cultivate relationships with his creatures. And relationships in a sinful world require time and patience. They also require unimaginable sacrifice, for God would even give *himself* to have an eternal relationship with us.

So much of Scripture is captured in a little prepositional phrase that signals

---

1   Vern S. Poythress, *Redeeming Sociology: A God-Centered Approach* (Wheaton, IL: Crossway, 2011), 24.

divine-human relationship: *with us*. All throughout the Bible, there is an ongoing theme of God reaffirming his desire to be *with* his people. In Exodus, God gives Moses and the Israelites precise instructions for building the tabernacle. He says, "And let them make me a sanctuary, *that I may dwell in their midst*" (Exod. 25:8; emphasis added). When the tabernacle was superseded by the temple, God spoke to Solomon, uttering a familiar promise. "Concerning this house that you are building, if you will walk in my statutes and obey my rules and keep all my commandments and walk in them, then I will establish my word with you, which I spoke to David your father. And I will *dwell among* the children of Israel and will not forsake my people Israel" (1 Kgs. 6:12–13). What a rapturous promise: that the God of all things would dwell *with* his people! But how much more jaw-dropping is the Incarnation, when the Son of God wrapped himself in flesh and took on a human nature? Then, truly, we encountered *Immanuel*, the "with us" God. Christ is the new temple, the person in whom we gather to meet with God. And one day we will be with God in uninterrupted fellowship. John tells us, "I heard a loud voice from the throne saying, 'Behold, the dwelling place of God is *with man*. He will dwell *with them*, and they will be his people, and God himself will be *with them* as their God'" (Rev. 21:3; emphasis added).

In short, God wants to have a relationship with his creatures. He wants to be *with us*. He does not *need* to have a relationship with us, since God has forever had the most fulfilling of relationships in himself.[2] But his love of relationship has overflowed and brought about the creation of his image bearers: little relational beings that reflect their relational God. For God, relationship is primary, not problem solving.

Now, that doesn't mean God isn't in the business of solving problems. In fact, he's the greatest problem solver and does more than we can even imagine to address the ills of the world. But if relationship is primary for God, if *love* is primary (1 John 4:8), then we must change the way we think about God interacting with a broken world.[3]

So, back to the question I posed a few paragraphs ago: Why did God not simply have Paul believe in Christ from his youth? Perhaps it was because the tough events and decisions in Paul's life would be critical components of his deepening *relationship* with God. Paul would look back on his church persecution with horror and

---

2   See chapter 1 in Michael Reeves, *Delighting in the Trinity: An Introduction to the Christian Faith* (Downers Grove, IL: IVP Academic, 2012).

3   This was a point made by St. Augustine. God must be tri-personal in order for love to be primary. If God were unipersonal, then power would be primary for God, rather than love.

guilt, but also with overwhelming gratitude for God's grace. Why would God choose *him*, of all people, to be an ambassador for Christ? The wonder and gratitude that Paul would have felt would then lead him into deeper, loving communion with God.

God ordained to work through process and relationship in Paul's life, just as he does in ours, because love is primary for him. In contrast with a world bent on quick problem solving and maintaining comfort, Scripture suggests that God's greatest concern is not to shape a world that conforms to a human understanding of perfection: a world that is sinless, painless, and pure. Yes, God is righteous; he is peace; and he is perfection. And if maintaining *our* understanding of these things were God's greatest concern, he could have prevented the fall of Adam. But in God's deep and mysterious providence, he didn't. This only makes sense if God is ultimately concerned with relationships.

Weakness and Suffering as Opportunities for Christ-Conformity

Now, given that God works through process and relationship, we need to view our physical and spiritual hardships—our weakness and suffering—not as travesties but as *opportunities*. Opportunities for what, exactly? Opportunities for profound spiritual growth, profound shaping to the image of Christ. This is so hard for us today because our instinctive response to weakness and suffering is to escape. Our instinctive response to anxiety is to find some way to get the criminal out of our lives in hand cuffs. We don't want the house guest. In fact, for many of us, the idea that anxiety could even be considered a house guest sounds certifiably insane! But putting "anxiety" in the same sentence with "opportunity" fits much more with the drift of Scripture.

Paul is such a great example of this. Just consider some of the incredible physical hardships that he experienced. In 2 Corinthians 11:24–30, he runs down the list.

> Five times I received at the hands of the Jews the forty lashes less one. [25] Three times I was beaten with rods. Once I was stoned. Three times I was shipwrecked; a night and a day I was adrift at sea; [26] on frequent journeys, in danger from rivers, danger from robbers, danger from my own people, danger from Gentiles, danger in the city, danger in the wilderness, danger at sea, danger from false brothers; [27] in toil and hardship, through many a sleepless night, in hunger and thirst, often without food, in cold and exposure. [28] And, apart from other things, there is the daily pres-

sure on me of my anxiety for all the churches. [29] Who is weak, and I am not weak? Who is made to fall, and I am not indignant? [30] If I must boast, I will boast of the things that show my weakness.

Paul was no stranger to struggle and strife. Every epistle he penned shows that weakness and suffering were his bread and butter. But look at how he ends the list of trials: boasting in things that show his *weakness*. The hardships that Paul experienced revealed his utter reliance on God for all things. In that utter reliance, Paul had the *opportunity* to build his relationship with Christ, a relationship that stood upon Paul's recognition of weakness. We see this in the following chapter, where Paul reflects on his "thorn in the flesh" (a fitting analogy for those of us who struggle with severe anxiety):

> So to keep me from becoming conceited because of the surpassing greatness of the revelations, a thorn was given me in the flesh, a messenger of Satan to harass me, to keep me from becoming conceited. [8] Three times I pleaded with the Lord about this, that it should leave me. [9] But he said to me, "My grace is sufficient for you, for my power is made perfect in weakness." Therefore I will boast all the more gladly of my weaknesses, so that the power of Christ may rest upon me. [10] For the sake of Christ, then, I am content with weaknesses, insults, hardships, persecutions, and calamities. For when I am weak, then I am strong. (2 Cor 12:7–10)

This sounds *so* backwards to us! Content with weakness, insult, hardship, persecution?! Why would we ever be *content* with such things? The short answer is this: true and lasting strength is only found in God, and when we are overwhelmed by weakness, we have no confusion about that basic fact. We see with utmost clarity that a relationship with the living God is utterly foreign to the world of godless problem-solving. *Weakness is the way to relationship.* Weakness is an opportunity for relational growth. But for Christians, this weakness is always tethered to *hope*. That's why Paul can "boast" about his weaknesses. No one would boast about weakness without any hope of redemption. To do so would be quasi-sadistic, evoking a strange love of affliction. Instead, Paul is lifted up by hope.

J. I. Packer wrote a little book titled *Weakness Is the Way*, in which he unpacks the wisdom of Paul's second letter to the Corinthians.[4] At one point, he reflects on

---

4   J. I. Packer, *Weakness Is the Way: Life with Christ Our Strength* (Wheaton, IL: Crossway, 2013).

Paul's ability to face the trials of his life with Spirit-given hope.

> For all that Paul is writing out of a situation of weakness and, without doubt, a sense of weakness more intense than we meet in any other of his letters, he is not lapsing into self-pity or voicing gloom and doom, but he is expressing his sense of ongoing triumph in Christ in the face of all obstacles. And he is declaring his sure and certain hope of glory when his course through this world reaches its end. It is this hope for his personal future—a hope which, to echo Bunyan's Mr. Stand-fast, lies as a glowing coal at his heart—that determines his attitude toward all the pressures of the present.[5]

Weakness tethered to hope—that's the way to relationship with God. I know that's a bitter pill to swallow for anxiety sufferers. But it's the only pill we have, and we must trust that God has good things in store for us not *in spite* of this but *because* of it. God makes no mistakes; he has divine purposes for our bitter pill.

"Weakness tethered to hope—that's the way to relationship with God."

Now, pause with me for a moment to see something critical about this Pauline paradigm—weakness tethered to hope as a way to relationship. It's not simply "the way things have to be" in a broken world. In fact, it's not even a *Pauline* paradigm; it's a *Christian* paradigm—it's modeled on Christ himself. Weakness is the way to divine relationship because *Christ* is the way to divine relationship, and Christ became weak for our sake. He cut a path for us in the wild brush of the world, and that path leads *through* suffering and *into* glory. Weakness and suffering aren't obstacles to be navigated around, just as anxiety isn't something to be gotten rid of; instead, they are a planned means of Christ-conformity. They are footsteps on the footpath of Christ, and it's *him* that we follow. David Powlison even goes so far as to say that "suffering is a means of grace."[6] Grace! And why is that? Because it's been ordained by God to draw us closer to Christ himself, and it does that by making us *like* Christ

---

5   Packer, *Weakness Is the Way*, 99–100.

6   David Powlison, *God's Grace in Your Suffering* (Wheaton, IL: Crossway, 2018), 87.

in his suffering, even in his death (Phil. 3:10). "The living faith that embraces Christ is formed in the crucible of weakness. The courage to carry on and the strong love that cares well for others are formed in the crucible of struggle."[7] This crucible of struggle is not something to be avoided; it's something to be embraced—not because we enjoy suffering and weakness but because we know that through them we are being called and crafted to the shape of our Lord, our elder brother, our savior.

When you think about it, this is a huge relief. People spend exorbitant amounts of time, energy, and money trying to avoid weakness and alleviate suffering. But weakness and suffering aren't going away anytime soon. They're long-term guests on this side of paradise. We live *with* them, not *around* them. All of the Christian life is about learning to live *with* and *through* weakness and suffering—anxiety included—in a way that follows the beaten path of Scripture, the beaten path of Christ. As Packer put it,

> Weakness . . . meaning inability finally to control our life situation relationally, circumstantially, financially, healthwise, and so on, despite all that our therapeutic present-day culture can do for us, will be with us as long as life in this world lasts. Our Lord Jesus Christ lived in poverty through the years of his ministry and, having been despised and rejected, as Isaiah phrased it, he was "crucified in weakness" (2 Cor. 13:4). This tells us what kind of life road we as his disciples must be prepared to travel. Paul, depending on the risen Christ, found strength to live with weaknesses and shows us how to do the same. But our weaknesses will not go away any more than his did . . . [8]

In our weaknesses and suffering, we look to Christ with hope. Even better: we rely on the comfort of the Holy Spirit, who gives us hope in Christ and lifts us up to our heavenly Father. On this side of paradise, *human weaknesses is the way to divine relationship*. The irony that we so often overlook is that the outcome of weakness or suffering or anxiety isn't helplessness; it's *hope*. And "hope is indestructible. Hope refuses to give up. Hope never caves in."[9] Do you know why? Because hope isn't a human aspiration; it's a divine gift. We see this in one of the most beautiful little prayers Paul offers on behalf of the Christians in Rome: "May the God of hope

---

7   Powlison, *God's Grace in Your Suffering*, 91.

8   Packer, *Weakness Is the Way*, 87–88.

9   John Mark Comer, *My Name Is Hope: Anxiety, Depression, and Life after Melancholy* (Portland, OR: Graphe, 2011), 206.

fill you with all joy and peace in believing, so that by the power of the Holy Spirit you may abound in hope" (Rom. 15:13). God *is* hope. He's the source. Through the power of the Spirit of God, you will *have* hope. In other words, you will have God himself! Weakness is a footpath to the forever hope of God our giver.

"On this side of paradise, human weaknesses is the way to divine relationship."

Changing the Way We Approach Anxiety

Let's recap. This approach to weakness, suffering, and anxiety is counterintuitive to us, so we need to rehearse it continually until it sinks in.

The long-term guest of anxiety is not in our lives by his own bidding. God is *always* using anxiety to build our relationship with him. In a myriad of ways, anxiety is always a tool in the hands of the triune God. That's the refrain of this book.

This means that we need to exchange a 21st century problem-solving mentality for the ancient truth of divine-human relationship. The former has us asking, "How can I get this to stop?" The latter encourages us to ask, "What are you teaching me, Lord? Please show me." I have uttered that prayer so often, and let this be an encouragement to you: *God has answered every single time.* He has answered through Scripture, since that is where God speaks to us.

The real paradox of anxiety (and of weakness and suffering more broadly) echoes the paradox that Paul voiced in 2 Corinthians 12:10. We've looked at this truth before: *Weakness through anxiety is strength in the Lord.* While anxiety seems to cripple us, it has the potential to give us spiritual wings, allowing us to rise above a materialistic view of the world, helping us to see the spiritual purposes that God has for the hardships at our fingertips. When anxiety makes you weak, ask God questions that can make you strong. "What are you teaching me, Lord?" He always answers.

Anxiety, for some, is a short-term guest that God ushers out of our lives when he's used it for his good purposes. But for others, it's a long-term guest. What I've tried to show in this chapter is that this isn't bad news. In fact, it's very good news, for through anxiety your relationship with God can grow in untold depth. And that's the best we can hope for on this earth: an ever-deepening, faith-based, hope-filled relationship with the Father, Son, and Holy Spirit. Living *with* anxiety, then, doesn't mean living in tormented isolation. If our hearts are tuned to Scripture, if we prayerfully rely on the Spirit's guidance, living with anxiety can mean living *closer* to God, not further away from him. And there's nothing better than that. As odd as it sounds, I'm happy that anxiety has been a long-term guest. If he hadn't come to stay, my relationship with the Lord would be as shallow as a rain puddle.

Theology: Where Hopeful Suffering Comes From

In the last chapter, we saw that the Word entered the world to hear and heed God's speech on our behalf. He went down to the dust, as we should have, but he rose from the dusty grave, as we long to. Nothing can silence the eternal speech of God.

The wonder of the Incarnation, however, is not just in the salvation it offers in the future; it's also in the *hope* that it brings right now. As we talked about anxiety as a long-term guest, we saw how we suffer with hope. Christians are hopeful sufferers. Ever since the Word came into the world and took our sin upon himself, we have walked on the suffering footpath of Christ with hope in what God is doing and what he will do. The Great Story of Scripture ends with hope, with a looking forward. The end of the story has been written, but we haven't turned to those pages yet. Soon, my friends . . . *soon.*

In the book of Revelation (21:1–7), we read these words from the eternal Word of the Father, spoken in the potent breath of the Holy Ghost:

> Then I saw a new heaven and a new earth, for the first heaven and the first earth had passed away, and the sea was no more. [2] And I saw the holy city, new Jerusalem, coming down out of heaven from God, prepared as a bride adorned for her husband. [3] And I heard a loud voice from the throne saying, "Behold, the dwelling place of God is with man. He will dwell with them, and they will be his people, and God himself will be with them as their God. [4] He will wipe away every tear from their eyes, and death shall be no more, neither shall there be mourning, nor crying, nor pain anymore, for the former things have passed away." [5] And he who was seated on the throne said, "Behold, I am making all things new." Also he said, "Write this down, for these words are trustworthy and true." [6] And he said to me, "It is done! I am the Alpha and the Omega, the beginning and the end. To the thirsty I will give from the spring of the water of life without payment. [7] The one who conquers will have this heritage, and I will be his God and he will be my son.

These seven verses are a bottomless well. So much is promised here. We could draw out bucket after bucket, and the whole world would grow tired before we even thought about the well running dry of hope. It's no accident that the eternal Word of the Father tells us "these words are trustworthy and true." *Trustworthy*—hasn't that always been at the heart of the Great Story, and in the smaller stories of our lives: the trustworthiness of God's speech? And here we're reminded: Yes, *trust* these words. Set your life on them. Build your house of hope here.

We're still in the midst of the Great Story, of course. We still have great need of hope. And God has given that hope to us in his word, in Scripture. In Scripture, we find the unfolding promises of God presented with perfection, promises on pages. And we need that because we're still struggling. We're still on the footpath of Christ: weakness and suffering leading up to glory. We walk on that path with hope precisely because God's words are trustworthy. God's words hold out hope to us.

Hope, I've found, always falls in the hands of belief. I think about my father's death a lot—almost every day. I was eighteen at the time. At that age, watching your father die of cancer right in front of you will leave a scar that never goes away. I think about the last moments he had before his final breaths. What was he thinking? What was he feeling? Did he want to say anything else to us? So many questions without answers. But the solace I've found since then is in the simple truth that not even death could take away the *choice* he had to believe. Death ravages our lives. It leaves paths of debris all over the place. But it can't take that choice away—the choice to believe, the choice to *hope*.

"At the end of our life, we'll have that one choice: to believe or not believe; to hope or not to hope."

At the end of our life, we'll have that one choice: to believe or not believe; to hope or not to hope. No amount of evidence can prepare us for that moment. No apologetic argument will silence every doubt. *It will be a moment governed by faith.* Satan won't be able to control your answer, nor will any doctor's terminal diagnosis. *It will be a moment governed by faith.* Your life goes on into eternity if you hope in the Word that's come in the flesh, in the speech of God for *you*, in Christ. No matter who you are or what you've done, that is where the Great Story will come to a halt (not an end, but a halt). You will have two paths, and you'll have to choose, knowing, mysteriously, that the all-controlling speech of God is somehow sovereign over that choice: to hope or not to hope. *It will be a moment governed by faith.*

Don't bring your worry to that moment. Don't bring your fears or your doubts. Don't bring your analysis. *Bring your resolve to hope.* That's all you need in the face of death.

And what's waiting for you after the end? Well, the Great Story offers an "un-ending." Do you notice how the focus of Revelation 21:1–7 is on something eternal? The focus is on God dwelling *with* us. The eternal God, who has no end, will be our ending. He will dwell with us, and we with him, and death will turn to a memory, evaporating in the burning light of God himself. Our hope, my friends, will blossom into the eternal presence of the speaking God—the one with whom we will commune forever, speaking and being spoken to. The Great Story began with words, and it ends with words, too. It ends with words that *must* be heard, words that *cannot* be silenced, words that *will* drown out the racket of our past rebellion—and also our past weakness, suffering, and anxiety. That's our un-ending ending. Grasp that tighter than anything else; squeeze it with the hands of your soul; never let it go. *You know your ending.*

The reason you can't ever let it go is that you're not there yet. We haven't yet been brought to death's door. Maybe it will be later this afternoon. Maybe tomorrow. May in twenty-five years. But not yet.

And here's the thing: When you're living in the land of *Not Yet*, suffering is not the anomaly; it's the norm. J. I. Packer reminded us of this earlier in the chapter. But—and please remember this—it's not the norm in the sense that suffering is merely *common*. It's the norm in the sense that we discussed earlier: *suffering is the path that God himself has laid out for you.* Sounds terrible, doesn't it? What sort of God would set out a path of suffering for the ones he wants to spend eternity with? Answer: The sort of God who knows first-hand that suffering is going to shape you, the sort of God who wants you to walk down the same, divinely trodden path that his Son walked down. Because at the end of that path is *glory*.

This message isn't very popular. It's not a podcast favorite. But it's the plain teaching of Scripture.[10] Let me end this chapter by setting that out before us. What I offer in the next several paragraphs, if you read it prayerfully, will revolutionize how you view suffering, including an anxiety disorder.

A Revolutionary Approach to Suffering

The first thing we have to come to grips with is our palpitating, live-giving relationship with Jesus Christ through the Holy Spirit. That *relationship* is always primary. We have to start there. Hold onto that for a minute.

Next, let me describe that relationship with the word *always*. It's not "always with Jesus" or "always safe" or "always at peace." Truth lives in all of those expressions. But there's a different *always* I have in mind. It's an *always* that comes from the mouth of the Apostle Paul in 2 Cor. 4:8–11.

> [8] We are afflicted in every way, but not crushed; perplexed, but not driven to despair; [9] persecuted, but not forsaken; struck down, but not destroyed; [10] always carrying in the body the death of Jesus, so that the life of Jesus may also be manifested in our bodies. [11] For we who live are always being given over to death for Jesus' sake, so that the life of Jesus also may be manifested in our mortal flesh.

Now you know where the title of the book comes from. Anxiety certainly strikes you down—down to the depths, to the dark, where it's just you and God. As I said in the first chapter, anxiety *crushes* us. We're truly struck down by it, spiritually and physically.

Thank God for conjunctions. "But" is the essence of the gospel. We're knocked to our knees by anxiety . . . but. We're face down in the dirt and near death . . . but. Our soul is lacerated, and all the hope is bleeding out . . . but. We. Are. Not. Destroyed. Never—not even at death. No matter how many times your anxiety strikes you down, you will not be destroyed. You're going to find your feet again, and rise—not because you pull yourself up by your bootstraps, but because *God* will pull you up so that you're closer to his Son.

With this in mind, look at the *always* that Paul utters. We're *always* carrying in our body the death of Christ. Did you get that? The death of a two-thousand-year-old Nazarene is *always* in your back pocket. It goes with you everywhere. *Everywhere.*

---

10   I owe this section to the wonderful reflections set out by Richard Gaffin in his article, "The Usefulness of the Cross," *Westminster Theological Journal* 41, no. 2 (1979): 228–46.

Not such a gleeful message, I know. But look at what Paul says about why.

"So that the life of Jesus may also be manifested in our bodies." There's another paradox for you (the gospel is full of them): carry around death in your body so that you can manifest life in your body?! What sort of logic is that? Divine logic, it turns out. And Paul keeps going. Are you ready? Why do we do this? *Because those of us who are on this side of death's door are given over to suffering and death for Jesus's sake.* But again, why?! Why? The logic is baffling, but the final reason is plain: *So that the very life of Christ shows up somehow in our flesh.*

This is really tough to grasp—that's the way divine logic works. So, slow down with me to review what Paul's saying. There are two instances of *always*, and both are tied to Christ. The first *always* is the death of Christ and his suffering (the next passage we look at will clarify that part). The second *always* is the life of Christ. But it's not a mere spiritual life. It's a life that shows up *in* or *through* our bodies. In other words, somehow the resurrection life of Jesus Christ shines through torn and tattered bodies. We always carry around the death of Christ, but not just to be somber or pitiful. We carry around the death of Christ *so that* the life of Christ will pierce through the holes in our battle-worn frames.

Other passages of Scripture make it plain, in fact, that our suffering as Christians isn't really *ours*. It doesn't belong to us. When we suffer, it's the suffering "of Christ."[11] Most people think of suffering *on behalf of Christ*, that is, persecution. That's certainly a reality, but when Saul (soon to be re-named Paul) was trotting down the Damascus road and was engulfed by a blinding light, he saw that what he'd been doing to followers of Christ he'd actually been doing to Christ himself: "And falling to the ground, he heard a voice saying to him, 'Saul, Saul, why are you persecuting me?' And he said, 'Who are you, Lord?' And he said, 'I am Jesus, whom you are persecuting'" (Acts 9:4–5). In a profound and mysterious way, Christ *shares* the persecution of those who suffer for his name.

But that's not what Paul is talking about in 2 Corinthians 4:7–11. Paul has in mind Christian suffering more broadly. He's focused on carrying around the death of Christ *in his body*—the fragile, weak, mortal vessel of his life. All of his physical and spiritual suffering in that body—his *Christian* body—is, as Gaffin puts it, "the *locus* of the life of Jesus. Paul's mortality and weakness, taken over in the service of Christ, constitute the comprehensive medium through which the eschatological life of the

---

11   Gaffin, "The Usefullness of the Cross," 234.

glorified Christ comes to expression."[12]

Here's my point (and Paul's . . . and Gaffin's): whenever we suffer as Christians, that suffering is the *means* through which God has chosen to manifest the resurrection life of Christ. And this whole process is encapsulated in the word *conformity*.

Here's how Paul puts it in his letter to the Philippians. He tells us point blank why he's suffered. What's the purpose of it all? Here's his answer: "that I may know him and the power of his resurrection, and may share his sufferings, becoming like him in his death, that by any means possible I may attain the resurrection from the dead" (Phil. 3:10–11). *Like Christ* in suffering and death leads to *like Christ* in resurrection. Conformity to Christ's suffering and weakness and death is the path to receiving glory and strength and life.

"Conformity to Christ's suffering and weakness and death is the path to receiving glory and strength and life."

And here's the kicker: that's the only way we receive true, eternal, impervious resurrected life from our savior. Gaffin writes, "the power of Christ's resurrection is realized just *as* the fellowship of his sufferings and conformity to his death. It tells us of the forming and patterning power of the resurrection; the resurrection is a conforming energy, an energy that produces conformity to Christ's death. The impact, the impress of the resurrection in Paul's existence is the cross."[13] That's our impress too. It's mine. It's yours. It's the impress of every Christian. You must understand this before we go any further: *for Christians, the purpose of all spiritual and physical suffering is conformity to Christ's death and—through that alone—the ushering in of Christ's resurrection life.*

Far from being deflating, that news is invigorating. It's empowering, because you can't avoid suffering on this side of paradise. It's inevitable. Everyone suffers. *But* you and I don't just bear with suffering; we don't just *endure* it. We revel in it. We enter it with eyes scanning the horizon for the light and life of Christ, because

---

12   Gaffin, "The Usefullness of the Cross," 233–34.

13   Gaffin, "The Usefullness of the Cross," 234.

we know it's coming. It has to. It must. That's what God has promised. I told you this would revolutionize your approach to suffering. If you're suffering from anxiety right now, start scanning the horizon.

As I end this chapter, I want you to continue thinking of anxiety as a *medicine of conformity leading to life* because that's exactly what it is. Remember the C of our CHRIST acronym: we *consider the feelings as spiritual medicine.* Anxiety isn't something to be avoided. It's not something to be drugged into submission. It's not even something to "get past" or "defeat." It's something that God is *using.* Pick up that little word with both of your ears: *using*—not just dealing with or managing or working around, but *using.* Your anxiety, my anxiety, is a tool in the hands of someone who knows how to raise the dead.

That, my friends, is why we're *hopeful* sufferers. We suffer with a smile because we know that death-defeating life is coming our way. We suffer with hope because we know that *especially* in this, in suffering, Christ's resurrected life is going to bloom, and no weather of the soul can lay that flower of hope back down in the soil.

Reflection Questions and Prayer

1. Has anxiety been a long-term guest for you or a short-term one?

2. How have you tended to deal with anxiety: have you tried to eliminate it or learn from it? Think of a specific example you can share with others. Or write it in your journal. (If you don't keep a journal, I strongly encourage you to do so. It helps you keep track of where you were and where you're going.)

3. How do you feel about weakness being a means to relationship with God? Be honest. What fears to do you have about this? What's lying behind your fears? Talk with a friend or pastor to dig down as deeply as you can.

4. What challenges do you confront when trying to find *hope* in the midst of anxiety? What are some biblical passages you could pray through in those moments? (See the appendix, "Words Worth Uttering," for suggestions.)

5. How does the biblical view of weakness as a means of Christ-conformity contrast with the way many other people deal with anxiety today? What are the implications (both for us and for those who reject Christ)?

6. What are some of the world's approaches to suffering and death? How does each one compare to Paul's understanding in 2 Corinthians?

7. Talk to at least two other people this week about how they view anxiety

and suffering. What's the purpose of it? How does their answer compare to what you've learned in this chapter?

Prayer

God, I know that you will use
All things for my good and growth.
Use my anxiety.
I know it may be with me for a long time,
But you will be with me forever.
Help me to know this in my core.
Help me to put on the paradox
That weakness is strength,
That to be fragile to the world
Is to be indestructible in Christ.
Let my question always be,
"What are you teaching me?"
And when I ask this,
Make my heart sensitive to your answer
As I pour over your word.

Remind me always that while anxiety is *with* me,
You are *in* me.
And you are always working,
Through every detail and daydream,
Every thought and feeling,
Every breath,
Every millisecond.
You never stop.

God of life,
You went through death . . . *for me*.
You struggled and sweat and bled.
Your joints ached. Your adrenaline surged.

Your heart raced.

And you faced the darkest door on our behalf.

You opened death's door.

And you walked through it.

Now, you're calling us to you.

We don't flee from suffering.

We run straight at it

Because you're standing right behind it

With open arms,

Longing to give us life through death.

Please, God, help me to be patient.

In the swells of anxiety and suffering,

Help me to stare at you.

Help me to be utterly convinced

That my suffering is not a weapon of the devil;

It's a *tool* of my loving Lord.

Use it, please. Right now.

Use it to draw me into your presence.

Use it to draw me to my knees.

Use it to lead me through your death.

Shape me.

And paint your hope on my eyes,

So that I cannot open them

Without seeing it.

Reader Resource: Taking a Break from the Long-Term Guest

We all have breaking points with anxiety. There are moments when we feel utterly spent, when we just can't take anymore. These are moments that trigger us to ask the long-term guest of anxiety to leave. But these are also moments that reveal our limits and our need for rest. It's okay to seek out times of rest amidst your anxiety. In fact, we need to be intentional about this.

In one of my counseling sessions, I recounted a close call with panic on the New Jersey boardwalk one summer night. My counselor asked me what else I had done that day. "I was 'out of it' for most of the day and a little hyper-vigilant . . . and then I took a three-mile run and felt pretty tired, but other than that there wasn't anything special going on." Her response: "It sounds like you pushed yourself too hard. Having a tough day with nerves, adding a three-mile run, and then turning right around to go to the boardwalk may have been too much."

I didn't like the thought of that. It made me feel restricted at the time. But the more I considered what she said, the more it made sense. I'm different from other people. And that's *okay*. Other people can run a marathon, meet up with friends, and then leave for a vacation in the same day. Other people are world travelers. I'm not. I can't do tons of activities sequentially without rest. I need space. I need down time—to read, regroup, and pray. When I don't get these things, I push myself to a breaking point, and that's when panic sets in.

What about you? What are some triggers for your anxiety, things that you need to recover from? Be intentional about planning some down time for yourself so that you can regroup and face whatever anxiety lies ahead with Christ-conforming courage. Write down your answers for the chart on the next page to help you in this. I've given you some ideas from my own experience.

Trigger # 1   Social engagements

- I can do social engagements in spurts. I love interacting with people, but it takes a toll on my nerves, too. So, I have to allow space in my schedule to decompress. Doing things once or twice a week is fine, but when it gets to be more than that, I feel myself growing more and more irritated with the long-term guest of anxiety.

Trigger # 2   Travel

- I enjoy seeing new places, but travel is also hard for me. I prefer to go to familiar locations and deepen my relationships with those I love. Too much travel is a trigger for me, as is the thought of flying, which I revealed at the end of the last chapter.

Trigger # 3   Conflict

- I'm a conflict-avoider and have always resonated with Matthew 5:19. Being close to discord and conflict even affects me physically. It ties my stomach in knots and makes it difficult for me to swallow. I can be part of conflicts when needed, but I also have to make sure I recover with Scripture reading and prayer.

CHAPTER 6

Fear and Faith: Strangers or Relatives?

KEY IDEA: Fear is something God can use to build your faith.

We have come a long way since chapter one. There we learned that anxiety crushes us, leading us to live life on a leash. That leash brings us to develop patterns of behavior that we might use to take baby steps of faith, all while relying on CHRIST (the acronym we unpacked). The last chapter focused on treating anxiety as a long-term guest. Once we understand that anxiety might be living with us for a while, we can study it more closely. We can look at our fears, for instance, and ask how they are shaping and building our faith. That's the goal of this chapter. And as in every chapter, I'll be reminding you that God is using our anxiety to do great things. How? By bringing our weakness center stage, conforming us to Christ in *his* weakness so that his resurrection life might shine through our bodies.

Strangers or Relatives?

In the last chapter, I gave you two images to mull over: the criminal and the house guest, two portrayals of the same referent. I'd like to do the same in this chapter, but with two different referents. On the one hand, we have *fear*. He's pale and lanky, glazed with nervous sweat, and always jittering when he speaks. He seems ready to bolt at the drop of a pin. Then, on the other hand, we have *faith*. He's quiet but confident, respectably humble, and always quick to listen. These two could hardly be more different. Befriending one seems to leave the other in isolation.

But what if these two know each other? What if they're not strangers? More than that, what if their relationship goes deeper than familiarity? What if they're relatives? I want you to be open to that idea in this chapter. Rather than treating fear and faith as polar opposites, I want you to think of them as relatives who often come to visit you together. Form an image in your mind that you can take with you for this chapter: the odd relatives who show up at your door for an unplanned visit. Do you have the image? Good. Now, let's look at a Bible verse that brings these two relatives to our doorstep.

The verse we'll look at is Exodus 14:31. Let's set the scene. The Egyptians are chasing after the Israelites, cracking whips on chariots and digging heals into horses because they've just realized that they let their slave labor wander into the wilderness. The almighty God of the great plagues has now visibly appeared to the people as a pillar of fire and cloud, coming between his people and their enemy. After the people cross through the parted Red Sea, walls of water to the right and left, they stand and watch God throw the Egyptians into confusion. As chariot wheels sink into the sand, as horses cast off their riders and flee in panic, the Egyptians are struck with wide-eyed fear. "Let us flee from before Israel, for the Lord fights for them against the Egyptians" (Exod. 14:25). Indeed, *the Lord* fights for them.

Moses then stretches his hand over the sea. The walls of water break. The surging power of the waves closes in on the Egyptians, crushing and drowning. Imagine the jaw-dropping silence of the people as the white-water hisses back into place—a loud period on the sentence of God's judgement. Then comes our verse, "Israel saw the great power that the Lord used against the Egyptians, so the people feared the Lord, and they believed in the Lord and in his servant Moses" (Exod. 14:31).

Look at the order of the people's response: *fear first, then faith*. Here are the two relatives, one setting the stage for the other. Fear, in other words, prepared the people for faith, for belief, which was a righteous response to a holy God. This is reaffirmed later when the people are standing before Mount Sinai, where God has descended in smoke and fire. As God talks to Moses in the tongue of thunder (Exod.

19:19), the people beg him to intercede for them. They were "afraid and trembled, and they stood far off" (Exod. 20:18). There's our first, shaking, sweat-glazed relative. In response to their fear, Moses tells them, "Do not fear, for God has come to test you, that the fear of him may be before you, that you may not sin" (20:20). Once again, fear is in place to *help* the people respond righteously to a holy God.

Notice that there are two types of fear, or maybe our first relative has a split personality. First, there's quivering fear, fear that's ready to flee, to bolt in terror. Moses (and God, especially in 1 John 4:18), says "no" to that kind of fear. Perfect love will not let that sort of fear stay. But then right after this Moses mentions a second kind of fear, what we might call *reverential fear*, "fear of him." Moses says "yes" to this kind of fear. In fact, he says that God *intends* for this kind of fear to be "before you." Why? "That you may not sin." Reverential fear, apparently, can guard us against sin. And that's an important part of faith, since the life of faith is a life of righteousness, a life that repents of and flees from sin (1 Cor. 6:18; 2 Tim. 2:22). Are you starting to see the family resemblance between fear and faith?

Now, I'll admit that this sounds a bit primeval in today's culture: that God would use fear to bring his people to submission. In conjures up images of a wrathful God who's only concerned with power and punishment. But we must remember that God is *using* fear to develop the people's relationship with himself, just as he *uses* our anxiety to conform us to the image of Christ. As we saw in the last chapter, relationship is primary for God. He doesn't bring about fear because he loves to wield power; he brings about fear because he loves his *people*.

"God doesn't bring about fear because he loves to wield power; he brings about fear because he loves his people."

Fear, in other words, is a providential *tool* in the hands of God. And that's really what we've been seeing all along with anxiety, fear's stepchild. Fear is not an end in itself. That's why in the New Testament John can say, "There is no fear in love, but perfect love casts out fear. For fear has to do with punishment, and whoever fears has not been perfected in love" (1 John 4:18). In a perfect relationship, there is no fear. But because on this side of paradise our relationship with God is not perfect, a kind of fear (reverential fear) is a regular tool in the hands of God, preparing us for faith and giving us a tangible reason to steer clear of sinful habits and decisions.

The good news of the gospel is that Christ has dealt the first kind of fear, the fear of terror and judgment, a lethal blow. We don't fear death or damnation because the cause of death and damnation—sin—has been swallowed up in Christ's victory (1 Cor. 15:54–57)! The fear that we once felt was unavoidable has been crushed by Christ. Now we have a new spirit within us, "a spirit not of fear but of power and love and self-control" (2 Tim. 1:7).

We must read the story of the Israelites—and the story of our own lives—in the light of Christ's work if we want to understand how the split personality of fear is related to faith. The reverential fear of the Israelites in Exodus served a relational purpose, but the fear of terror and judgment is what Christ would ultimately destroy. In fact, the way in which the fear of the Israelites led to a holy and faithful relationship with God was the work of Christ, before his incarnation. The Son of God has always been our mediator. So, when the fear of the Israelites led them into relationship with God, there is a very real sense in which *Christ* was leading them into relationship with God, for it is only through him that we can have a lasting relationship with the Father and Holy Spirit (John 14:6; 1 Tim. 2:5).

In short, reverential fear preceded the Israelites' faith, as it often does in our own lives, but now Christ has taken the place of our fear of judgment and death. We cling to him in hope and trust, knowing that the earthly fears we encounter (and we encounter many of them) can't overcome or even overshadow the eternal *relationship* that Christ has secured for us in the power of the Holy Spirit.

For much of our lives, fear will precede faith. Fear will also serve the purpose of preventing sin. As the Exodus story implies, God has a history of using our fear to lead us into relationship with himself. But know this: ultimately, faith overcomes the second kind of fear—the fear of terror, judgement and death—for that kind of fear is from the fallen world, and Christ has overcome the world (John 16:33). My dear reader, Christ has overcome the uncertainty and timidity of anxiety. Christ has overcome the cold sweats, the pinhole throat, the difficulty swallowing, the hyper-vigilance, the heat spells, the heart palpitations, the shortness of breath. Christ is standing on the other side of our anxiety and asking us never to take our eyes off him, and the Spirit holds up our chin when we try to look down.

A Positive Take on Fear and Anxiety

Now, bring this a little closer to our anxiety. Let me start with a hard truth: *It's pain-fully difficult for us to let what we know affect how we feel.* Nowhere is this more obvious than in our struggle with anxiety. The feelings scream at us with deafening decibels; they drown out every other sound; they demand our undivided attention. In these circumstances, it's ridiculously difficult to let what we know affect us. We want the feelings to go away so that we can think rationally. But what if the feelings are there for a higher purpose? What if the fear-inducing symptoms we encounter are tools God is using to bring us to faith? That's what I've been saying from the outset. Recall the "C" in the CHRIST acronym—*consider the feelings as spiritual medicine.* The feelings we have are not just terrors; they're *tools.*

The ugly feelings of anxiety, all of the nerve-wracking symptoms, are tools in the hands of God. We don't use tools by getting rid of them, but that's such a common approach to anxiety in our day. We're so bent on eliminating anxiety that we completely ignore the possibility that we might not simply be eliminating an evil. We might *also* be eliminating a relational tool that can bring us to deeper faith. My point is this: We use tools by taking them up and working with them. And this is related to what we discovered in the previous chapter. We're not trying to kick the criminal of anxiety out; we're trying to learn how God will shape us *through* our residence with a long-term guest.

Let me encourage you as you deal with your anxiety today. I offer a simple truth: *Christ is on the other side of your feelings.* Faith is going to follow your fear, just as it did with the Israelites, just as it did for all of God's people throughout history. Faith will follow. Faith *will* follow. Repeat that to yourself as long as you need to for it to become default. Fear is not detached from God's purposes; nothing is. Fear is always a stage in the divinely governed process that builds our faith.

This leads to something very strange: as Christians, we can meet anxiety with *enthusiasm* (I'll show this in a case study at the end of the chapter). Remember James's words, "Count it all joy, my brothers, when you meet trials of various kinds, for you know that the testing of your faith produces steadfastness. And let steadfast-ness have its full effect, that you may be perfect and complete, lacking in nothing" (James 1:2–4). Anxiety is certainly a trial, but we can count it *joy* because we know to whom it is leading us: Christ. Anxiety *cannot*—please hear this—it *cannot* ultimately destroy you. It has only the potency to strike you down, but that will just make you stronger in your faith. For the Christian, faith will *always* follow fear.

Here's something you might try, something that I've tried many times. It sounds a bit insane at first, but biblical faith can look that way. Abraham didn't look sane when he picked up his life and walked toward a nameless country! When you feel anxious, rather than saying "No" in your head, say, "Yes." When I feel anxious, my impulse is to say, "No, no, no! Not again. Please God, not here! Not now. No!" I still react that way many times. And one author suggests that this impulse is precisely what can make anxiety worse![1] When we flee from fear, we panic if we're not running fast enough. But what if we said, "Yes"? What if we didn't run? What if we stayed? It's counterintuitive, I know, but because of the power of God's Spirit working in us, we can take the greatest obstacle in our life and say, "Yes. Good. God, use this." You can say this with utter confidence because you *know*—not *think*, but *know*—that God is working . . . right now. While your breath shortens; while your throat tightens; while you start feeling removed from reality—the divine surgeon is at work on your soul, making an incision, sewing his Son into you with the thread of his Spirit. He's binding you to himself. He's using your fear, your anxiety, to bring you into deeper relationship. The needlework of the Lord is the salvation of the soul. Because you know that, you can say, "Yes." And have no doubt: God will always teach you when your heart is willing and open to him. He's always ready to guide you into the faith that lies just ahead of your fear.

"The divine surgeon is at work on your soul, making an incision, sewing his Son into you with the thread of his Spirit."

Fear Building Faith

Let me be blunt with you: The fact that fear leads to faith will take months, maybe years, to sink in. And it's something we have to relearn every time we forget that we're weak—and that happens all too often. I would even go so far as to say that it's very difficult for us to have faith *without* fear being present in our lives. It's not impossible, but it's very difficult. Why? Because fear, and its attendant physical symptoms, is like fire burning away the dross of sin. Remember the adjusted Hemmingway quo-

---

1   Barry McDonagh, *Dare: The New Way to End Anxiety and Stop Panic Attacks* (BMD Publishing, 2015).

tation I brought up in a previous chapter? "Anxiety burns the fat off our souls." On this side of eternity, we'll always have something that needs burning.

Now, I want to be careful here. God isn't out to scare us into loving him. He uses our fear to draw us into relationship with himself, but this is no sadistic game on his part. He uses us as we are, and we *are* creatures who have a damaged and brittle faith. We're constantly in need of spiritual instruction because we're constantly wayward in our walk with him. As Robert Robinson wrote in "Come Thou Fount of Every Blessing," we are prone to wander, prone to leave the God we love.

"When my mind feels free of fear, my heart feels free of commitment."

Like everyone else who deals with an anxiety disorder, I've gone through ups and downs—moments where it's difficult just to function and perform routine tasks, and other moments when anxiety seems absent. Without fail, here's what I've noticed: *Whenever anxiety leaves my life, waywardness sets in.* When my mind feels free of fear, my heart feels free of commitment. As comfort creeps into my life, slowly and silently, a canyon opens in my soul, putting space between my behavior and the purposes of God. It becomes more difficult to pray, more difficult to cultivate godly motivations, more difficult to put others above myself. In short, when I'm not tormented by anxiety, I become tormented by something else: my own sin. Satan himself seems to wait for my anxiety to dissolve, and then he sends in his minions, tempting me in every direction.

Charles Spurgeon reflected on this in his writing on spiritual warfare. Freedom from anxiety is a sort of joy, a triumph over the hazards our minds introduce or perceive. Yet, he says,

> If we are joyous and triumphant and are something in the frame of mind that David was in when he danced before the ark, then Satan knows how to set his traps by tempting us to presumption—"My mountain standeth firm, I shall never be moved"—or else to carnal security—"Soul, take thine ease, thou hast much goods laid up for many years"—or to self-righteousness—"My own power and goodness

exalted me."[2]

I've noticed that I'm especially vulnerable to idolatry when I'm free of anxiety, and it can take the form of nearly anything: writing, coffee, exercise, sweets, praise from others—things that I get more excited about than communion with God.[3] *Anything* with behavior-shaping power that brings us more joy and passion than our relationship with God is an idol. How right John Calvin was: our hearts are idol factories![4] When I'm closed off from fear, I'm wide open to idols. So, in a strange sense, I've come to appreciate my anxiety as a means of building spiritual defense and circumspection. God is using something that I hate to do something that I love.

Anxiety as a Spiritual Directive

Anxiety, in this sense, is what I call a *spiritual directive*. Again, this is linked to the "C" from our acronym: *consider the feelings as spiritual medicine*. You might even think of it as an *aid* in spiritual warfare. That's counterintuitive to most of us, since we believe that anxiety is an *attack* on us as Christians. Indeed, it can be. Christ himself warned us of anxiety as a threat to trust (Matt. 6:25–34). But in God's mysterious providence, he uses the evil of the world for his good purposes. As Romans 8:28 says, God uses *all* things for the good of those who love him—anxiety included.

Now, how does this work, exactly? How is anxiety a spiritual directive? Let me try to illustrate by recapping some of what we've noted thus far. Anxiety is potent. As I said when I first experienced it, anxiety has *crushing* power. Everyone who struggles with an anxiety disorder knows this all too well. But that power always pushes us in one of two spiritual directions. In fact, these are the only two spiritual directions that exist: towards God in trust and love or away from him in distrust and fear. Satan himself, as the supreme doubter of God's words, stands at one end. The all-knowing, wholly good, triune God stands at the other end.

Here are a few things I want you to soak up. First, anxiety will always move you in one of these directions. We always respond to anxiety in some way. We're never static. As spiritual creatures made in God's image, we're dynamic and relation-al, always moving and developing in relation to someone, whether that's God in his

2   Charles Spurgeon, *Spiritual Warfare in a Believer's Life*, ed. Robert Hall (Lynnwoood, WA: Emerald Books, 1993), 102.

3   Tim Keller's book on this continues to be very helpful: *Counterfeit Gods: The Empty Promises of Money, Sex, and Power, and the Only Hope that Matters* (New York: Viking, 2009).

4   John Calvin, *Institutes of the Christian Religion*, 1.11.8.

goodness and mercy, or Satan in his evil and corruption. It's never a question of *if* you will move in response to your anxiety; it's simply a question of *which direction.*

Second—and please hear this!—*Satan is a liar.* In John's Gospel, Jesus says, "He was a murderer from the beginning, and does not stand in the truth, because there is no truth in him. When he lies, he speaks out of his own character, for he is a liar and the father of lies" (John 8:44). When you move towards Satan in distrust and fear, you are simultaneously moving towards falsehood; you are moving towards the way things are *not.* What exactly is the *lie* that we're talking about when it comes to anxiety? It's the lie that your physical experience is for your demise, that anxiety can *only* lead you into bad places, and that you should therefore run from it. That is a lie. It's a lie that Satan himself hopes you believe, and one to which we often give ourselves. But Romans 8:28 says the opposite: *everything* that you experience is ultimately for your *good.*

This lesson sounds very simple, like a Sunday school basic, but those of us who struggle with anxiety know how hard of a lesson it is to learn. In a panic attack, for instance, your body goes on high alert. It tells you to run, to flee, to get help because you're going to die; you're going to stop breathing; you're going to pass out at the wheel and drive your car off the road. You're going to seize up in public and everyone's going to stare at you. You're going to . . . . And, in fact, I know people who have passed out from panic attacks. It can happen. And you'll survive. The message that anxiety sends is not suggestive; it's direct and abrasive; it oppresses us physically and spiritually. In the midst of that direct oppression, it takes great spiritual strength to say, "No. I see the lie. This anxiety is *not* going to lead me to a bad place. It's going to lead me to a *good* place because God works for my good. God, what are you teaching me? Show me." And the spiritual strength we have in saying this is nothing short of a gift from the Holy Spirit, our helper and comforter (John 14:26).

Third is the refrain I've been singing throughout the book: God providentially controls our anxiety for our good (Rom. 8:28) by enabling it to push us in his direction, and to shape us to Christ. This is where we embrace Spirit-given trust and love. When I'm anxious, the spiritual fog in my life lifts. The distractions disappear. The idols burn up and turn to dust. Even while the symptoms are painful and disconcerting, I see straight ahead of me to the God of truth. I know with utter certainty what must take priority in my life: prayer, meditation on God's word, sacrificial action for those I love (and don't love), and worship. And here's the best part: I *act* on those priorities. When the distractions fall away, action-based faith rises to the surface.

Paul writes in Ephesians 2:8–10, "For by grace you have been saved through faith. And this is not your own doing; it is the gift of God, not a result of works, so that no one may boast. For we are his workmanship, created in Christ Jesus for good works, which God prepared beforehand, that we should walk in them." There is no greater joy and motivation than that which comes from walking with God, from acting in accordance with our identity as followers of Christ. This is not only because when we do so, we're walking in the truth (2 John 1:4), living according to the way things really are, but because we're focused on a relationship that is eternal.

Do you know that—not just know it conceptually, but know it in your bones? Anxiety tries to make us forget this again and again and again: you and I are in an *eternal* relationship with God, a relationship that not even death can break. Because of this, we're called to be "heavenly minded." Paul admonishes us in Colossians 3:1–3, "If then you have been raised with Christ, seek the things that are above, where Christ is, seated at the right hand of God. Set your minds on things that are above, not on things that are on earth. For you have died, and your life is hidden with Christ in God."

Now, being heavenly minded can mean several things, but one of them is this: Keep your mind fixed on the eternal destiny that God has prepared for you, communion with him. That means looking at anxiety not as a barrier to be removed, but as something that pushes us to Christ-shadowing weakness, something that warms the clay of our souls so that we can be shaped to Christ's image. Anxiety turns us into vessels ready to be filled with his resurrection life. It's this Christ conformity that redirects our lives, that makes us reassess our priorities and values so that we can walk with God in trustful, loving communion.

In short, anxiety is a *spiritual directive* in the sense that it has great power to push us in a Godward direction, the end of which is unending communion with him.

Can You Have Faith without Fear?

On this side of paradise, can we really have faith without fear? Yes, it's possible. Some of us have experienced it for a time. But it's far more common for God to *use* fear to draw us closer to himself. We're still walking the long street of sanctification. Holiness is a pilgrimage, not an errand.

What's more, there's a holy fear that should always be with us, that reverential fear that I mentioned earlier. "The fear of the Lord is the beginning of wisdom" (Prov. 9:10). There's a godly reverence that all Christians are called to embrace as we work out our salvation with fear and trembling (Phil. 2:12). So, fear is not itself a pure evil. Reverential fear of God is a biblical mandate. And when we experience something *other* than reverential fear, we can trust that God is using it as a spiritual directive, and that in the end he will destroy it. Until then, we know that it will draw us to a place of weakness. The world rushes *away* from this, but we rush *toward* it. We follow in a long line of brothers and sisters who find *God's* strength in *their* weakness. As Paul said, when we are weak—when we are crushed, humbled, brought low— then we are strong (2 Cor. 12:10).

My anxiety-ridden friends, I hope and pray that anxiety will be just a season for you, that your winter in the tomb of trial will bring a resurrection spring. But for those of us who seem to be dealing with anxiety for the long haul, we have to remind ourselves daily that this is not a *bad* thing. In fact, it's the soil in which God will sow many seeds of hope. We don't enjoy anxiety, and we can plead with Paul that God would pull out this thorn in our flesh. But God may have the same answer for us that he did for the Apostle: "My strength is made perfect in your weakness." No matter how long our anxiety lasts, no matter how many seasons of it circle through our life-calendar, God has ordained to use it *for* us, not against us. Anxiety has unparalleled power to draw us into deeper trust and love with the Father, Son, and Spirit.

So, on this side of paradise, we may not have faith *without* fear. And when our fear disappears, our fervency for the things of God may dwindle. Apart from fear, you may find, as I did, that you drift easily in the wrong direction. Your anxiety may turn out to be an anchor for your soul, not a hole in the hull of your comfort. After twelve years of battling it myself, I can honestly say I'm thankful that God has kept it in my life. It keeps my soul in God's harbor. Without it, I chase after every breeze.

A Case Study

Now, to help remind myself that I'm still in this struggle with you, and to show you how this understanding of fear and faith can help, I believe God gave me a sort of case study on the very morning that I wrote this chapter. I offer it to you here.

I'll start with a confession: I woke up at 5:00am and drank too much coffee. Those of us who suffer with anxiety *really* have to be careful with caffeine intake. Caffeine jolts your system and puts you on high-alert. In the language of an anxiety sufferer, caffeine can bring you pretty close to the edge of panic if you're not careful, and if you don't balance caffeine intake with exercise. I hadn't been balancing those two, so you can imagine how I felt: amped, jittery, and intense. That lead to some clear writing for an hour, but then I got in the car to go to work. Enter fear, pale-faced and sweating.

As I drove down the highway through the dense fog, my shoulders began to rise. The pesky pinhole throat sensation showed up, and I could feel hot adrenaline beginning to course through my legs and chest. Then came the difficulty swallowing, and an internal dialogue ensued.

"You know these feelings. They're as old as you are. You're going to be okay. . . . In fact, weren't you just writing about the relationship between fear and faith a few minutes ago? Time to test the theory! You've got the fear right now. You can feel it—that unwanted, long-term guest of anxiety. Now, what about the faith?"

The feelings were growing stronger in the midst of this dialogue, and I felt closer and closer to panic. Panic tells you to run the other way, to get out of the situation. A little whisper from the past said, "Slam the breaks! Pull off to the side of the road already! You're going to seize up any second!"

At this moment, I thought, "Isn't this *exactly* what I want to help other people with? Haven't I just been encouraging people to see the positive side of fear, to see fear as a tool? I'm not going to run from it. I'm going to run *into* it. This is the moment when the internal dialogue changed and took on a Jacob-wrestling-with-God scenario. I'm not saying that my anxious feelings were God—but I did feel as if I was in a wrestling match that was meant to build and shape my faith, just as Jacob was (Gen. 32:22–32). In my mind, I pictured two versions of myself sparring with each other in a wrestling ring. I wasn't getting rid of this fear. No, no. With God in my corner and the shaping of my soul at stake, I stepped into the ring and called fear out. All of this was happening internally as I drove down the highway (makes you wonder what other souls are dealing with when you're commuting to work alongside them!). Here's how the conversation played out.

Me: "Let's go! Get in the ring! I'm not wasting this opportunity. Come on."
Fear: "Fine by me. Let's do this."

Our arms locked as we threw each other around the ring—red-faced and wild. He pushed; I pulled. He grabbed my shirt, and I grabbed his. We shifted feet and circled each other, looking for the best move we could make. Then he ran at me. I hugged his chest and threw him down on the floor.

Me: "That's it? That's what you're coming at me with? The same old pinhole throat, adrenaline veins, and heat swells?

Fear: "You're weak and you know it!"

Another series of spins and circles and punches—all the awkwardness of a middle-school brawl. As I kept the image in my head, I noticed something remarkable: the feelings began to subside. The adrenaline started to recede a bit. I was stepping back from the ledge of panic. Fear was trying to get out of the ring. But I wasn't finished.

Me: "No, no, no! Get back in this ring! If I'm going to have a good shaping workout for my soul this morning, I'm gonna make it count!"

I pulled fear back into the ring and pushed him around a few more times, watching him lose his strength. My anxious feelings receded even more. I was beginning to feel more normal. And now my mind was clearing as I realized what was going on: *this* was textbook spiritual warfare. Satan would have loved nothing more than to see me seize up in panic, call an ambulance, and doubt that I could ever drive to work again. In fact, I'm sure he was spurring on my sinful desire for more caffeine earlier, which got the whole thing started in the first place.

But this battle belonged to the Lord, and he'd won through me. Fear had served its purpose, had built and strengthened the muscles of my faith, had shown Christ's resurrection life in my weak body. Fear and faith, the odd relatives, had met and served *God's* greater purpose for me: the purpose of shaping me to his suffering Son!

I was elated. I was praising God. In the midst of *my* poor decision to have too much coffee, God had orchestrated a spiritual skirmish and walked me through every second of it! He'd used my anxiety as a tool, just as he'd done a thousand times before, but I was still surprised at how powerful the experience was, how much soul-shaping had taken place in the span of ten minutes. For the remainder of my commute (which is about an hour), I was focused, calm, and just ecstatic to have witnessed the resurrection life of Christ overthrow the death-dealing feelings of anxiety! Christ won, and so I had won with him. My soul was quiet and satisfied. Faith was standing in the ring victorious, while fear was having his wounds dressed on the sidelines. What a match!

Theology: Finding Yourself in a Story

That little case study is a concrete example of what it's like to live life in the context of the Great Story. I'm sure thousands of other drivers across America experienced similar feelings that morning (anxiety disorders affect some forty-million Americans each year, after all), and they probably responded very differently. The same feelings in one person can evoke remarkably different responses in another. Why? Because of how we *interpret* them! Interpretation is huge. We talk about hermeneutics as a biblical discipline, but it's also a *life* discipline. Everything in our world needs interpreting, and God has given us the interpretation in his word. Thank God for his speech!

From God's word, I know that he uses anxiety and fear to shape my faith, so I could run *towards* it and not *away* from it on my morning commute. And once I made the decision to do that, I had a front-row seat to the spiritual shaping that God would do. But this whole scenario would have been impossible unless I had taken a certain approach to my fear and anxiety, unless I had a certain interpretation of my feelings. I embraced a spiritually-purposeful, Christ-conforming interpretation, and that made all the difference.

More broadly speaking, what I did on my morning commute was simply *find myself in a story*, in the Great Story. I interpreted my present experiences and even bodily sensations in light of what I know from the characters, events, and teachings of Scripture. Everyone, in fact, has to do this. Everyone is interpreting his or her life as a part of a story—whether that's the complete, hope-filled, restorative, Christ-conforming story of Scripture or the fragmented, distressing, grief-stricken short stories of the world.

"Everyone is interpreting his or her life as a part of a story."

This story that we find ourselves in isn't over. The pages are all written, but we can't turn to them yet. We can't turn to them until God calls us home or Christ returns. But we can't let that "not yet" element keep us from owning the story on a daily basis. This isn't just *a* story or even *the* story; it's *our* story. It's *our* history, *our* happening—our tale and our turn, our life and our death.

That's why I've taken the ending of each chapter to retell it. I know you've picked up this book to read about anxiety, and I hope you're getting the help you seek, but even more than that, my prayer is that you firmly grasp the Bible's *context* for interpreting what you're experiencing right now. The fears and the sensations you have are not accidental. They fit perfectly into the script that we all must read in our own way: the script of Christ-conformity, the script of moving *through* weakness and suffering to strength in the Lord. My reader, we need to own that script. We need to clutch it in both hands and call out from it each day, from our morning commute to our nighttime routine.

My experience for over twelve years has been an anxiety disorder. I don't know how long you've been dealing with anxiety, but I do know that both of us have to put all of that anxiety-ridden time and experience on the pages of our script. We have to read our experience in that context. More than that: we have to write our stories into that story, letting the script of Christ-conformity change how we act in the future. Everyday we have to ask ourselves, *how do I understand and cope with my anxiety in light of the Great Story?* Take some time right now to write out your answer to that question.

If it makes you feel any better, I didn't embrace this script before I was diagnosed with an anxiety disorder; I learned it along the way, as I went to seminary and read more of God's word. I wish I'd grasped this so much earlier. I really do. But I'm laying it out for you here in hopes that you might find yourself in its pages sooner than I did.

Reflection Questions and Prayer

1. How do you tend to respond when anxiety starts to affect you physically? Are fear and faith still strangers for you in those moments? Would you be willing, the next time, to work through the feelings and see how deeply related fear and faith can be? It only takes one concrete moment to make a breakthrough.

2. What are other places in Scripture where *fear* seems to come before *faith*, or where fear and faith are treated more like relatives and less like strangers?

3. How do you respond to the biblical idea that faith comes *after* fear? If the idea makes you frustrated, explain why. Dig into your soul a little bit and uncover what's there. What do you want instead?

4. What positive effects can fear have on our faith more broadly?

5. What happens to your spiritual life when you're free from anxiety? Do you find that you continue to grow closer to the Lord or further away from him?

6. Describe a time when you experienced a *reverential* fear of God. How did that affect your spiritual life? Was the effect short term, or did it last longer than you expected?

7. How has your own experience with anxiety helped to push you either *further from* or *closer to* God?

8. In what ways have you seen God shape your soul through anxiety? Think of a specific example and share it with a group or a friend.

9. Believing that anxiety is a *tool* in the hands of God requires that you trust in God's sovereignty. What are the main obstacles to developing this trust right now?

Prayer

Lord, though I hate it,
I know that fear and anxiety
Are spiritual directives.
Anxiety turns my shoulders
So that I am square with you.
You are my direction, Lord.
Use my anxiety to show me
When I need to turn around,
To trust you and your great love
Above every feeling,
Every thought,
Every whisper from the devil.
He is a liar.
You *are* truth.
Grow in me.
Silence his lies with your promises.
Help me to work through the feelings
To follow your voice.

Oh Lord, I know that you have used

The fear of your people

To bring them to faith.

That is all I want: *faith*.

I know this is a gift of your Spirit.

Holy Comforter, please . . . give it to me.

Let my heart always be open

To the path that fear is pointing to

As long as that path is beaten out

On the dust of Scripture.

Keep me ever reading your word,

Ever hearing your voice,

So that I can walk through fear

To faith.

As I rise and walk through the day,

Remind me that you have told a story.

It's a wondrous story. It's the Great Story.

And you've put me in its pages.

I forget.

I forget *so* often that I'm a word in your story.

I believe the lie that I'm *just here*.

That the world around me is *just here*.

Help me to see that this is a lie.

Help me to embrace the context

You have called me into.

Bring me to trust

That your hands are holding me,

That your hands are shaping me,

That your hands are healing me,

That your voice is leading me.

And when I don't trust you,

Put a pick and shovel in my hands.

Help me to dig with diligence,

To mine for the trust

That is buried beneath my blindness.

CHAPTER 7

The Shortcomings of a Purely Rational Approach

KEY IDEA: A purely rational approach to anxiety is ignorant of spiritual warfare.

N ow we know a bit more about the relationship between fear and faith, and that should make us challenge any approach to anxiety that seems to ignore its spiritual purposes. In this chapter, we address one of those, the most common one, in my opinion. It's what I'll call *the way of pure rationality*.

The Way of Pure Rationality

The way of pure rationality is our attempt to use reason *without* any conscious regard for God's word. It's a use of reason that momentarily ignores God's speech in an attempt to get rid of the fear, doubt, and physical oppression of anxiety. The keyword in this approach is usually *why*. "Why am I feeling this way?" "Why am I anxious?" "Why does driving at night bother me so much?" "Why do certain social settings feel imprisoning?" "Why do I start to hyperventilate when I hear people talking about flying?" Why? Why? Why?

Now, let's not rush past the obvious benefits of asking these sorts of questions. We're made in the image of an ultimately rational God. There's a biblically prescribed use and function for reason in the Christian life. And we rely on reason more broadly simply to walk through the world each day.

But here's the problem: when rationality becomes the *only* approach we take to anxiety (pure rationality), the greater spiritual purposes that God has for us—i.e., fear and weakness serving as opportunities for Christ-conformity, anxiety working as a spiritual directive—are pushed out of the picture. We become rational calculators and assessors rather than servants of Christ who look at pain and adversity as tools in the hands of God. Our goal becomes pinpointing and eliminating anxiety, not prayerfully facing and using it.

When I first developed my anxiety disorder, I can't tell you how many times I or loved ones practiced the way of pure rationality. Family members would repeatedly ask, "But why are you anxious? What's making you feel this way? There's nothing threatening you." The fact that I didn't have answers to those questions made me feel even more anxious! Sometimes I wanted to snap back: "I don't *know*! I'm just anxious all the time!"

"When it comes down to it, reason is not the panacea for the soul; Christ is."

Now, we might respond by thinking, "Well, there's always a reason. *Something* must be causing my anxiety." Yes, there's always a reason for what occurs in the world—from planes coursing through the blue sky to dusk particles drifting through the morning air. That doesn't mean we can know what it is. But more to the point: we can't address the *why* question outside the context of the Great Story. In other words, it's not just a matter of asking *why*; it's a matter of asking why *in light of what we know about God's purposes for our suffering*—suffering as a spiritual directive, suffering as Christ conformity, suffering as a means for manifesting the resurrection life of God's Son in our bodies. In contrast with this approach, the textbook response of pure rationality is to ignore the Great Story and search for *purely* physiological or situational explanations of our anxiety. And make no mistake, many times there are plain reasons for our anxiety, and addressing those reasons can have a profound effect on us. Causality and reasoning are not evils; they are gifts from God and of great value.

But to isolate those reasons from the greater spiritual purposes that God has for the details of our daily life is to do ourselves a great disservice and to ignore the most important events in world history: Christ's death and resurrection. When it comes down to it, reason is not the panacea for the soul; Christ is.

Consider a few things with me. First, what if anxiety is fundamentally irrational? Or, what if we're not able to perceive a clear cause or reason, because our lives and personalities are so complex and multifaceted? Certainly, we try to look for reasons by leaning on the body of Christ. I'm a firm believer that we can and should seek the help of others, especially well-trained Christian counselors and pastors, when digging up the roots of our anxiety. But even then, we may not be able to pinpoint exactly *why* anxiety is an issue for us in purely physiological or situational categories. This was precisely my predicament when I first dealt with anxiety. There didn't seem to be a clear situational cause for it. There were things that made me anxious, of course, but these were things that hadn't made me anxious before. Why the sudden change? I had no idea—neither did my doctor, though she offered a physiological explanation. At a later point, my counselor helped uncover some potential physiological and situational causes, but these were not always consistent. I felt lost. Was my brain just broken?[1]

I felt lost because I wasn't living in the right story. I wasn't able to understand the events and feelings in my life within a purposeful context—a context that not only made use of my suffering, but (and here's the hard truth) *required* it. Suffering as Christ-conformity isn't the anomaly in the Christian life; it's the norm. It's the path we're on, whether or not we realize it. Your feet have to fall on suffering, because that's where Christ's feet fell, and no servant is greater than his master.

I didn't grasp this when I began combating anxiety. Instead, I tried to use pure rationality. And note this: when rationality offers no insight, rationalists often become *empiricists*. In other words, if reason can't solve the problem for us, then something else measurable, and often physical, can. Hence, doctors will look at your family history and the chemical functions of your brain (empirical data). They'll explain your anxiety as something to which you were genetically predisposed. For instance, my mother has struggled with anxiety in her life. Therefore, I was prone to developing an anxiety disorder. That's the explanation.

Or perhaps they'll blame anxiety on the brain: you're not producing enough

---

1   I recommend a helpful little article by Rebecca Carrell, "When the Brain Betrays the Body," *Fathom Magazine*, May 20, 2019, https://www.fathommag.com/stories/when-the-brain-betrays-the-body.

serotonin. You need the help of SSRIs (selective serotonin reuptake inhibitors, such as Paxil or Prozac) to correct your brain's chemical functions.[2]

Now, please hear me: I'm not discrediting rationality, genetics, or empirical data based on how our bodies function. As I've already said, reason is a gift, our genetics have an obvious role to play in our medical history, and the complex processes of our brains may show deficiencies as compared to a "normal" functioning brain. These things are all helpful and valid resources for us. That's not what I'm taking issue with here. And, to be candid with you, I've been taking medication for years, and it has been, on the whole, a great blessing to me. So has counseling and the wisdom of medical professionals. The problem with these approaches (rationality, genetics, empiricism) isn't what they offer. It's what they *don't* offer.

Notice that none of these approaches has any room for *spiritual purpose*. None of them considers Christ-conformity. None of them looks at anxiety as a spiritual directive at work in our relationship with God. With pure rationality, faith is, at best, marginalized and, at worst, completely ignored. The spiritual component of anxiety is left by the wayside.

That's not a minor problem! But many people can turn it into one by being pragmatic: "The medicine works, so what's the big deal? My anxiety is getting better. I'm getting my life back." The problem for Christians is that this approach discounts something that the Bible says is utterly critical: *spiritual warfare*.

The Way of Spiritual Warfare

We live during a time when people have made every attempt to *de-supernaturalize* the world. Wizards, dragons, and trolls have been put on the same terrain as angels, demons, and the devil. The unspoken assumption for most people today (including many Christians) is that spiritual warfare is an outdated way of dealing with problems that science and modern medicine are better equip to handle. Spiritual warfare is more of an afterthought for many Christians, something that their pastor has to remind them of; but it rarely takes center stage in their assessment of the situation. It's more of a catch-all category for anything that doesn't fit into the boxes of science, medicine, and psychology.

The problem is that spiritual warfare *does* take center stage in the Great Story of Scripture. Remember that we need a context to interpret our experience.

---

2   SSRIs help regulate the function of the nerve cells in your brain. They prevent those cells from taking back the serotonin they release in transmitting messages to your brain. This leaves you with more serotonin. Serotonin is a chemical our brains produce, serving a variety of functions, among them is emotional wellbeing and happiness.

If your context is the Great Story, then spiritual warfare can't be an afterthought; it has to be primary. We have to *start* our assessment and interpretation of the problems we encounter by considering the spiritual purposes those problems are serving (Christ-conformity) and the attempts of an adversary to thwart those purposes.

We've already been looking at the spiritual purposes that anxiety can serve in our lives. But we haven't explicitly considered one of the most basic facts of Scripture, one of the central tenets from the Great Story: *every one of us is born into a cosmic and personal war for our soul.* The Apostle Paul is direct with us: "For we do not wrestle against flesh and blood, but against the rulers, against the authorities, against the cosmic powers over this present darkness, against the spiritual forces of evil in the heavenly places" (Eph. 6:12). Cosmic and personal spiritual war—that's what every single person in this world is up against at this very moment. The real travesty of the situation isn't that we're often losing spiritual battles; it's that we're mostly ignorant of them.

Why? As noted above, we live in an age dominated by rational and empirical thinking. Our default perspective on the world is a de-supernaturalized perspective. What's true must be what we can understand or sense with our body. Anything beyond the reach of the mind is functionally treated as non-existent. That poses a grave threat to Christians who worship a God who is (1) an incomprehensible being and (2) a Spirit. Our minds will never wrap themselves around the fullness of God, and we cannot empirically verify God's presence with us, though he is omnipresent. In fact, he is our very environment *for* existence (Acts 17:28)!

All of this puts Christians in a precarious position: The God who sovereignly rules over all things has told us plainly in his word that we're all in a spiritual war, and yet the world we inhabit tells us that God and this "spiritual world" of ours are basically imaginary. What do we do? *We choose.* We choose everyday, even every hour. We choose whose voice we accept as authoritative. We choose whose voice is true. We choose whose voice will ring in our ears. We choose. Is it the voice of God in Scripture, who tells us we are in grave danger, or is it the voice of our collective culture, which encourages us to keep sauntering through the world like tired dogs?

The decision that we make each day and hour varies. But there's something else that doesn't: the attacks of our spiritual nemesis. You see, Satan doesn't care whether or not we acknowledge him. In fact, he gets on quite well when we don't. Think of it in common military settings. What sort of target is the most vulnerable? The one that's wholly ignorant of attack, the country that carries on as if no one really intended it any harm. Contrary to the popular expression, ignorance isn't bliss; it's death. To be ignorant of our spiritual war is to be most open to attack and destruction. This is our position if we treat spiritual warfare as an outdated myth. This is our position if we take the way of pure rationality.

> ## "Satan doesn't care whether or not we acknowledge him. In fact, he gets on quite well when we don't."

Spiritual warfare isn't mythical or marginal; it's prevalent and pervasive. What does this mean for those of us who suffer from anxiety? It means that there's no such thing as *mere anxiety*. We noted in an earlier chapter that our anxiety is always being used. Ultimately, it's used by God in his sovereign purposes, but, secondarily, it's used by Satan himself and his host of evil malcontents. If God can and does use our anxiety as an opportunity for Christ-conformity, then Satan has the opposite goal of helping anxiety undo us. God can use our anxiety to weave the fabric of our faith; Satan can use anxiety to unravel it.

I know—it's difficult for us to make spiritual warfare our default context for interpretation. We're prone to dismissing it as peripheral and sporadic, something that happens now and then, on the margins of life. We think spiritual evil rears its head at high school shootings and terrorist attacks, but not during the quiet moments of the morning when we're anxious about starting the day—perhaps not even during a panic attack, which we explain away as a physiological problem, something doctors help us deal with. In terms of our spiritual situation, we're all too often the ignorant country, attributing our suffering to anything and anyone but the real enemy. When we do that, we're essentially making ourselves targets of our spiritual nemesis.

Where We Look in Warfare

Pure rationality is the use of reason without conscious regard for what God has revealed in Scripture. It's the use of reason *alone*, in isolation from the truth that we're caught up in a great spiritual war, in isolation from the truth that God has great purposes for our anxiety: to conform us to the image of his own Son so that the very resurrection life of God might burst through our bondage and testify to the God who *is* life.

The way of pure rationality isn't an option for us. We have to let it go. And because it's become a habit, we have to *keep* letting it go. We have to *train* ourselves to let it go. It will take years of practice . . . years. So, settle in for the long haul, and get ready for God to draw you closer to himself.

But let's get even more practical. If we need to take the way of spiritual warfare instead of the way of pure rationality, how do we actually confront the anxiety in our lives? What do we *do* with anxiety when it hits?

We already have some answers from the previous chapters. We can start by asking the sorts of questions that prioritize God's Christ-conforming purposes for us. Rather than asking *why* when we feel anxious, we can ask, "God, what are you teaching me?" This approach prioritizes the spiritual meaningfulness of our anxiety. To find an answer to that question, we need to hear the voice of God. But we don't hear the voice of God in some mystical, subjective sense; we hear it when we open the good book. In Scripture, we encounter the voice of God, made audible to his people by the power of the Holy Spirit in us. *When you ask God what he is teaching you, look for the answer in what he has already said.* And let me encourage you: he always delivers. I've never had a time when I went to God's word asking that question and walked away without an answer. That doesn't mean the answers are simple or easy to implement. But they are on the page somewhere.

To put this in the context of battle imagery again, which Paul takes up in Ephesians 6, in spiritual warfare, we need a sword and a shield. There are other necessary parts of our armor that Paul discusses, but let me just focus here on the sword and shield. The sword is the word of God. This is what you use to cut through the lies of anxiety. When everything in your body screams at you—when the fight-or-flight instinct is roaring—you have a weapon in your hands, a weapon in your heart, if you meditate on Scripture. Remember the use of Psalm 9:9–10 from a previous chapter? That's just one example of the thousands of passages we can speak in the face of anxiety. Psalm 23 is also very powerful. At the back of this book, you'll find a list of passages that I've turned to in my own battles.

The shield of faith is equally important. Let's be honest with each other. We don't naturally confront anxiety with faith. We confront it with fear, with terror and panic, with frustration and despair, with pills—but not faith. Faith says, "There is *nothing* that the devil can do to me, for I already belong to Christ. If I am to suffer right now, it is my spiritual medicine, working for the good of my salvation." Faith is the Spirit-given response to adversity of all shapes and sizes, anxiety included. One group of words that I've kept close to my heart comes from the Heidelberg Catechism (question and answer 1). For me, it's the quintessential response of faith and hope, drawn right from the well of Scripture.

Q. What is your only comfort in life and in death?

A. That I am not my own, but belong—body and soul, in life and in death—to my faithful Savior, Jesus Christ. He has fully paid for all my sins with his precious blood, and has set me free from the tyranny of the devil. He also watches over me in such a way that not a hair can fall from my head without the will of my Father in heaven; in fact, all things must work together for my salvation. Because I belong to him, Christ, by his Holy Spirit, assures me of eternal life and makes me wholeheartedly willing and ready from now on to live for him.

Such a beautiful and biblical response! In Christ, we're set free from the tyranny of the devil, including all of the means and measures he takes to cause doubt and despair.

In addition, we can recall the CHRIST acronym and link it with our discussion here. The sword of God's word and the shield of faith are related to the C and the R. We *consider the feelings* of anxiety as spiritual medicine and lean on God's word for strength in our weakness. And we also *remember the promise* of God's eternal presence by rehearsing that truth in what God has said to us. This is a faith exercise. We remember and believe, remember and believe, remember and believe. It parallels physical weight lifting. It's tiring and difficult, but over time the repetition results in strength. Our muscles tear in the moment, but as we rest they rebuild.

And added to the sword of God's word and the shield of faith is something more profound than we can imagine: we have the sympathy of God himself in Christ Jesus. That's the H from our CHRIST acronym. *He knows.* Look once more at what the writer of Hebrews says. This should baffle us when we consider that this is the Son of God, the Lord of *all.*

Since then we have a great high priest who has passed through the heavens, Jesus, the Son of God, let us hold fast our confession. For we do not have a high priest who is unable to sympathize with our weaknesses, but one who in every respect has been tempted as we are, yet without sin. Let us then with confidence draw near to the throne of grace, that we may receive mercy and find grace to help in time of need. (Heb. 4:14–16)

In the heat and terror of anxiety, amidst all of its crippling effects, sometimes the greatest sentence we can utter is the simplest: *He knows.* Do you feel shortness of breath? He knows. Do you feel despair that weighs you down? He knows. Do you feel crushed? He knows. In God's amazing mercy and grace, he's taken on our human nature in Christ and is able to sympathize with us in our weakness *in every respect*, except for sin. He knows. And therefore, you are not alone. You are suffering in the presence of God. You are suffering with Christ in order that you might be raised with him (Rom. 8:17).

In a previous chapter, I mentioned feeling the greatest burden lifted when I first read another person's account of panic attacks. It was in *The Anxiety and Phobia Workbook* by Edmund Bourne, given to me by a counselor. In it I found a short, concise description of the feelings I was having. All at once, I remember saying out loud, "YES! That's it! That's what I feel!" I found such relief in that. Why? It was just another person's description, words on a page. Why was it so powerful? Because it meant that I wasn't alone.

There's great power in human sympathy: the sharing of our experiences. But how much more potent is the sympathy that the Son of God himself gives to us! What's more, Christ not only sympathizes with us; he offers ultimate and eternal hope to go with that sympathy (the R in our CHRIST acronym). He not only says, "I know," but also "It's okay. I'm with you. I'm *always* going to be with you—even after death." Christ doesn't just meet us where we are; he takes us where we need to go. He lifts us up in the power of his Spirit and carries us to spiritual safety. *Remember the promise of his presence.*

There's much more we could say about this, but before we end the chapter and move on to other issues, I want to summarize what we've covered.

The way of pure rationality—the use of bare reason without conscious attention to what God has said in Scripture—can't be our approach to anxiety if we want to grow closer to God. The way of pure rationality will try to *eliminate* anxiety; the way of spiritual warfare will make every attempt to *use* it. There's a huge difference! While reasoning is a great tool that we all have at our disposal, it is not *the* tool.

As I said earlier: reason is not the panacea for the soul; Christ is. And as the eternal Word in the flesh, Christ calls his people to look at the words of his Father. So, we need to take up God's word and hear his voice amidst the spiritual war we're fighting.

Always remember that your anxiety has a context: it's a powerful tool, a spiritual directive, that affects your relationship with God—either moving you towards him or away from him. I want you to take up the practice of viewing anxiety in that context, not in a purely physiological one. When you do, I have no doubt that God will start to work mightily in your heart and mind, bringing you to the hope and consolation that can only be found in him. As Augustine wrote so many years ago, we are restless until we find our rest in God. So, let us prayerfully ask for that, with complete confidence that the God of rest will give it to us.

Theology: The Triune God of the Great Story

We find ourselves in a story. That's what we focused on in the previous chapter. But finding ourselves in a story isn't all that helpful unless we know who's telling the story. We need to know who, exactly, is narrating. What's this story teller like? It may seem as if a question like this isn't all that practical, but I promise you it is. Why? Because the trinitarian nature of our story teller—Father, Son, and Spirit—can help us particularize our prayers and grasp the rich personality of God. That goes a long way in helping us with our anxiety.

"The trinitarian nature of our story teller can help us particularize our prayers and grasp the rich personality of God."

Growing up, I don't remember the doctrine of the Trinity being a focal point in our church. Jesus Christ and salvation by faith alone, the infallibility of Scripture, the need for repentance and continuing sanctification—these were staples of the sermons I heard, mostly by my late father. The idea of communion among the divine persons, of the Trinity being the basis of love (the greatest human faculty), of God having one will and yet three distinct persons—I don't remember hearing much of this. Perhaps my memory is just poor. Either way, the Trinity was not a central concept for my faith until I went to seminary.

What was the effect? Well, functionally speaking, I tended to view God as unitarian rather than trinitarian. There was Jesus—the one who gave his life for me and rose from the dead—and there was the Spirit, who seemed more like a nebulous cloud than a divine *person*, hovering in the background of reality. But the Father seemed to be the real referent whenever the word "God" was mentioned. So, when I heard "God," I thought of the Father, and then Jesus and the Spirit worked their way into my thinking later. I really didn't know how to relate to and worship a triune God. The doctrine of the Trinity seemed more like a mathematical conundrum than a staple of biblical teaching. So I left it alone.

I didn't know it at the time, but the doctrine of the Trinity does a whole lot to help you relate to God. It does that by helping you see more specifically *who* each of the divine persons is and *how* you can communicate with this one God more effectively. It shows, in other words, how the threeness of God serves the oneness of God, and how both of those truths serve your relationship with him.

For me, knowing that the Father, Son, and Spirit were each divine *persons* made a world of difference. A distant heavenly being somehow bound up with Jesus and the Holy Spirit? That was tough to grapple with. But the word *person*—a keyword for the doctrine of the Trinity—has such rich connotations in human language! I could immediately grasp God's immanence—his closeness—by that word. Certainly, God is not a person in the sense that we are (which is a basic teaching in the doctrine of the Trinity), but there is overlap to help us understand something of the nature of God. Let me spell out how the word *person* enabled me to draw nearer to God.

First, of course, you have to figure out what a divine person is. Based on the teaching of Scripture and my own study of theology, I understand a person to be "one who speaks." That applies to God and to humans in distinct ways. For persons as speakers, *communion* is central, which makes a whole lot of sense based on what we said earlier in the book about who God is and who we are.[3] But the divine persons are more than this. They are persons who speak *with an incommunicable property*. I know, I know—that sounds stuffy and abstract. But hear me out. The Father, Son, and Spirit can't simply be "ones who speak," since that would make them really indistinct from one another. They would just be three variations of the same thing. And if they're not distinct from one another, then the persons are an illusion: that's

---

3   I unpack what this means more fully in *The Speaking Trinity & His Worded World: Why Language Is at the Center of Everything* (Eugene, OR: Wipf & Stock, 2018).

the ancient heresy of *modalism*—the idea that the Father, Son, and Spirit are really just different *modes* of one God. No—the persons are distinct; they each have something that marks them as identifiably different, even though they share the same essence. That marker is an incommunicable property ("incommunicable" because it cannot be transferred or "communicated" to anyone else). For the Father, that marker is being eternally unbegotten; for the Son, it's being eternally begotten from the Father; and for the Spirit, it's eternally proceeding from the Father and the Son. Now, before you throw your hands up in boredom from the abstraction, let me show you just how personal and concrete this is! It really does have implications for how you relate to God.

As noted, the Father is a *person* in communion with the *persons* of the Son and the Spirit. He is the person who is "eternally unbegotten," as theologians have put it. But he is also the person who eternally begets the Son and "spirates" or sends out the Holy Spirit. He is a *person* in communion with the other persons. There is no such thing, strictly speaking, as "the Father by himself." You can't isolate the Father from his Son and Spirit. There is something profoundly relational and familial here—going well beyond our understanding.

Why is that helpful? Well, think of it this way: that relational, familial portrait of God bleeds into our earthly experience and helps us draw nearer to him. The eternal Father, in fact, is the original Father of whom every earthly father is but a dim reflection. We think of earthly fathers as originals upon which we generate a metaphor for God as our eternal Father. But the opposite is the case! As Herman Bavinck put it, "This name of 'Father,' . . . is not a metaphor derived from the earth and attributed to God. Exactly the opposite is true: fatherhood on earth is but a distant and vague reflection of the fatherhood of God (Eph 3:14–15). God is Father in the true and complete sense of the term."[4] That's huge!

Fatherhood: I could grasp that, and my longing for it was especially strong after my earthly father died from cancer at age 47, when I was just 18. I missed my father (and still do). I longed for the stability, guidance, and direction that fatherhood provided. And the doctrine of the Trinity showed me that I could *never* really lose fatherhood, for I could never lose my heavenly Father! He was always going to be there. He was always going to be speaking to me through his word. He was always going to be listening to me when I prayed and worshiped. We can't lose our Father—

---

4   Herman Bavinck, *Reformed Dogmatics*, vol. 2, *God and Creation*, ed. John Bolt, trans. John Vriend (Grand Rapids, MI: Baker Academic, 2004), 307.

our earthly fathers, certainly, but not our heavenly Father.

The Son, also, is an eternal *person* in communion with his heavenly Father and the Holy Spirit. His personal property is being "eternally begotten." This is linked with the Son being the eternally perfect image (Col. 1:15) or exact imprint of the Father's nature. As the writer of Hebrews puts it, "He is the radiance of the glory of God and the exact imprint of his nature, and he upholds the universe by the word of his power" (Heb. 1:3). What does this mean, exactly? Many things! But for now let's focus on the Son being an image of what we cannot see in the Father. The Son is the one through whom the glorious splendor of God comes into focus. The Fatherhood of God is blinding and overwhelming (in the best possible sense), and the image of that God accommodates the radiance of our Father to our limited capacities. That was the full-orbed beauty of the incarnation. The eternal image of God became a temporal image of God, so that Jesus could say to his disciples, "Whoever has seen me has seen the Father" (John 14:9). You want to know what God is like? Look at the Son. You want to experience the fullness of God in your limited life? Look at the Son. You want communion with God? Go *through* the Son, who, as we've seen, can sympathize with us in every way (Heb. 4:15). I'm a son looking for a father. He's *the* Son of the *the* Father. I run to him in order to commune with God. I speak to him, and he speaks to me through the word and even intercedes for me right now with the Father (Rom. 8:34)! I not only speak with the Father and hear from him; I speak with the Son and hear from him, and he speaks *for* me. Such wondrous and rapturous communion!

Lastly, the Spirit is a *person* in communion with the Father and the Son. His property is being "eternally spirated" from the Father and Son, or "eternally proceeding" from them. Again, note the personal richness. The Father and the Son are united in the Spirit, who goes out from them in love and power. This happened at creation, where the Spirit and Word (the Son) worked jointly to create all things from the mouth of the Father. And it happened in recreation, where the Spirit and Word work jointly to remake us at the behest of our Father. As the one proceeding from the Father and Son, the Spirit is also called our "comforter" and "teacher" (John 14:26). And he teaches us what he has been given from the Father and the Son. Do you see how trinitarian and *personal* the communication is?

The doctrine of the Trinity helped me grasp the *persons* of the Godhead in ways I had never considered. And it did this in a profoundly communicative way. In other words, it taught me that God is a *speaking* God—one God in three persons—

who is always communicating with me and beckoning me to communicate back! And this is not three separate persons with warring wills on my behalf. Rather, this three-personed God has *one* will for me—one loving, sanctifying will for my life. I had never known God in that way before. It put communication at the center of who God is and who I am, and that's made a world of difference.

"The doctrine of the Trinity taught me that God is a speaking God who is always communicating with me and beckoning me to communicate back!"

Let me apply this to the concrete practice of prayer. How does the doctrine of the Trinity help our prayer life? I like to recall an article I read by my former professor, Carl Trueman. Here's what he had to say about prayer and the Trinity. Note the focus on the persons in union (one will).

There are actually some immediate practical benefits that come from a proper Trinitarian understanding of God. For example, think of how it enhances prayer. The Bible teaches that Christ is the One who intercedes for us. If we think of Christ and the Father as being in some kind of opposition to each other, then the success of Christ's prayer always depends upon his persuasive powers and the willingness of the Father to be persuaded. Perhaps today the Father will listen to Christ, but tomorrow he might change his mind. That serves to undermine our own confidence in our prayers. Our prayers are tenuous enough anyway, without adding a further weak link in the prayer chain by misunderstanding the relationship between the Son and the Father.

If, however, Father and Son are one God and will precisely the same things, then we know that the Son's intercession must succeed. When he prays to his Father, he is merely asking for that which the Father desires to give him. What tremendous practical confidence that gives to believers when they come to the Lord in prayer. As Christ takes our prayers, perfects them, and presents them to the Father, he asks for nothing that the Father is not already eager to grant in abundance.

The Spirit also plays his role. As the bond of union with Christ, he is intimately connected to our prayers, and—as Paul so beautifully yet mysteriously states—he too intercedes for us in our weakness. The same applies to his prayers: as he is God with the Father and the Son, he joins them in the holy confluence of intercession and divine will.[1]

What a beautiful encouragement—to know that the three persons of the Godhead want the same things for us!

My prayer life has also been enhanced by recognizing the distinct work of each person. Most often, I pray *to* the Father, *in* the name of the Son, and *by* the power of the Holy Spirit. The Spirit gives me the words I need (Rom. 8:26–27). The Son carries them with his atoning work into the presence of my heavenly Father (Rom. 8:34), and the Father hears them and acts in accordance with his eternal plan (1 John 5:14; Eph. 3:11). Each divine person, though they are one and share the same will, have played different roles in our redemption. I recognize those roles when I pray.

I also pray to each person distinctly. This helps me to focus on what each of the divine persons has done and is doing in me. In other words, it helps me as a human person make a more direct connection with a divine person, even though the divine persons cannot be separated and all work in unity. Do I need a sympathizer? I call on Christ. Do I need comfort? I call on the Spirit. Do I need fatherly guidance and love? I call on the Father. I know each of the divine persons shares the same will, and that when I pray to the Spirit, the Father and Son are listening in. But it can be profoundly helpful for us to focus on a particular person when we're in the midst of distress or turmoil . . . or triumph, for that matter. The concreteness of each person in the Godhead is a gift we have been given so that we might grasp God with both hands.

As we end the chapter, let's bring this to bear on anxiety. Anxiety is driven by panic. Panic is the oxygen for the flame of anxiety. And in the height of panic, we grasp for something particular, something concrete, something to draw us into the present (recall the I from the CHRIST acronym). There have been times when I struggled to cry out to "God" (the general noun) in the midst of anxiety, but I could cry out to a specific *person*. I could say, "Christ, commune with me now. Show me you're with me. Let this suffering draw me closer to you, who suffered for me.

---

1   Carl R. Trueman, "Trinitarianism 101: Evangelical Confusion and Problems," *Modern Reformation* 23, no. 6 (November/December 2014): 16–19.

The dust of the earth covered your blood-stained body. I'm dust right now. I'm diminished. And I cling to you. Grab my hand." Or, "Spirit, give me your comfort and peace. You have both stored up in great barns like grain. I just need a few kernels—just a handful of the grain. My hands are open. I hold nothing back. Please, put peace in my palms and comfort in my heart." Or, "Father, I doubt you. I don't know why, but I do. I doubt your fatherly care and the depth of your adoption. I doubt your promises—every one of them true! I doubt your patience. I even doubt your presence! I'm so embarrassed . . . please be patient with me and help me to trust you. Help me to lean on your shoulder, as Christ did. Help me to rest in you, as the Spirit does. Help me to know beyond every shadow of doubt that you are perfectly present and always faithful to wait for my faithlessness to pass."

These are a few ways in which the doctrine of the Trinity has been a blessing to my spiritual life. There are many more, but I leave you with this: don't settle for a general understanding of God. Get concrete. Dig into the dirt with your fingers and nails, squeeze the sanctity of doctrine until you can utter it in the throes of an anxiety storm. That's what the doctrines are here for, after all—for you to *use*. And this doctrine, in particular, is at the heart of who God is, who the story teller is. If we're going to find ourselves in the Great Story, we need to find ourselves in the Great Story Teller.

Reflection Questions and Prayer

1. Have you used the way of pure rationality in your own battle with anxiety? If so, what has been your experience (positive and negative)?

2. Consider some ways you have been tempted to de-supernaturalize the world you live in. Discuss these ways with someone else. What effect has one of these ways had on your spiritual life?

3. How often do you make spiritual warfare the context for interpreting your experience? When you do so, how do you end up interpreting and responding to the difficulty before you?

4. Consider a recent moment of anxiety you've encountered. Apply the CHRIST acronym again and take notes on what this experience can teach you in relation to your own spiritual warfare.

5. What are some passages that you think would be helpful to rehearse in the midst of anxiety? How do those passages relate to the letters of the CHRIST acronym (particularly the C, H, and R)?

6. Consider keeping an anxiety journal, in which you apply the CHRIST acro-

nym to each moment of anxiety you encounter. Discuss what you've found with your pastor or a fellow Christian. Keep the journal long-term and see how you develop in your approach to anxiety.

7. What difference does the doctrine of the Trinity make in your own spiritual life? Discuss this with a fellow believer.

8. What's another example of a doctrine (besides the doctrine of the Trinity) that you've found helpful in your battle with anxiety?

9. The word *person* helped me grasp God in ways I hadn't before. What words have done this for you in your own spiritual life?

10. Think of a time when you experienced intense anxiety. When you began panicking, what helped you to stop? Was it staying busy? Was it thinking "good" thoughts? What biblical teaching can you make concrete in your life so that you can use it when you confront anxiety? Discuss your ideas with a pastor or friend.

Prayer

Almighty God,
My mind is churning.
I'm trying to reason my way out of this.
And I know you have reasons—
Relational reasons—for this anxiety.
So, pull me closer to yourself.
Show me what you want me to see.
Speak to me in your word,
And bring it to my memory now.
In you I live, and breath, and have my being.
In *you.*
Not even the devil himself can take me
From the nail-pierced hands of Christ.
I know, my Lord, that *you know.*
You know exactly how I feel right now.
You *know* . . .
So please, Christ, fill me with your Spirit.
If I am to burn with fear,

Let me burn for you,
Like a candle
That illumines all around it.
In my burning, broken state,
Use me to encourage others,
That I might truly be an ambassador
For your quiet kingdom of hope.

Father, Son, and Spirit
Persons unparalleled,
I know so little of you.
But take what little I know
And multiply it beyond measure
So that I can rest secure
Simply in hearing your name.

Reader Resource: Spiritual Warfare Vs. Pure Rationality

For nearly every explanation that a purely rational approach to anxiety offers, there is an explanation linked to spiritual warfare (oftentimes *indirectly*, though direct links may be there too). What elements of spiritual warfare do you see hiding behind the following types of anxiety? Discuss your thoughts with a pastor or fellow believer. Remember that identifying an element of spiritual warfare with a type of anxiety does *not* translate into easy problem solving. Someone who deals with social anxiety isn't helped in the slightest when someone says, "Just stop caring what people think of you." We need grace and prayer to handle these issues with kindness and sensitivity—not to mention humility.

CHAPTER 8

Always Dealing with Feelings

KEY IDEA: Focusing on the purpose of our anxious feelings can help us let God use them.

Experience
The feelings of anxiety

Scripture
Matt. 26:36–46

Theology
Communion with God

A nxiety demands reinforcement. Every season, every holiday, every week, every day, every hour, every minute—we need reinforcements. We struggle to keep fighting. Sometimes we're in the trenches from morning 'til evening. We don't just fight the war against anxiety; we live it. It becomes our norm. And it's exhausting, for both the mind and the body. So, while you might think that discussing the feelings of anxiety is overkill at this point, I promise it's not. I'm giving you some reinforcements, because I know you need them. I know *I* need them, too.

In this chapter, let's hone in on the C of our CHRIST acronym. The way of spiritual warfare means that we need to find some way to deal with all of the horrible feelings that come with anxiety. In my experience, they come in swells. We manage things well for a while, take some behavioral or physiological risks (e.g., being more spontaneous, having more coffee or sugar), and then deal with the aftermath. With each swell, we learn more about our own anxiety, how it makes us feel and what it pushes us to do.

Throughout the book, I've rehearsed the anxious feelings that I encounter, and I'm guessing you're familiar with them. These are the textbook symptoms, though you may have a few of your own to add:

1. An overt awareness of your own breathing
2. A sense that your throat is closing up
3. Adrenaline in your arms and legs
4. A tingling sensation in your extremities
5. Increased heart palpitations
6. The sneaking suspicion that your mind might just break at any moment
7. A sense of sickness and anemia that you can't pin down or reason away
8. De-realization or disassociation: the sense that you're slightly removed from reality

And the feelings, of course, lead to corresponding tendencies:

1. A desire to stay where you're comfortable
2. A hatred of travel
3. A hatred of disruption to routine
4. Difficulty focusing

We have to do something to deal with these feelings. One way to deal with them, of course, is to try to find a way to eliminate them, perhaps through medication. With roughly 40 million Americans diagnosed with a general anxiety disorder, there's no shortage of medication: Prozac, Xanax, Klonopin, Ativan, and a never-ending list of new ones to test out.[2] I'll deal with medication in another chapter. For now, I want to emphasize the fact that we have to face the feelings, interpret them, and work through them. This is part of Christ conformity, part of how God uses the anxiety in our lives to do great things. It's never a comfortable process. The feelings of anxiety are hot, but it's in their heat that our souls become malleable, easily shaped. Apart from anxiety, we can grow cold and calloused. But in the midst of these terrible feelings, we soften.

Here's another example from my own life. I left work on a darker, rainy November evening and took a different way home so that I could meet my wife at her parents' house. We were going to have a date night, so I was excited to get there as

---

2   "Facts and Statistics," Anxiety and Depression Association of America, accessed August 23, 2019, https://adaa.org/about-adaa/press-room/facts-statistics.

soon as I could. The different way that I took happened to be the Pennsylvania turn-pike, which happens to have horrendous traffic on Friday afternoons, which happens to make me feel anxious and trapped. Within a few minutes of going 40 mph on the highway, I was feeling waves of heat, each one pushing me closer towards panic. My long-term guest was in the room, staring me down. These feelings—I knew what they made me want to do (lock up and stop breathing) and what eventually happened with all of them (they dissipated). But in the moment, I was really struggling. I need-ed reinforcements.

It was at that point that I did something I hadn't planned on doing. I felt as if the anxiety were washing over me like waves, each one trying to push me under the white water of panic. But at the same time, I knew that God *always* uses my anxiety as a kind of spiritual medicine (C = *consider the feelings as spiritual medicine*). I'd been using the CHRIST acronym for over a year at that point. If these hot waves of anxiety were going to keep washing over me, I decided to *lean into them*. I don't know how else to describe it. It was like letting the feeling have its full effect while I said internally, "Yes. Yes, go ahead. Wash over me. Purge me. Wash out every speck of self-reliance and sinfulness." And as I let it happen, I suddenly felt a little bit calmer. Don't get me wrong: I was still going through all of my nervous ticks (rubbing my finger nails, shaking my foot on the floor, gripping the steering wheel like an Indy race car driver). But something lifted. Something let go.

This was the first time I had ever "rolled into" my feelings of anxiety. I don't really know how to tell you how to do it because . . . well, I don't really know how *I* did it. But I think there's something to be said for *facing* the feelings rather than *fleeing* from them. I noted in an earlier chapter: There's something to be said for *staying*, for not fleeing right away. When we roll *into* the feelings of anxiety rather than *away* from them, the light of Christ conformity starts to burn brighter. And we can follow that light.

To Face or Flee

We spend much of our time trying to *flee from* the feelings of anxiety. And who wouldn't? Who wants to feel like an alien in their own skin? No one! We want out! But those feelings don't leave us alone just because we flee from them. They might leave for a while, but they come back. Again. And again. And again. If we face them, we can learn about them. If we flee from them, we can't. In fact, when we try to flee from them, we can become even more panicked. This was one of Barry McDonagh's points in his popular book *Dare: The New Way to End Anxiety and Stop Panic Attacks Fast* (not exactly the goal of the book you're reading). McDonagh noted that our attempt to flee from panic is the very thing that induces more panic. We long to get away from anxiety, but when we turn to run and find our feet frozen in the mud, we snap. And you know what follows: brown-paper-bag breathing and wishes for imminent death.

This is one of the hardest lessons for us to learn as anxiety-ridden creatures in the twenty-first century. We have been trained by the broader culture to make decisions based on a series of simple formulas: LIFE + PAIN/DISCOMFORT = UNHAPPINESS. Subtract the pain and discomfort, and you're left with the greatest desire for most people: a life of *happiness*, a life of *comfort*. Be candid with yourself. You know that *this* is what you want 99% of the time.

But then there's that 1%. There's that clear but disconcerting truth that life is not about comfort and happiness, because these things *end* at some point. Even though the pursuit of happiness is considered a *right* by Americans, the Great Story tells us something quite different. It tells us that God himself, the eternal Son who came to us in the flesh, did not consider happiness a right. He considered it a *blessing*. And there's a big difference.

"If happiness is a right, then we immediately feel jaded when we don't have it."

If happiness is a right, then we immediately feel jaded when we don't have it. We feel wronged. We feel cheated. And we fall into the mire of self-pity. And the broader culture is waiting and ready to offer us a host of ways to get the happiness we've been cheated out of. This makes sense, because if happiness really is a *right*, then life is problematic without it. And we want to solve our problems.

But if happiness is a *blessing*, then it's not a right; it's a gift. Gifts are not required. They aren't deserved. They aren't merited. Gifts are *given*. When we're given a gift, we say, "Thank you." When we're given a right, we don't say anything. We act as if things are going *as they should*. Justice is being held. Things are the way they're supposed to be. We say "thank you" for blessings; we say "it's about time" for rights.

My reader, happiness is not a right. In the Great Story, happiness is *always* a blessing, a gift. And that happiness—of which we only get a taste on this side of paradise—comes from one place: communion with God. Every instance of happiness in our lives is but a reflection of the eternal happiness we find in the presence of the Father, Son, and Holy Spirit. That's what it means to be a creature made in God's image. I've quoted Geerhardus Vos many times before, but it bears repeating because the truth is so critical: being made in God's image means that we're everywhere and always *disposed for communion with him.*[1] Communion with God is the wellspring of our happiness because communion with God is highest purpose for living. We live and breathe and move so that we can commune with God.

Now, the problem is that we continually confuse the concept of blessing with the concept of higher purpose. Instead of putting communion with God at the center of our lives, we put blessing there. That's why we're bent on moving up the rungs in our career path, on buying single-family homes, on storing up for retirement. We're bent on blessing. But if you're bent on blessing, you'll always be predisposed to hold a grudge against whatever is keeping it from you, including God himself. Ironically, being bent on blessing often means being bent *away* from the one who gives it to you. We can't keep confusing blessing with purpose. We can't. Or things or never going to change for us.

Things start to change when we realize that our higher purpose of communion with God is attained by *one* means in the Great Story, and only one: Christ-conformity. If we're going to be in communion with God, then we have to be made like him. We have to be shaped and impressed and molded to the image of Christ. We have to be sculpted, not satisfied; shaped, not sheltered. That's not a popular message today. But it's the message of the Great Story.

Now, what does it mean, practically, to be made like Christ in our anxiety? We've already discussed a few different ways in the previous chapters—the most important of which is a heavy reliance on the speech of God, which was always the calling of God's people. Let me give you the same answer in a different word, though it might make you wince a little: *resigning.* Resigning can be captured in a lot of our body language: open palms, bowing on our knees, lifting up our hands in prayer. Resigning is resolving, in all circumstances, to the truth that God knows what's better, both for his eternal plan and for your little place within it. To be made like Christ, we have to resign ourselves to his control. I believe that's what I did when I "rolled into"

---

1   Geerhardus Vos, *Reformed Dogmatics*, vol. 2, *Anthropology*, ed. and trans. Richard B. Gaffin Jr. (Bellingham, WA: Lexham Press, 2014), 13.

my feelings of anxiety on the turnpike that day. I resigned. I resolved to let God be in control, *even if that meant that the feelings weren't going to leave.* Resigning ourselves to God's will is the ultimate way to face the feelings of our anxiety and to let God work through them. And Jesus gave us the perfect example, as he always does.

Jesus Facing the Feelings in Gethsemane

Jesus faced some tidal waves of anxiety during his time on earth. The one that I think of most often happened in a peaceful place, a garden.

> [36] Then Jesus went with them to a place called Gethsemane, and he said to his disciples, "Sit here, while I go over there and pray." [37] And taking with him Peter and the two sons of Zebedee, he began to be sorrowful and troubled. [38] Then he said to them, "My soul is very sorrowful, even to death; remain here, and watch with me." [39] And going a little farther he fell on his face and prayed, saying, "My Father, if it be possible, let this cup pass from me; nevertheless, not as I will, but as you will." [40] And he came to the disciples and found them sleeping. And he said to Peter, "So, could you not watch with me one hour? [41] Watch and pray that you may not enter into temptation. The spirit indeed is willing, but the flesh is weak." [42] Again, for the second time, he went away and prayed, "My Father, if this cannot pass unless I drink it, your will be done." [43] And again he came and found them sleeping, for their eyes were heavy. [44] So, leaving them again, he went away and prayed for the third time, saying the same words again. [45] Then he came to the disciples and said to them, "Sleep and take your rest later on. See, the hour is at hand, and the Son of Man is betrayed into the hands of sinners. [46] Rise, let us be going; see, my betrayer is at hand." (Matt. 26:36–46)

There's a lot to unpack here. But let's start with the feelings: *sorrowful, even to death.* In another gospel account, we read that Jesus is "greatly distressed and troubled" (Mark 14:33). On another occasion, he was in such emotional agony that his sweat became "like drops of blood" (Luke 22:44). These are heavy feelings . . . deep feelings. We often feel anxious because we're afraid death could be approaching—even if the fear we're confronting has been blown out of proportion. But Jesus actually *knew* he was close to his death. That's a whole new level of distress.

In the midst of these feelings, Jesus identifies a focus, stays engaged, and talks (notice the I, S, and T of our CHRIST acronym). But he combines these three elements in *prayer.* His focus is our heavenly Father, he stays engaged by asking the same question repeatedly (and resigning himself to the same answer), and throughout this process he's obviously talking, voicing the deepest concerns in his soul, drawing what is inside to the outside.

But what I want us to gaze at for a few minutes is the *pattern* of Jesus's prayer. He *asks* and *resigns himself* to the Father's will. "If it be possible, let this cup pass from me . . ." Three times he brings the request before his Father. And three times there is a submission of will. "Not as I will, but as you will." How simple that submission looks, but how hard and dense it is! It's packed with *relationship*, with years of faithful service, of prayer and action, of trust and passion. Submission to God's will is never a light thing, but think of it here! The Son of God incarnate, bowed in his earthly body before the Father he's known from eternity—his human nature pulsing within him, asking for a different way. This is *Godtalk*. This is *God* talking to *God!* This is divine self-speech unfolding before us so that we might see the weight of what's happening! God is offering *himself* to *himself.* Think about that for a minute.

But this is also happening so that we might see the pattern our elder brother sets for us. It's a pattern of resigning; it's an exchange of will. Christ does not fight against his Father's wishes. He asks. And then he submits. This is the trademark of steadfast faith in God's love. The verifier of faith is action. A commitment and resolve must someday hit our walking feet. We have to *act* on the faith we have. The good news is that God himself will act in us to do what he's planned (Phil. 1:6)! *He's* ultimately responsible for the faith-action we take.

If we desire to be conformed to Christ through our anxiety, we have to be resolved to resign. That's the path that Jesus himself stomped out for us in the grass of Gethsemane. It's not a path of comfort. It's not a path of ease. But comfort and ease are not the aims of a person walking through the Great Story. Christ is. Christ-conformity is our aim because communion with God is our aim.

My reader, the feelings of anxiety will come. They'll come again and again and again. And each time, we'll have the painful opportunity to resign ourselves to God's will, to let him work *through* them to teach us whatever he wishes in that moment. That's not bad news; it's the best news, because it's offering the best result: Christ-conformity. As we stand in the trenches of anxiety and fight for life and godliness, the Father, Son, and Spirit are *in* us making us beautiful. There's pain in that because there's purging; there's refining; there's shaping. But we're being crafted into the most beautiful image that exists: the image of Christ.

"As we stand in the trenches of anxiety and fight for life and godliness, the Father, Son, and Spirit are in us making us beautiful."

My prayer for you in this chapter is that the Spirit of God would begin teaching you not to flee from your feelings. We always want to say "No!" when we sense those feelings approaching. But the power of God can turn our "no" into "yes." "Yes, come along. Come on in and stay awhile." Roll into those feelings. Through prayer, resign yourself to God's will *in* them, and he'll show you amazing things: about himself, about you, and about others around you who need the light and strength of Christ.

Theology: John Owen on Communion with God

In this chapter, we've talked about communion with God, and in the previous chapter, we discussed the three persons of the Godhead, God's trinitarian nature. Communion with God is actually bound tightly to the truth of his trinitarian nature. We commune with God because he *is* a communion of divine persons—Father, Son, and Spirit. It's not that communion is just a fitting action to take in relationship with God; it's that communion is at the heart of who God is, so when we commune with him, we're entering into the intimacy at the heart of God's identity. Let's explore this a bit more.

John Owen wrote much of communion with God, and his approach was both biblical and cautious. There's a certain way in which we need to approach communion with God. What is that communion, exactly? Here's Owen's answer: "Our communion . . . with God consists in his *communication of himself unto us, with our return unto him* of that which he requires and accepts, flowing from that *union* which in Jesus Christ we have with him."[2] Now, the logic of this statement can be reworked to help us understand what happens first.

1. *We are united to Christ by faith.* Notice that you *can't* have communion with God apart from Christ. There's no such thing.
2. *God communicates himself to us.* God has always done this, in fact. He's revealed himself both in the world around us and in Scripture. He's a speak-

---

2   John Owen, *Communion with the Triune God*, ed. Kelly M. Kapic and Justin Tayler (Wheaton, IL: Crossway, 2007), 94.

ing God.[3] But we can't hear or process his speech when we have a rebellious or callous heart. We need Christ, who offers us a new heart (Ezek. 36:26), one that pumps the blood of faith into the soul's arteries.

3. *We respond to him with words and actions that he accepts.* Put in the language of "sacrifice," this means that we come to God in brokenness, with contrite and humble hearts. "The sacrifices of God are a broken spirit; a broken and contrite heart, O God, you will not despise" (Ps. 51:17).

Now, the feelings of anxiety do many things to us, but they're remarkably powerful when it comes to brokenness and contrition. How quickly we feel broken and lowly when the feelings of anxiety hit! That's important, because those feelings put us in the perfect place to offer ourselves to God, to give him what he "requires and accepts." That may be as simple as asking your spouse what you can do to help clean up the house, or running an errand to make someone else's life a little easier. It may mean getting your hands dirty. Christ, remember, did tasks that dirtied his hands. Washing the dusty feet of twelve grown men is hardly an act fit for divine royalty (John 13:1–5). Christ did it because it needed to be done. Why? To show his disciples how they should act towards others (13:14–15).

As we end this chapter, I want you to bind together two things: your feelings of anxiety and your ability to commune with God. The former can put you in the perfect position to do the latter. When we resign ourselves to let God work through our feelings, we also situate our souls to enter into deeper communion with him. That's the greater purpose our anxious feelings can serve, if we roll into them instead of fleeing from them. Use the chart at the end of this chapter to work through the specific feelings you encounter.

Reflection Questions and Prayer

1. In your own life, what has tended to happen when you flee from the feelings you experience?

2. If you've ever tried to stand fast and face the feelings, what has happened? Talk to a fellow believer about your experience.

3. How does anxiety affect your prayer life? Do you tend to pray more or less when the anxious feelings hit?

---

3   For more on this, see *The Speaking Trinity & His Worded World: Why Language Is at the Center of Everything* (Eugene, OR: Wipf & Stock, 2018).

4. Write out a prayer that you can recite when the feelings hit next. Memorize it so that you're ready to use it in the moment. Then talk with a fellow believer or pastor about your experience.

5. Make a list of the feelings you commonly encounter with anxiety. Then brainstorm ways in which God might use those feelings to conform you to Christ. (Hint: what opportunities do the feelings present you with spiritually?) See the chart at the end of this chapter.

6. Using the same list of feelings, brainstorm ways in which you think God might use each feeling to draw you into communion with him. What can each feeling lead you to do that would be acceptable to God?

7. Communion with God should be the highest goal we have, but it often gets replaced by other things, by idols. Think of a few idols in your own life that tend to replace communion with God. If you need some help identifying them, remember that an idol is basically anything that gets you more excited than your relationship with God.

Prayer

My Father,
You heard the words of your Son
Going up from Gethsemane.
You saw him resign himself.
You looked with eternal love
On the one who was offering himself
On our behalf.
God, I want to conform to that.
I want to be shaped to Christ.
But I'm often afraid.
I'm scared of the pain.
I'm scared of the discomfort.
I'm scared of the embarrassment.
Make my heart willing.
Help me to speak to you in those moments,
To resign my own will to yours,
To roll into the feelings I encounter,

Knowing that you are faithful

To shape me through them.

You're making me into something beautiful.

Give me faith to believe that

In the little moments,

When I want to flee

And remain the same.

Help me to face the feelings,

To fall into your hands,

To trust your craftsmanship.

Use my feelings of anxiety

To set me free in you.

Reader Resource: Working through Anxious Feelings

It helps to have a system in place to work through the anxious feelings you encounter. Here's a system that I've always found helpful. I'll give you an example from my own experience to flesh this out.

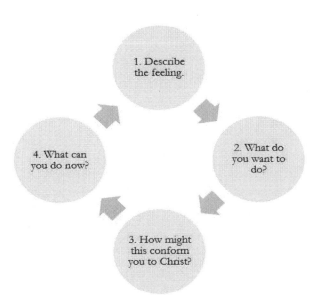

The first step is simple: just describe the feeling you have. Bring it out into the open. For me, one of my most frequent anxious feelings is the sense that my throat is closing up. I call it *pinhole throat*. It feels as if I can't swallow or breathe easily. That's the way it *feels*, however, not the way it *is*. I have to remind myself of that constantly. Step two: be candid about what you want to do. When my throat feels like it's closing up, I want to shut my eyes and be in a comfort zone. I want to breathe freely, without so much effort. I want to be comfortable again. Step three: think about how this feelings might be conforming you to Christ's character in some way. My pinhole throat makes me feel weak and debilitated. It makes me feel trapped. In Gethsemane, I have little doubt that Christ felt trapped. Why else would he ask for the "cup" to pass from him? His human nature did not long to suffer pain and torment. He pleaded with his Father . . . multiple times. I plead with my Father, too. But Christ then submitted, so that's what I have to do. I say, "God, if you want me to feel this way right now, it's okay. I'll keep the long-term guest of anxiety in my living room. I don't want him here; I'm asking you to kick him out, but I submit to the truth that *you* know what is best for me. You're using this to build me, to strengthen me, to focus my heart and mind on the only eternal source of hope and joy: yourself! Spirit, please grant me patience and help me to focus right now. Direct my attention to the needs of others. Help me to lay myself down in the service of others." Step four: start taking action on your prayer. I find that talking to someone else (the T from our CHRIST acronym) is one of the best ways to draw my focus away from my feelings and onto someone else.

Give this a try with one of your own anxious feelings. What do you discover about yourself? What do you discover about conforming to Christ? Talk with a fellow believer or with your pastor to help you see how conformity to Christ might be working itself out in these feelings.

CHAPTER 9

The Priority of Prayer

KEY IDEA: Prayer must be constant in our battle with anxiety.

Experience
Our prayer life

Scripture
1 Cor. 10:13

Theology
Prayer and communion

The last chapter puts us in a good place to dwell on the priority of prayer. This also gives us a chance to focus on the T of our CHRIST acronym: *talk*.

In our distracted age, consistent and prolonged prayer is a rarity. I start praying for my spouse, and in a matter of seconds, I've stopped. Instead, I have a song from a Disney movie overtaking my concentration. I'm starting to mouth the words (with three little kids, I find Disney songs get pressed into my memory with minimal effort). I try again, and an issue at work takes over. I try a third time, and an idea for something I'd like to write jumps into the foreground. I try and try and try. You know what I'm talking about. After a few attempts, often I just stop fighting and give in to the distractions.

In the grand scheme of things, we take this struggle to concentrate fairly lightly, don't we? We blame it on the rise of smart phones and then settle back into whatever song we were listening to, whatever app we were browsing, whatever worry was consuming us. "Sure, prayer is hard, but what else can we do?" That sort of reasoning would seem very strange to other Christians in church history.

I've heard it said that Martin Luther once reported being so busy and overwhelmed that he had to pray for three hours a day instead of one. How foreign that logic is to us! When we get overwhelmed, we pray less, not more. Luther, it seems, knew that he needed communion with God more than anything else—a need we still have today, because we always have it. His logic helps us see the centrality of prayer in the context of spiritual warfare, and we've already talked about how anxiety is a clear part of that warfare. Prayer is not about petitions; it's about lifeblood—it's the stuff of divine-human communion. When the feelings of anxiety hit, pushing us into weakness, brokenness, and humility, we draw on strength in the Lord through prayer. For that reason, prayer isn't just an appropriate habit for Christians; it's a measure of how important communion with God is to us.

Let me take a moment to explain why. There's a biblical teaching that's at the heart of prayer, but we might not see it so easily. It's the teaching that humans are made in the image of God. We talked about this a bit in the context of the Great Story, but we need to remind ourselves of it here in relation to prayer. Now, scads of literature have been written about what it means to be made in God's image, and this isn't the place to get into a technical theological discussion. But I want to present what I believe this means because it has implications for our prayer life.

Geerhardus Vos, the Dutch Reformed theologian whom I've quoted numerous times in previous chapters, said, "That man bears God's image means much more than that he is spirit and possesses understanding, will, etc. It means above all that he is disposed for communion with God, that all the capacities of his soul can act in a way that corresponds to their destiny only if they rest in God."[1] Slow down with me and focus on that word once more: *communion*. Being made in the image of God means that we are disposed for *communion* with him. We long for it; we dream of it; we chase after it. It's in our blood. A longing for communion with God is the very thing that makes us human. I want to relate this to language first, and then to prayer.

"Words are not mere expressions of thought; they are threads that bind together to bring us closer to each other."

---

1   Geerhardus Vos, *Reformed Dogmatics*, vol. 2, *Anthropology*, ed. and trans. Richard B. Gaffin Jr. (Bellingham, WA: Lexham Press, 2014), 13.

For years I've been writing about the nature of language and how it's related to the nature of God. Do you know what I noticed? The word *communion* is central to both. In fact, I call language *communion behavior*.[2] Why? Because language is something that we do to commune with another person, and to commune with God himself. Words are not mere expressions of thought; they are threads that bind together to bring us closer to each other. And do you know why words work, why they're effective? Because God is a being who communes with himself, and we are creatures made to commune with him. Language is effective because of who God is and who he made us to be. Words work because the fabric of all things is geared towards communion.

Now, why am I talking about the nature of language in a book about anxiety? Because if what makes us essentially human—our being image bearers of the triune God—is our being disposed for *communion* with God, and if language is *communion behavior*, that means we should be constantly using language to deepen our relationship with God, to increase our loving dependence on him in all areas of life. And what better way to do this than through prayer!? What better way to commune with the God who talks than to talk back?

For many of us, this is a very different way of looking at prayer. Prayer is not wishful thinking or an opportunity to pour out our anguish in the midst of great trials and physical turmoil. Certainly, we ask God for things with the hope that he will give us what we need (Matt. 7:7; 21:22; Mark 11:24; John 14:13–14), and we're always welcome to join the psalmists and lay our hearts bare before the God of love. But prayer is more than these elements. Prayer is a continuous *dialogue* with God. It is an ongoing, intimate, honest, faith-based conversation between you and the Lord of all things.

Now, the phrase "Lord of all things" is especially important for someone who struggles with anxiety. I opened this book by talking about how anxiety crushes us, exposing our utter weakness and dependence. But there's a corresponding positive side to that crushing, and we've touched on this several times in the previous chapters: once you've been crushed by God and made weak, you can rely on his unparalleled strength. This is what Paul meant when he said that when he is weak, then he is strong. The weakness that anxiety ushers into our lives is spiritually beneficial

---

2   See "Imaging Communion: An Argument for God's Existence Based on Speech," *Westminster Theological Journal* 77, no. 1 (Spring 2015): 35–51; "Words for Communion," *Modern Reformation* 25, no. 4 (August 2016): 5–8; "Closing the Gaps: Perichoresis and the Nature of Language," *Westminster Theological Journal* 78, no. 2 (Fall 2016): 299–322; and *The Speaking Trinity & His Worded World: Why Language Is at the Center of Everything* (Eugene, OR: Wipf & Stock, 2018).

(even medicinal; remember the C of our CHRIST acronym) because it sets us up to cling to the eternal source of unchallengeable strength: God himself. The paradox of anxiety-induced weakness is that weakness leads to communion and strength, not to isolation and hopelessness. But for this to happen, we must commune with God through prayer . . . *regularly*. We have to make prayer a holy habit, not an occasional occurrence.

And God actually *delights* in our prayer. That's one of the reasons why it's commanded of us (1 Thess. 5:16–18). It's not just that God arbitrarily requires it. Nothing that God does is arbitrary. He requires prayer because it please him, because he delights in it. And why does he delight in it? Because he delights in communion, in relationship.

In this light, prayer—as communion behavior that binds us to the Father, Son, and Holy Spirit—is not an addendum to our identity as Christians. It's not something we make an effort to do while accepting the sad fact that we probably won't carry through. It's tempting to do that on an everyday basis, but we need to resist. Prayer is lifeblood. We *need* it, precisely because it taps into the very thing that makes us human. We need it to be a habit, a routine kneaded into the dough of daily life. When it's not, when prayer dissolves, then distance ensues—distance from God, which also creates distance between his intended purposes for our lives and our ability to carry out those purposes. The distance comes not just because we're doing something "wrong" in a broad sense; it comes because by discarding prayer we are moving away from our God-given identity. Our identity is "communion-seekers." When we leave communion behavior aside and don't have consistent dialogue with our Lord and maker, we functionally forget about all the riches of our spiritual inheritance (Eph. 1:3). And that makes us look for riches in other places. Put in stark terms, the absence of prayer turns into a door for idolatry. It leaves us open to seek fulfillment, purpose, and meaning in something *other than* God. And we simply aren't made to do that.

"If you don't chase the speech of God, you'll chase something else."

Walking through Anxiety with Prayer

Our need for prayer works itself out in a particular way in the context of anxiety. We've been looking at how anxiety is a tool in the hands of God, who uses it to shape us to the image of Christ. This approach to anxiety foregrounds the spiritual purpose of our experience, and prayer has a vital role in this: it directs our spiritual feet, telling us where to go, when to wait, and what to look for in the world around us that might offer opportunities for Christ conformity.

Let me offer you some words I treasure to help you understand what I mean. I lost my father to cancer when I was eighteen. When you lose people close to you, their possessions take on a certain sanctity—especially what they touched. I mentioned earlier in the book that when I first encountered anxiety, I brought my father's Bible with me everywhere. Inside the cover of his Bible are written several quotes. One of them is ascribed to a man named Wellington Boone: "You cannot go where you have not prayed." Think about that for a moment. I mean it: stop reading this book and think about those words.

What might he mean? In the context of our discussion, I think he's saying that prayer is a means of spiritual trail blazing. Prayer cuts through the bramble and brush of our own sin, confusion, and misguidance. By opening us up to dialogue, it makes a way for us to walk in faith. That's the nature of dialogue, isn't it? When you begin a conversation with another person, you don't know what he or she will say next. You have your guesses, but ultimately it's a mystery. Analogously, when we pray to God for peace or rest from anxiety, we don't know exactly what God will say when we open his word to listen for his voice. We do know a great deal about God's promises, and we can trust in those with full confidence. For instance, no matter what your prayer is, you can know (not hope, but *know*) that Christ is with you in that very moment (Matt. 28:20). But you don't know the way in which God will apply his particular words to your life situation. You don't know what action or thought God might be calling you to so that he can shape you more to the image of his Son. And here's the rub: If you don't pray, you never will. Prayer with God is about communing with him and looking for his Spirit-led speech to us in the pages of Scripture. If you don't chase the speech of God, you'll be clueless of God's divine purposes for you. Even worse, if you don't chase the speech of God, you'll chase something else.

Note a few things here. First, prayer isn't simply talking to God and then sitting in silence, waiting for a divine voice. While I don't put limits on the way in which God can commune with his creatures, I will say that God has already given us a living and active word from himself (Heb. 4:12). We don't have to go searching for God's voice. He's already delivered it to us. Hearing God's voice isn't a matter of opening our soul to mystical union; it's a matter of opening a book to hear a voice that never stops speaking. We already have a living and active word from God. What more do we want?

Second, prayer is a means to *progressive* intimacy with God. If prayer is a means of spiritual trail blazing, we won't make any trails without it; we won't go further and deeper in our relationship. As Boone said, we cannot go where we have not prayed. Without prayer, you won't make a trail; you won't go deeper into the forest of divine relationship. You won't reach destinations that will drop your jaw in awe and worship. You'll just stay where you are. You'll be stagnant. And in spiritual terms, "stagnant" is a near synonym for "dead."

Third, prayer is always a way out of anxiety, but let me clarify what I mean by that. In 1 Corinthians 10:13, Paul writes, "God is faithful, and he will not let you be tempted beyond your ability, but with the temptation he will also provide the way of escape, that you may be able to endure it." God's "way of escape" can take many forms, but it can always take the form of prayer. It's not that your anxiety will dissipate as soon as you start uttering words. But it will bring your mind to focus on something other than your feelings. It will also present another opportunity for you to show yourself that God is real, that he's present. That little truth is hard for us to believe and so easily forgotten! We need thousands of reminders—tens of thousands, especially when the bodily sensations of anxiety are pulsing through us.

Whenever you're in the midst of anxiety, you can always commune with the God who is controlling every fiber and particle of the world around you. You can always use prayer as a bridge that leads away from anxiety to the safe haven of the almighty God. Again, this doesn't mean that when you pray, your symptoms of anxiety go away immediately. It means that you can hold your ground and persevere with the power of God (Eph. 6:13). And I've found that the symptoms *do* eventually go away as I continue to focus on my speech with him, even if that speech is going on in my head.

Let me give you an example. My anxiety often keeps me from leaving the familiar and doing things that break routine—I still struggle with my imprisoning patterns (see chapter 2). I once went to a Rutgers basketball game with my father-in-law and two brothers-in-law. I love basketball, so everyone assumed this would be fun and relaxing for me. But it was hard. As all anxiety-ridden people do, the week before I rehearsed all of the ways the day could play out: me passing out in the car and having to go to the hospital, me not being able to breathe as we sat in the arena, me drawing the attention of other people as I hyperventilated. You get the idea. (Almost every scenario ended up with me not being able to breathe and laying in a hospital bed.) I had to work very hard to think positively, to trust in the presence of God.

I ended up bringing a pocket-sized Bible with me. Inside the cover was a card I had written to help guide myself, statements I would repeat in my head. They were an earlier manifestation of the CHRIST acronym.

C - What you are feeling right now are only symptoms—spiritual medicine. The *bitter* is making you *better*. (2 Cor. 12:10)

H – Christ knows *exactly* how you feel right now. You're closer to him *because* of this. (Heb. 4:15)

R - No matter where you are, God has already decided to take you to the safest place. Nothing can separate you from him—not now, not *ever*. (Matt. 28:20)

I - Take a breath and start enjoying the world God put you in at this moment. Find a focus. Look at the birds. (Matt. 6:26)

S - Stay engaged with your surroundings. God is there. You're living *in* him. (Acts 17:28)

T - Keep talking; focus on the people around you, not yourself. (John 13:34)

These points were essentially my way of rehearsing biblical truth. You'll find similar tactics in secular anxiety books, but they'll usually represent the way of pure rationality—a use of self-argumentation that leaves out God's spiritual purposes for your anxiety.

So, with the Bible and my card of notes in my left breast pocket, I took the hour and a half trip to the Rutgers stadium. The day was mostly fun, not anything like the horrors I imagined. But there was one moment during the game when I felt a brief heat flash, a sign that usually threw me into panic. I took a deep breath and walked down to the edge of a balcony. I started talking to God in my head. I started praying.

God, you are here.

You are here in the sounds—

The conversations, the laughter,

The squeaking sneakers.

You are present all around me,

Whether or not I sense you.

You are even inside my heart and mind.

I am your home.

But I treat you as a guest

Who comes only on occasion.

Please, God, help me to sense your presence

In the house of my body.

Help me to relax

And enjoy this game I love.

Help me to talk with my family

And learn how I can be praying for them.

Help me to engage with my surroundings,

To fixate on the world you have made,

And to focus less on my own feelings.

In the name of Christ I pray. Amen.

Remember Boone's words: *You cannot go where you have not prayed.* That was where I prayed. And now I could go there with full assurance that I would arrive. This didn't mean that no effort was required on my part. I really had to focus and stay engaged; it took constant effort. But I didn't end up having a panic attack. I could even enjoy myself a bit. Eventually, I stopped thinking about my anxiety, and the feelings started to fade. I felt good enough to do something ridiculously child-like: I ordered an ice-cream sundae for dinner—which my family has never let me forget! In that moment, I was happy to be childlike, to smile, to laugh with family, to commune with others, and through them, to commune with God. I was happy just to talk.

My point is that communing with God through prayer isn't something merely beneficial, something we check off our list of spiritual chores. It's a life-sustaining, heart-forming, and physically engaging conversation between you and God. And you can go wherever you pray.

Theology: Prayer and Communion

I've said it so many times, but we have to turn this into a refrain if we're to make it our default response: Anxiety can play a spiritually beneficial role in our life. In God's providence, it moves us towards communion, and one of the ways it does this is by pushing us to pray. In my own life, this has been a profound application of Romans 8:28. The ultimate "good" for those who love God is deeper communion with him. And we need prayer to have that. Remember Owen's definition of communion from the previous chapter: God communicates himself to us, and then we respond to him with words and actions that he accepts. We come before him with a broken, contrite, and humble heart. And as we utter words from our heart, we draw nearer to the God who has specific plans for us. He uses his words to shape us: call it *Son-shaping*. While this Son-shaping is focused specifically on Christ, it's also *God-shaping*. We are becoming more like Christ, which can only draw us into deeper communion with God, since Christ is God. Son-shaping is really God-shaping.

What does this look like, exactly? Think of the concrete actions and behaviors of Christ.[3] Think about how he turned down bread in a death-dealing desert. Think about how he took pity on a prostitute. Think about how he stood up for mercy (Matt. 9:13; John 8:1–11), not just justice. Think about how he pulled children up on his knees (Luke 18:16) and pushed hypocritical sacrifice down to the dust (Matt. 9:13). Think about his self-control and patience when spit met his skin, when hair was ripped from his beard, when whips cut through his back. *That* Jesus—he's the one you're conforming to. He's the one you and are shaped after. We pray so that in all of the tiny particulars of our life, we might be moved and molded to *him*.

The sad truth for many Christians is that prayer only re-enters our lives when tragedy or trauma step in. When we live in darkness and doubt, prayer becomes a lifeline. What anxiety can remind us of is that prayer is a necessary constant. It squares our shoulders to God. It shows us where to step in a thousand concrete situations. We can't abandon it when our health improves, or when our lives feel relatively trauma-free. Continuous dialogue with God is our spiritual oxygen. And this is precisely because we were born for communion with him.

I encourage you to develop a daily prayer routine, to keep a prayer journal, or to have some other means to keep yourself accountable to this. Paul Miller has several good suggestions in *A Praying Life: Connecting with God in a Distracting World* .

---

3   I have written down some ideas for this in a short post: "What Do You Do with Your Anxiety? Let God Use It," September 25, 2019, http://piercetaylorhibbs.com/what-do-you-do-with-your-anxiety-let-god-use-it/.

Whatever way you choose, remember this: your communion with God has a gravitational pull on your spiritual life. When you're communing with him, your closeness will help you perceive the world as a child bound for eternity with him. When you drift apart from him, your farness will lead you to see the world as someone without the hope, healing, and purpose that only God can offer. Pray, my friends. Pray always.

Reflection Questions and Prayer

1. How does prayer fit into your daily routine? If it doesn't yet, how can you make it more regular?

2. What sorts of activities tend to get in the way of your prayer life?

3. How does viewing prayer as a type of communion behavior put you in a better place to develop dialogue with God? In other words, how does the idea of communion behavior shape the way you might pray?

4. Develop a list of people in your life who need prayer right now (that's everybody, by the way). Write down what you can pray for, and then make a habit of checking in with those people to see how God is working.

5. Write out a prayer that you would pray in the heat of anxiety, and memorize it. You can use the list of points from earlier in this chapter, or you can use the CHRIST acronym. The point is to be able to pray through biblical truths as a default response to anxiety.

Prayer

God, we were made for communion with you.
That is who we are.
And you call us into holy conversation.
Help us not to turn a deaf ear to you.
Help us to speak and to listen
As we hear your voice in Scripture.
Let our hearts learn that nothing
Is greater than our dialogue with you.
In a world that is bent on pulling us away,
You are always with us, always listening.
Help us remember that, although we cannot see you,
You are the most real,

In our anxiety, help us turn to you,

And never turn away,

When anxiety fades.

Reader Resource: Prayer Log

We've talked about how God can use our anxiety to direct our focus elsewhere, away from ourselves and onto others who need prayer and encouragement. Take a few minutes to fill out the table below. Write down five people you could pray for, a Scripture passage that can lead your prayers, and what, specifically, you're asking God to do on their behalf. Write down the date, and then check in with that person a month later to see what God is up to. If nothing has changed, keep praying and check back in another month. Every prayer is answered, but the timeline for fulfillment is something we don't have access to. So, keep checking.

Person	Scripture	Request	Date Asked	Check In

CHAPTER 10

Dealing with Medication

KEY IDEA: A balanced approach to medication helps us to use our anxiety.

I n the previous chapter, we looked at how vital prayer is in dealing with our anxious thoughts and feelings. In this chapter, I want to get into one of the most common ways that people try to deal with the feelings of anxiety: medication. This is a *very* sensitive topic, especially for Christians, so I write carefully and prayerfully. In the following chapter, I'll get into three other elements that have a major effect on our feelings.

Harmful Approaches to Medication

Let me start with some wildly popular but false and unbiblical approaches to the idea of taking medication for anxiety. We'll call the first way *the lack of faith* approach, and the second *the idol* approach.

You've probably heard the lack of faith approach before. It goes something like this: "If you *really* believe in God and trust in the promises of Scripture, then you shouldn't *need* to take medication. Your anxiety is a faith problem. Seek out your sin of unbelief, build your faith, and your anxiety will fade. Taking medication is a manifestation of distrust." I know this approach all too well because it was my own approach when I first started dealing with anxiety. And it's appealing because a lack of faith is often the root of many spiritual problems, and the remainder of our problems stem from indwelling sin! So, this looks like an approach that covers all our spiritual bases. If you're dealing with anxiety, it's always worth examining your faith and the sin in your life that might be causing you spiritual distress. Those are *always* helpful habits.

However, this approach seems to ignore the plain truth that God has very often used *secondary causes* as a means of achieving his purposes in the world. A secondary cause is anything that God uses to accomplish something apart from his direct involvement. God is always the primary cause because he's all-powerful and governs every fiber and fleck of reality. He's the source of all purpose. For example, God is the one who created the grass and governs its growth (primary cause). He upholds all things by the word of his power (Heb. 1:3). Yet, he's put in place the process of photosynthesis and the various elements of weather (sunshine and rain) to help the grass to grow (secondary causes). Here's another example. God is the ultimate healer (Exod. 15:26; primary cause), but he's also given medical wisdom to us so that various illnesses can be treated (secondary causes).

Now, it's critical that we never detach secondary causes from the primary cause. We don't ever take Advil and then say, "Well, Advil helped my headache, not God." The secondary causes are only effective because of the Lordship of God, the primary cause. But neither do we discount the secondary causes. The *lack of faith* approach to medication is guilty of doing this. It says, "Secondary causes don't apply to you taking medication for anxiety." Frankly, I see no biblical support for that position. God has always used secondary causes to accomplish his purposes, and the taking of medication is no different.

The other harmful approach to anxiety medication is to treat it as an idol, to take a *good* thing and make it a *god* thing. It can be very tempting to use medication as an end-all, a final answer for the distressing feelings that come along with anxiety. The medications for anxiety are extremely potent. We can numb ourselves to feelings even if that's not our intention at the outset. So, yes, medication can become an idol. And notice the double-harm that comes from this: (1) it encourages us to ignore God completely (since he's not part of solving the problem anymore), which is what all idolatry aims to do, and (2) it removes Christ-conformity from the equation. The idol approach to medication seeks to *eliminate* anxiety rather than *use* it. I've been arguing throughout the book that our anxiety is one of the most formative spiritual tools in the hands of our great physician. We can learn *so* much from it and be conformed to Christ in amazing ways. But we short-circuit that spiritual process when we become overly dependent on medication, or when we take too much medication and become zombie-like. I've had the latter experience with Paxel. When the dose is too high, you start sleeping through life. You don't engage with tasks and people around you very well, and you start coasting through each day like a train on the tracks.

At this point, I can't emphasize enough how important it is for you to be in contact with a wise and sensitive medical doctor who knows about your faith. Along with your pastor, who is in charge of your spiritual shepherding, your doctor should be helping you make the decision as to whether or not you should take medication, and how much. Your doctor can also help you monitor your experience so that you can make adjustments, and good doctors and pastors will help you identify other factors that may be contributing to your anxiety. For instance, my doctor has helped me see that exercise is not optional for me; it's a necessity. If I don't run at least three or four times a week, my anxiety is bound to get worse. She's also helped me notice the impact of caffeine on my anxiety. I've gone through seasons where I drank way too much coffee in order to get more work done, and that's always led to a major battle with my nerves. I explained to my doctor that I get up very early in the morning so that I can get writing done, so a cup of coffee in the morning is okay, and it keeps me alert when I'm driving to work. But beyond that, the caffeine does more harm than good. My point here is that medication is not the *only* factor in dealing with your anxious feelings. It might be one factor, but there are many others.

A Healthy Approach to Medication

Now, those are the two most common harmful approaches to medication (the *lack of faith* approach and *the idol* approach). Both are spiritually destructive. The first reduces the complexity of sin and suffering; the second reduces the glory and Lordship of God in our lives. We need a different approach, a balanced approach.

I'd like to introduce an approach related to what Mike Emlet has referred to as the *Goldilocks principle*.[1] It avoids both of the harmful approaches discussed above. Remember that we need an approach to medication that (1) recognizes medication as an aid but not an end in itself (an idol); (2) appreciates the place of secondary causes in God's world; and (3) still gives us plenty of opportunities to let God use

---

1 Mike Emlet, *Descriptions and Prescriptions: A Biblical Perspective on Psychiatric Diagnoses and Medications* (Greensboro, NC: New Growth, 2017), 1–2, 95–98.

our anxiety for Christ-conformity.

So, what is the Goldilocks principle? As the name suggests, it's a principle of balance. For Emlet, it's a way of looking at psychiatric diagnoses without being overly critical (*the lack of faith* approach) or blindly trusting (*the idol* approach). But I'm applying Emlet's general principle for approaching psychiatric diagnoses to the actual taking of medication as well. The approach is very simple:

No medication: constant suffering, unchecked spiritual and physical damage

Too much medication: constant comfort or zombie-like states, unchecked spiritual and physical laziness

Some medication: opportunities for suffering and Christ conformity within a controlled environment

For the first few weeks of my battle with anxiety, I took the first path: no medication. What did I get? In two weeks, I lost 30 lbs. and was virtually isolated from all people, even those I loved and trusted the most. I was non-functional and couldn't partake in the smallest activities of a "normal" person. I was dead in the water.

Then I went on the other path: too much medication. I went into a zombie like state where I almost forgot what it was even like to be anxious. I was dazed and distanced from the people I loved most. I grew spiritually and physically lazy. In a different way, I was dead in the water.

Finally, after *years* of working with counselors and doctors, juggling different doses and different combinations of medication, I found the path that I'm currently walking: some medication. I can still get anxious and have opportunities for Christ conformity on a weekly basis, but I'm functional in terms of daily routines with my family, friends, and professional life. Medication isn't an idol for me, but it's not a sign of my lack of faith either. In the end, medication has ended up reflecting my weakness and need for the Lord—in all of his primary *and* secondary causes—and also given me the support I need to focus on living a life for *his* sake.

Is the balance difficult to maintain? Sure! At least, it can be. But pursuing the Goldilocks principle for taking medication has meant that my suffering with anxiety serves my spiritual growth. One of my favorite quotes from Emlet's book is the following, which summarizes a lot of the terrain we've covered: "Too much suffering can be 'hazardous' to spiritual growth and too little suffering may be 'hazardous' to spiritual growth."[2] We need balance.

"Medication has ended up reflecting my weakness and need for the Lord and also given me the support I need to focus on living a life for his sake."

I'm not saying that everyone who suffers from anxiety should take medication. Far from it! I encourage people who are dealing with it to see if medication is truly necessary, in consultation with their pastor and primary physician. Medication is not a necessity for everyone, and the decision to take it shouldn't be made lightly. It requires prayer, biblical meditation, soul searching, and wisdom from the body of Christ. If, in that process, you end up choosing to take medication, I want you to know that you're not a faith-failure. You didn't *lose* the battle with anxiety. You're just taking another step and learning more about what this battle will look like for you.

Dealing with the feelings of anxiety is a huge concern for people today, and we need to keep talking about it. If you take nothing else from this chapter, I hope you take that much. For details on the medications that are being used today and their potential effect on us, I would refer readers to chapters 11–13 of Emlet's book. Use the reflection questions at the end of the chapter to continue the conversation with yourself, your pastor, and others you know who are struggling.

Theology: Body-spirit Image Bearers

We've talked about how we image God in our disposition for communion with him. Yet, one important part of our being image-bearers has been left out up until this point. We are *body*-spirit image bearers. What does that mean? It means that our bodies are not some outer shell that constantly gets in the way of our spiritual growth. Our bodies are woven into our spiritual development. God did not create us as spirits and then decide to add flesh as an afterthought. He made us *embodied*. There's an intimate connection between the body and the soul, and that connection was put there by God himself. It's not just our souls that have eternal value, but our bodies as well.

---

2   Emlet, *Descriptions and Prescriptions*, 77.

The most important theological evidence for this is Jesus's *bodily* resurrection. Jesus didn't raise from the dead "in spirit." He was raised in the flesh (Luke 24:39; Acts 2:30–31). His flesh—*our* flesh—is not some rotting cover that we're all waiting to shed. It's part of God's good creation. It was *after* God created our bodies that he pronounced creation "very good" (Gen. 1:31). This has a few implications for us as we struggle with anxiety. Let's look at just one of them for now. We may touch on other ones in the next chapter.

Perhaps the greatest implication is this: *we can't assume that what we do to and with our bodies is detached from our spiritual well-being and development.* As a "good" part of God's creation, our bodies underwent a change when Adam sinned. They became *fallen bodies*, bound to *fallen souls*. Redemption, however, comes to us on both fronts, as we see in Christ's own resurrection. His *body* was raised from the dead. His body, in other words, needed to be restored. Redemption is holistic. But if that's the case, then that means our development as image-bearers is holistic, too. Development—growth in holiness—covers both our spiritual life and our physical life, often in ways that weave the two together. To put it in concrete terms, a refusal to exercise is not simply a body decision; it's a soul decision. It's part of how we're being conformed to Christ.

Why am I saying all of this? How you treat your body can have a profound effect on the well-being of your soul. This comes to our attention when we talk about how we *feel* after doing something unhealthy. Eat a quarter pound of gummy worms, wash them down with soda, and then cram a few cookies. How do you feel? That feeling isn't just an effect on your body; it affects your ability to engage with the world. And isn't that what our souls enable us to do (along with our minds)? If we can't engage with the world in a way that honors Christ because we're tired, malnourished, or driven over the edge by a sugar-rush, then the problem we've created is clearly not just physical. It's spiritual as well.

This brings the Spiritual gifts that God gives out into the open, especially the gift of *self-control* (Gal. 5:23). That's a gift of the Spirit we'd rather not talk about, because it means saying "no" to ourselves in tough situations. But as Drew Dyck wrote recently, "People with greater self-control are more sociable, honest, and sacrificial. They have lower rates of depression, anxiety, substance abuse, and aggression. They even live longer. If you could bottle self-control, it would be one of the most valuable substances on earth."[3] Self-control is precious not because it's a human as-piration, but because it's a divine gift. And it's a divine gift that has a profound effect on our spiritual lives.

The sad thing is that many of us don't even have self-control on our radar. If we do, we're seldom linking it to spiritual development. We don't tie a lack of self-control to soul warfare as quickly as we do other vices such as lust, envy, or pride. In the battle for our souls, we seem to focus on larger, more threatening issues. But I'm convinced that a lack of self-control is one of the most threatening issues we face. It's a central battle, whether we admit it or not. "Unfortunately, most of us are oblivious to the battle, which virtually guarantees we will never win it."[4]

I don't want to go on a long diatribe against our ignorance of self-con-trol—mostly because I'd be condemning myself! But we need to remember that medication is not the only thing that's going to affect the feelings of anxiety. How you treat your body has a huge effect on those feelings, too.

In attempting to commune with God, we can't just think about spiritual practices such as prayer and worship. Those things are massively important! But be-cause we're *body*-spirit image bearers, our ability to commune with God is never *purely* a spiritual battle. It's a flesh-and-blood battle, too. While we don't wage war against "flesh and blood" (Eph. 6:12), that doesn't mean flesh and blood have to sit on the sidelines, unaware that a war is going on.

Self-control may be a gift of the Spirit (Gal. 5:23), but it's a gift that gets used in the physical world. As people who struggle with anxiety, we have to be very careful how we treat the *good* creation that is our body.

I'll end with an example. I have an insatiable sweet tooth. That doesn't mean I just have to "trim down" on my sugar intake; it means I can't control it very well at all. It's *insatiable*. I lack the self-control I need to have sweets in moderation. The older I get, the more convinced I am of this little, biting truth. So, at one point I made the decision to prayerfully step away from processed sugar: candy, cakes, and most desserts. That's hard, because *so* much of our food has sugar in it! As I strug-gled each day to step away from the Snickers bars and Swedish Fish, I noticed some-thing: my moods were becoming more stable. I wasn't quite as anxious as I normally was. After a few weeks, I even went down on my anxiety medication!

---

3   Drew Dyck, *Your Future Self Will Thank You: Secrets to Self-Control from the Bible and Brain Science* (Chicago: Moody, 2019), 23.

4   Dyck, *Your Future Self Will Thank You*, 65.

I never understood how potent sugar was before. Now that I've made an effort to cut most of it out, I can see how great an impact it's had on my body, and how great an impact it's had on my *soul*. My anxiety and my moods are connected to my sugar intake. My body is connected to my spirit. I'm a *body*-spirit image bearer of God. I wish I'd realized this so much sooner in my life, but now that I have, I'm praying that God will keep me from going back to my old ways.

Taking care of the *good* creation of our bodies plays a major role in the well-being of our spirits. What we've said here sets us up for a fuller discussion in the next chapter.

Reflection Questions and Prayer

1. What has been your approach to medication, or the approach of others whom you know? What have been the effects of your approach (or their approach)?

2. Discuss *the lack of faith* approach to medication and *the idol* approach with a group of people. What are their responses? What biblical passages do they bring up? Write them down and pray over them.

3. Has someone you know been accused of taking *the lack of faith* approach? How has that accusation affected them?

4. What are difficult points in finding a balance for the use of medication? Where do you have more room to grow in finding that balance?

5. How does the CHRIST acronym fit into the use of medication? Write out each letter and think about how medication relates to each point.

6. Talk to others about their experiences with particular medications. What have been some common physical and spiritual effects of a particular medication?

7. Some people take medication and then feel better, so they decide to stop taking the medicine. Discuss this with your doctor and with others who take medication. What has been their experience?

8. In what ways has the physical treatment of your body affected your spir-

itual life? How might self-control play a role in the improvement of your bodily health?

Prayer

God, we depend on you for everything.
You give us gifts beyond count.
You have taken your wisdom
And given pieces to mankind
So that they might live for you
And glorify your name.
Medication has been a blessing for us,
But it's also been a curse,
Because we turn good things
Into god things.
We idolize.
We make false gods.
And we give up Christ-conformity,
Conforming instead
To lesser things.
Give us wisdom in the use
Of your secondary causes.
Give us patience and endurance
For Christ-conformity.
Help us to keep your greater purposes
At the forefront of our hearts
So that we can act and live
In a way that draws every eye
To Christ.

Reader Resource: Body Check In

This may not be the most fun exercise to complete, but it's not meant to make you feel guilty. It's meant to make you more aware of your own habits. What are certain habits you have that are affecting (or not affecting) your body? How might those have an effect on your soul? Do some self-inspection. Then plan a proposed change: try to take *one* concrete action (taking too many will lead to failure and frustration). What do you notice? I've put in the example of sugar intake, but there are tons of examples you could substitute. Focus on what *you* deal with on a regular basis.

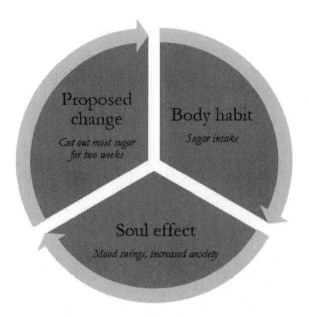

CHAPTER 11

Diet, Exercise, and Sleep

KEY IDEA: Diet, exercise, and sleep are critical in our battle with anxiety.

We ended the last chapter with a discussion of the biblical truth that we're *body*-spirit image bearers. This chapter will explore that in a bit more depth, bringing in our exercise and sleep habits. All of this is part of the larger conversation exploring how we confront the feelings of anxiety. Do we flee from them or face them and let God work? Do we let them shape our prayers, or do we leave prayer by the wayside? How does the treatment of our bodies interact with these feelings? In this chapter, I'm going to offer you an important triad that has a major effect on our feelings of anxiety. After this chapter, we'll focus on managing anxiety in the context of two central human relationships: marriage and family.

The Inside, the Outside, and the In-Between

When you think about it, there are only a few basic actions for humans: *eating, doing,* and *sleeping.* That triad fills our entire lives. When we aren't eating, we're doing something else, or we're sleeping. When we're sleeping, we aren't doing or eating. When we're eating (most of the time), we aren't able to do much else, and we definitely can't sleep!

Put differently, eating addresses what we take in (*the inside*); doing addresses what we put out (*the outside*); and sleeping addresses *the in-between*. These three elements are intertwined and have massive influence on how we feel, not just physically but also spiritually. After all, God made us with bodies. We're body-spirit image bearers. Ignore the spirit, and the body suffers. Ignore the body, and the spirit suffers.

Scripture is plain about the fundamental importance of these three elements. Take *the inside*, for example. One of the first provisions God made for his image bearers was food (Gen. 1:29–30). And the importance of that providence is paralleled by the curse that God put in place for their disobedience: a curse of the ground from which they would take their food (Gen. 3:17–18). After the fall, the lands that God's people seek out are often distinguished by what they offer the people in terms of sustenance. The Promised Land, for instance, was always described as a land "flowing with milk and honey" (Exod. 3:8, 17; 13:15; 33:3; Lev. 24:20; Num. 13:17; 14:8; and others). The fact that land was frequently identified in this way suggests how important it was. Food and drink are not small things to us. We might blow them out of proportion in 21st century first-world countries, but that shouldn't belittle the fact that they are more than just "things." They are *blessings* and *gifts* that God has given to sustain us. Like all else that God originally made, what we take into our bodies is *good* (though we don't always take in things that are actually good for us).

Later in Israel's history, Daniel famously chose to stake out his allegiance to the God of his fathers based on diet (Dan. 1:8–16). Out of all of the things that he could've protested against in that pagan empire, he chose what goes inside his body. Why? Because it had a profound effect. What happened when Daniel and his men ate vegetables and drank water? "They were better in appearance and fatter in flesh than all the youths who ate the king's food" (Dan. 1:15). Notice here that *the inside* is bound up with *the outside*. Because Daniel and his men took *in* what was good, they were able to put *out* what was good; that is, they were able to work well, with strength and power.

"Our ultimate sustenance is the presence of God himself. Food, in that way, points us to eternal sustenance."

What we take into our bodies really does have a life-changing effect on how we look and feel. But we're supposed to put that in a spiritual context. We're supposed to view food and drink in the context of the Great Story. Our ultimate sustenance, after all, isn't food and drink, which is temporal. Our ultimate sustenance is the presence of God himself. Food, in that way, points us to eternal sustenance. That's one of the reasons why, when Moses and the Israelites set up the tabernacle, they were to regularly put out "the bread of Presence" on one of the tables (Exod. 25:30; 35:13; 39:36). The bread of the presence symbolized *God's* presence with his people. God was the sustenance of his people because he was *present* with them. He dwelt in their midst. Jesus understood this so clearly. While his disciples often quibbled and cried about what they would find for dinner, Jesus said he had a different sort of food.

> [31] Meanwhile the disciples were urging him, saying, "Rabbi, eat." [32] But he said to them, "I have food to eat that you do not know about." [33] So the disciples said to one another, "Has anyone brought him something to eat?" [34] Jesus said to them, "My food is to do the will of him who sent me and to accomplish his work." (John 4:31–34)

Doing his Father's will and accomplishing his work might not, at first glance, appear related to God's presence. But the presence of God is manifested among creatures by obedience and holiness. Think about it. When God was going to dwell in the midst of his people via the tabernacle, the temple, and through the body of Christ himself, what was required of the people? Holy obedience to his will! The regulations for sacrifices, diet, and interpersonal relations that we read about in the Pentateuch were meant to set the people apart, to show that they were a kingdom of priests and a holy nation (Exod. 19:6). That holiness was a prerequisite for dwelling in the presence of a holy God. It was the same in the temple, which we can see in the dedication of Solomon (1 Kgs. 8:57–61), and it continues to hold for those who are in Christ. Those who are in Christ draw near to God, and he draws near to them (James 4:8). Why? Because they are *in* his Son, who is holy beyond measure (Rom. 3:24; 6:11; 8:1–2; 1 Cor. 1:30; 2 Cor. 5:17; Gal. 2:16; Eph. 2:10, 13; Phil. 3:9; 2 Tim. 1:9)!

All this is to say that in the context of our spiritual development, our eternal sustenance is our presence with God through Christ, in the power of the Holy Spirit (i.e., our communion with God). We live ultimately on God, not on food. But food is meant to be a reflection, a pointer, to the ultimate truth of our eternal sustenance: God's presence. Put differently, the power and sustenance our bodies receive through food and drink are under-girded by the power and sustenance of God's being with us. In this light, eating poorly is not merely a bad habit; in fact, doing so may cloud our ability to see the underlying purpose of food as a pointer to God. What goes inside our bodies can then become destructive, or it may become an idol—something about which we're more excited than God's being with us. This isn't meant to make us feel bad for eating a donut. I hate guilt trips (and I love donuts). But it should remind us that what we eat isn't peripheral to our spiritual life. There's a major connection there. Towards the end of this chapter, I'll talk about how this has worked itself out in my own diet (I already gave you one example in the previous chapter).

Scripture also has much to say about *the outside*, about what we do with our bodies. The book of Proverbs is especially focused on "the sluggard," the one who never does much.[1] What happens to us when we become lethargic, when we fail to exercise our bodies by doing the various sorts of work God has put before us? We become impoverished and needy. "A little sleep, a little slumber, a little folding of the hands to rest, and poverty will come upon you like a robber, and want like an armed man" (Prov. 6:10–11). That doesn't mean we shouldn't rest. God has called us to rest after his own pattern in Genesis (2:1–3), and we'll talk about another purpose of rest later in this chapter. But developing a *pattern* of lethargy will affect your soul. It will make you crave things that you will not get: "The soul of the sluggard craves and gets nothing, while the soul of the diligent is richly supplied" (Prov. 13:4). Now, what do we all ultimately crave? Remember the theology from a previous chapter: we crave *communion with God*. That's our deepest desire. But we won't get it by failing to care for our bodies. Instead, we'll just end up hurting ourselves, physically and spiritually. We'll get scraped and scratched by a fallen world, for "the way of a sluggard is like a hedge of thorns" (Prov. 15:19). As with *the inside*, however we treat *the outside* has profound effects on our physical and spiritual well-being.

What about *the in-between*? Does Scripture have much to say about sleep? Yes! God tells us that sleep has a huge impact on our well being. One of my favorite passages in this regard is Psalm 127:2, "It is in vain that you rise up early and go late to rest, eating the bread of anxious toil; for he gives to his beloved sleep." Sleep is a

---

1   For a fuller discussion, see Rev. Nam Joon Kimi's book, *Busy for Self, Lazy for God: Meditations on Proverbs for Diligence Living*, trans. Charles Kim and Pierce T. Hibbs (Philadelphia: Westminster Seminary Press, 2018).

gift of *love* from God to his people. But it comes after work, after labor, after we give enough to *the outside*. "Sweet is the sleep of a laborer, whether he eats little or much, but the full stomach of the rich will not let him sleep" (Eccl. 5:12). But perhaps the greatest testament to the necessity and goodness of sleep comes from our following the pattern of God's rest at the end of creation. Rest, you see, is not something that we thought up on our own. God had to show us *how* to rest. He designed us to rest, but he had to show us how to do it. We don't rest all the time. We don't rest for just 3 hours a day, either. We rest at the end of labor for the Lord, and we rest on the Sabbath, trusting that God himself is faithful to labor and care for us while we lay ourselves down in him. Once again, this notion of *the in-between* has a profound effect on us physically and spiritually.

My Experience

Now, I'd love to synthesize a host of articles and books and draw up a diet, exercise, and sleep-plan for you. That would take research, and I love research (because I'm a nerd). But that's not what I have to offer you. Others will offer that better than I can. What I can offer you is twelve years of experience on how these areas have affected my own battle with anxiety. This is my best effort to save you the time and trials of learning some of these things the hard way.

In terms of *the inside*, I've learned that sugar and caffeine have a dramatic effect on my anxiety. I've always struggled with sugar intake, and caffeine was something I took up in coffee once we had kids (not so surprising). I have to be *very* intentional and cautious with my sugar and caffeine intake, or else there are clear repercussions. It's like clockwork. On one side, several days of more sugar, a few extra cups of coffee throughout the week, and I'm on edge. I'm more easily set off by anxiety-inducing tasks, and the feelings of anxiety (hyper-vigilance, throat sensitivity, de-realization) begin creeping up on me. On the other side, cutting back on sugar seems to stabilize my moods and help me feel more relaxed overall. The same is the case with coffee. These two elements alone can be *really* hard to control, especially the coffee. I'm a morning person and get up around 5:00am each day. That can be tough without any boost from caffeine, but sometimes I've had to switch to tea or leave out the caffeine completely for a few days. This also provides a great opportunity for me to check my soul and see if something as insignificant as coffee has actually become an idol for me—something I crave more than the presence of God.

I'll be transparent with you. It's been easy for me to turn sugar and caffeine into idols. I know that sounds silly and a bit extreme, but be honest with yourself: do you look forward to your morning coffee more than your devotional time? Are you more excited about cake than communing with God through prayer? No one's above subtle idolatry. In fact, that sort of idolatry can be the most potent, since it doesn't seem like a big deal. We let it go, and then it becomes a bigger deal. It works its way into routine and pushes something else out, and then something else. And then it settles into the human heart and starts trying to nudge God off the throne (as if that were even possible!).

> *"No one's above subtle idolatry. In fact, that sort of idolatry can be the most potent, since it doesn't seem like a big deal."*

Positively, taking in more vegetables and protein, rather than processed carbohydrates, has had a profound effect on how I feel. I have more energy, more focus, and I'm more alert. Again, I'm not a medical professional or a dietitian. There are tons of books out there on these topics, and I invite you to do some of your own research. That's what I've had to do. But for me, personally, sugar and caffeine have been the greatest pressure points. Maybe they are for you, too. If not, take some time to think about what you eat (and when), and start experimenting with your intake. I promise you this: you'll be amazed at how much your diet affects your anxiety. It's not a triviality.

Regarding *the outside*, I've mentioned before that exercise is a necessity for me, at least 30 minutes of intense cardio multiple times a week. My doctor actually wrote me a prescription for this! I keep it near my desk. On a medical prescription form, she wrote out, "30 minutes of cardio, 5 times a week, indefinitely." That little prescription slip helps me take exercise seriously, as part of my medical care. I don't make five times a week too often, to be honest. But that little slip of paper is a constant reminder that I *need* to do this. And as with the diet, it's like clockwork: if I skip a week or two of exercise, the stress levels increase. I become more aware of my anxiety and struggle to focus on anything but that. Then I get back to running, cut down on caffeine, and things start to shift almost within a day.

The same goes for the *in-between*. When my wife and I had our first child, I started to drink coffee in order to deal with the lack of sleep. And for a few months, we were running on so much adrenaline, that I would usually only get 3–4 hours of sleep a night. I thought, "Wow! I've been wasting so much time in my life! I only need 4 hours of sleep to get by." So, I started getting up around 4:00 or 4:30am every day, to study and write. I got some articles written, and a few books, so I was excited to keep up the momentum.

But then I crashed. After several months of this, my nerves were shot. I had a relapse with my anxiety and had to start getting 7–8 hours of sleep consistently. I pushed too hard. I treated sleep and rest too lightly, and I paid the price. I've learned that my body *needs* a certain amount of sleep to function (usually at least 7 hours). I know that other people can function on less, and I'm quick to be jealous of them. But God has made us each unique. We have to be confident about walking the path that he's made for our bodies. If I sacrifice sleep now, I do so with the knowledge that I'll pay for it later. It's just that simple.

I don't know how much sleep you need, but most doctors recommend 8 hours. If you're not getting that much, you may have to change your routines. As with diet and exercise, this has a major effect on how we feel, how we deal with the anxiety that comes our way.

The spiritual gift that comes into focus in all three areas is something that Paul talks about frequently. It's something I introduced in the previous chapter: *self-control* (Gal. 5:22; 2 Tim. 1:7; Titus 1:8; 2:1, 6). As we've already noted, self-control is actually a *gift* of the Spirit (Gal. 5:22–23). It's listed among the "fruit" of the Spirit, those things which the Spirit of God produces in us by grace. That means, first of all, that self-control is something we need to pray for; we need to ask our Father, in the name of Christ, to give us that which he's already promised to bestow on us. Self-control, in the end, is not purely about will power. It's about God's power *given* to us. We need to pray for it regularly.

Yet, self-control is also something that manifests itself in our daily habits and choices. We face a hundred opportunities for self-control every day, in little moments. Think of them in the form of questions: should I have another cup of coffee? Should I have a donut or eggs? Should I eat a piece of fruit or Poptarts? Should I sleep an extra hour or get up to do my devotions? Should I read my Bible or keep perusing Netflix? These are matters of self-control; they are the tiny concrete opportunities where we can manifest the Spirit-given gift of self-control. I love what

Drew Dyck said about this: "While we may be tested in dramatic moments, the fabric of life is stitched slowly, through a thousand tiny choices that end up defining our lives. The difference of those accumulated decisions is dramatic. They can add up to a life crippled by sloth and sin or to one characterized by freedom and flourishing."[2]

We all need to work on this. For these three areas—the inside, the outside, and the in-between—self-control hovers at the center. This is another reminder of the plain truth that our anxiety is not just a physical issue; it's a spiritual one, and God may be calling us to do some hard work with self-control. That's not a fun message, but it's true for many of us. And know this, your self-control will eventually lead to *freedom*. As Dyck writes, "The Bible portrays self-control not as restrictive but rather as the path to freedom. It enables us to do what's right—and ultimately what's best for us."[3]

The point of this chapter is just to highlight what many of us know but often ignore: what you eat, what you do with your body, and how much you sleep *matters*. For people with anxiety, it matters *a lot*. Making some significant changes in one or more of these areas may have a major impact on your symptoms. I recommend that you start taking some notes in each area. Start becoming more familiar with your eating, exercise, and sleep habits. Then start seeking out advice and guidance to make changes. These changes are not just going to affect your physical well-being; they'll do a whole lot for your spiritual life as well. So, mind the triad, my friends. Mind it well.

Theology: Rest and Sanctification

I end this chapter with a bit of theology related to one of the elements in the triad: sleep and rest. What is the purpose of sleep and rest? The default answer for many people is something like, "To recharge your batteries," or "To do nothing so that you can be more effective when you have to start moving again." There's some truth to those answers, but Scripture has a unique perspective on rest, one that we probably don't think much about.

Let's start with the beginning of rest. After he created all things, God rested from his labors. "Thus the heavens and the earth were finished, and all the host of them. And on the seventh day God finished his work that he had done, and he rested

---

2   Drew Dyck, *Your Future Self Will Thank You: Secrets to Self-Control from the Bible and Brain Science* (Chicago: Moody, 2019), 29.

3   Dyck, *Your Future Self Will Thank You*, 20.

on the seventh day from all his work that he had done. So God blessed the seventh day and made it holy, because on it God rested from all his work that he had done in creation" (Gen. 2:1–3). He didn't rest because he was tired; God's strength is immeasurable. He didn't rest because he got burnt out; that's only a problem for limited creatures. Why did he rest? The short answer is, "He rested to give us an example."

God models everything for his people—not just what we should do but also what we shouldn't do. And rest falls into this category as well. On the seventh day of creation, God showed us how to rest. But he also tells us *why* we rest. Did you notice the reason for God blessing the seventh day and making it holy? He rested. Resting brought blessing and holiness. Of course, God's already utterly holy, so resting didn't make him any more holy than he already is. But this relationship between rest and growth in holiness certainly applies to us.

In fact, later in Scripture, God makes the relationship between holiness and rest even more explicit. In speaking to Moses, he tells him why the people of Israel are to keep the Sabbath. "And the LORD said to Moses, 'You are to speak to the people of Israel and say, "Above all you shall keep my Sabbaths, for this is a sign between me and you throughout your generations, that you may know that I, the LORD, sanctify you"'" (Exod. 31:12–13). God *sanctifies* his people in their rest. Why should the people rest? "So that you may *know* that I, the Lord, sanctify you." In resting, we learn how God is sanctifying us.

"In resting, we learn how God is sanctifying us."

This makes practical sense, when you think about it. Part of the reason why we're ignorant of the ways in which we need to be sanctified is that we don't stop. We're always busy; there's always more to do, more to entertain us, more to do for our kids, and our spouse, and our extended family, and our church, and . . . you get the picture. If we don't ever stop, if we don't rest, it will be harder to see, harder to *know*, that God is sanctifying us.

I have a hard time resting, especially sleeping. I mentioned that I get up around 5:00am every day, sometimes earlier if I can't sleep, to write and read. There's a constant grind once I wake up in the morning—so constant that it's hard for me to stop what I'm doing to help the kids get up and have breakfast. I break this habit on

Sunday mornings, when I sleep a little bit later and wake up with the rest of the family. Do you know what God recently showed me one Sunday morning? He showed me how little patience I have. As we were rushing to get the kids dressed and out the door to church, I found myself repeating commands and raising my voice with irritation. "Why do I have to ask you to get dressed six times?" I'm rushing because I don't want to be late for church. I'm paying no mind to the huge smile on my son's face as he jumps off of the coffee table, or to the wildness in my daughter's eyes as she sprints around the living room, or to my youngest daughter's arms that are flapping up and down because she can hear music. I'm trying to rush past these things so that we can get to church on time. It's not working, and I'm starting to lose my temper.

But because I had a bit more sleep that morning (and because my wife plays an important role in my sanctification, too), God helped me to stop—to stop yelling, stop trying so hard to bend everyone's will to my own, stop getting frustrated over something so small. I paused and took a deep breath. In my head, I said, "I'm not a patient man. But God, you are *so* patient with me. Would you please help me to have patience?"

That's sanctification in real life: it's concrete moments where you pause and know that the Lord is sanctifying you, drawing your attention to the holiness he gives. When we don't rest, it becomes very hard to find those moments.

Rest is not just healthy or a physical necessity; it's a spiritual tool for sanctification. In your rest, God is showing you that he is the one who will sanctify you. He will slow you down so that you can see him working.

I find that I'm much more likely to rest when I keep this in mind. I'm not just resting because my eyelids are dropping or because I can't think straight anymore. I'm resting because it's part of my holiness, my growth in becoming more like Christ. When you don't rest, you're not just hurting your body and mind; you're hurting your soul. If you want to see how God is sanctifying you, you need to sleep.

Reflection Questions and Prayer

1. What are your typical habits with *the inside* (food)? How do you think those habits are affecting your anxiety? What changes do you think you could make?

2. What are your typical habits with *the outside* (exercise)? How do you think those habits are affecting your anxiety? What sorts of exercise might help you to get more energy out or increase your heart-rate?

3.   What are your typical sleep patterns? If you need more sleep, what could you cut out in order to allow for that? Develop a consistent sleep schedule to help with this.

4.   After getting more sleep on a Sunday, pray and ask God to show you how he's sanctifying you. What does God reveal to you?

5.   How are each of the elements in the triad related to your own spiritual well-being? Try to be specific and share examples with a pastor or friend.

6.   Which of the elements in the triad tends to become an idol for you, or may become an idol if you aren't careful? What are some Scripture passages that you could memorize to help you combat the idolatry?

7.   Set aside time to rest on the next Sabbath. As you rest, pray and ask God to open your eyes to the ways in which he wants to help you grow in holiness. Write down those ways so that you can pay special attention to them in the next week and continually pray for growth.

Prayer

God, I know that the inside, the outside, and the in-between
Matter.
They matter to you.
They need to matter to me.
Help me to see food
As a pointer to your sustaining presence.
Help me to see exercise
As a way to labor for you.
Help me to see sleep
As the blessing of rest
Patterned after you.
Take these seemingly little things
And show me their weight.
Show me their gravity.
Help me to focus on the particulars
So that you can work great things
In the details of my day.
Amen.

Reader Resource: Tracking the Triad

For the last few chapters, we've been doing some self-study. Continue doing that here by becoming more aware of your habits with diet, exercise, and sleep. Where do you feel strong? Where do you have room to grow? The important thing here is that when you propose changes, don't propose too many changes at the same time. Start small. Gain a victory, and then build in another change. Over time, you'll notice a big difference. Again, I've filled this out with my own experiences to give you a sense of how specific and practical you can be.

	Diet	Exercise	Sleep
What are my current habits?	*I'm drawn to sugar and processed carbohydrates. I need more protein, vegetables, and fruit to increase my energy and focus.*	*I run 2–3 times a week, but when I get tired or lazy, I quit and tell myself I'll catch up later. But this turns into not catching up at all.*	*I usually get around 7 hours, but I cut this short a few days a week, which can lead to a vicious cycle of tiredness.*
What can I do to change?	*Pack protein and vegetable snacks when I go to work (nuts, cheese, carrots, broccoli). When I get a sugar craving, I can drink water or chew gum.*	*Bring workout clothes to work and go running on my lunchbreak. Aim for at least 4 runs a week.*	*Set my alarm a half hour later two days a week, to catch up on any lost sleep.*

Helpful Articles on Diet, Exercise, and Sleep

- Debret, Chelsea. "Understanding How a Plant-Based Whole Foods Diet and Exercise Improves Cortisol Levels." One Green Planet. https://www. onegreenplanet.org/natural-health/understanding-how-a-plant-based-whole-foods-diet-and-exercise-improves-cortisol-levels/.

- "Exercise for Stress and Anxiety." Anxiety and Depression Association of America. https://adaa.org/living-with-anxiety/managing-anxiety/exercise-stress-and-anxiety.

- Naidoo, Uma. "Eating Well To Help Manage Anxiety: Your Questions Answered." Harvard Health Blog. March 14, 2018. https://www.health.harvard.edu/blog/eating-well-to-help-manage-anxiety-your-questions-answered.

- Smith, Kathleen. "Anxiety and Sleep." Psycom. April 11, 2019. https://www.psycom.net/anxiety-and-sleep/.

- Star, Katharina. "How Physical Exercise Benefits Mental Health." VeryWellMind. November 7, 2019. https://www.verywellmind.com/physical-exercise-for-panic-disorder-and-anxiety-2584094.

- "Tips for Beating Anxiety To Get a Better Night's Sleep." Harvard Health Publishing. https://www.health.harvard.edu/mind-and-mood/tips-for-a-better-nights-sleep.

CHAPTER 12

Marriage and Anxiety

KEY IDEA: Your spouse shares the burden of your anxiety.

I
n this chapter and the following one, I'm turning our attention to relationships. We've dealt with the longevity of anxiety (a long-term guest), with the relationship between fear and faith, with spiritual waWrfare, with the feelings of anxiety, with the priority of prayer, with medication, and with the basic human triad. We've examined many parts of the CHRIST acronym. But now we have to turn our attention away from ourselves and onto others. We have to turn our attention to the *relationships* we take part in while we suffer with anxiety and are conformed to Christ by it.

If you're not married and don't ever plan to be, you could skip this chapter and the following one, but I think there's something here for you if you're willing to read on.

And the Two Shall Become One Flesh

We're disposed for communion with the God who communes with himself. But we're also disposed for communion with others. We're social. We're relational. As one of my favorite theologians put it when discussing the creation of Adam:

No matter how richly favored and how grateful, that first man was not satisfied, not fulfilled. The cause is indicated to him by God himself. It lies in his solitude. It is not good for the man that he should be alone. He is not so constituted, he was not created that way. His nature inclines to the social—he wants company. He must be able to express himself, reveal himself, and give himself. He must be able to pour out his heart, to give form to his feelings. He must share his awareness with a being who can understand him and can feel and live along with him. Solitude is poverty, forsakeness, a gradual pining and wasting away. How lonesome it is to be alone![1]

We were not created to be alone. We were created for communion. We were created for company.

"We were created for communion. We were created for company."

Now, that doesn't mean that everyone needs to get married. Jesus and the Apostle Paul were never married, after all. It's not a biblical necessity. But it is a biblical *blessing* for many people. Why? Besides the obvious benefit of combating solitude (which is healthy in small doses), there's something unique about marriage. And God tells us exactly what it is in Genesis 2:18–24.

> [18] Then the Lord God said, "It is not good that the man should be alone; I will make him a helper fit for him." [19] Now out of the ground the Lord God had formed every beast of the field and every bird of the heavens and brought them to the man to see what he would call them. And whatever the man called every living creature, that was its name. [20] The man gave names to all livestock and to the birds of the heavens and to every beast of the field. But for Adam there was not found a helper fit for him. [21] So the Lord God caused a deep sleep to fall upon the man, and while he slept took one of his ribs and closed up its place with flesh. [22] And the rib that the Lord God had taken from the man he made into a woman and brought her to the man. [23]

---

1   Herman Bavinck, *The Wonderful Works of God: Instruction in the Christian Religion according to the Reformed Confession* (Glenside, PA: Westminster Seminary Press, 2019), 170.

Then the man said, "This at last is bone of my bones and flesh of my flesh; she shall be called Woman, because she was taken out of Man." [24] Therefore a man shall leave his father and his mother and hold fast to his wife, and they shall become one flesh.

There's a lot going on here, but focus on just a few points. First, God isn't saying that Adam is "lonely." He just says that it isn't good for Adam to be "alone." What's the difference? If Adam were *lonely*, that would mean he was created with a problem, a malfunction. But that can't be the case because God already said in Genesis 1:31 that everything he made was "very good." Adam isn't lonely or even "lonesome" as Bavinck put it. He's simply *alone*. And God says that this "aloneness" is not "good." Why not, and what does he mean? Well, Adam *is* good as a creation of God, but the creation of humans isn't *finished*. It's not yet complete. There's nothing wrong with calling something that isn't completely finished "good." A builder who lays a solid foundation doesn't stand back and say, "That's terrible! The building isn't finished yet." Instead, he looks at the foundation and, if it's constructed well, he says, "Good." Something similar is happening with the creation of man. What God has made in Adam is good, even "very good." But it's not finished yet. Eve *completes* the creation of humanity. Without her, Adam would have been good, but humanity itself—the very meaning of what it is to be human—would be unfinished. Eve completes not just Adam, but the creation of humanity as a whole. Adam is unfinished without Eve.

Second, Adam needs someone *equal* to him. Bavinck wrote that Adam "must share his awareness with a being who can understand him and can feel and live along with him." Adam needs an equal. He needs someone "fit for him." Think of the joy and passion that flowed off his lips when said, "This at last is bone of my bones and flesh of my flesh" (v. 23)! It's as if he's saying, "At last! An equal! Someone I can pour myself out for and receive in full!"

Third, the equality of Eve and Adam is complemented by *intimacy*. Eve was taken from *inside* Adam! Don't interpret that the wrong way, as if God is saying that Eve is somehow inferior to Adam. No! This is an expression of intimacy. Eve was taken from a part of Adam's own body. She is *that* close to him. The expression "bone of my bones and flesh of my flesh" is one of intimacy, of unparalleled union. Adam and Eve match on the inside (bones) and the outside (flesh).

Fourth, verse 24 puts it all together for us: "they shall become one flesh." One *flesh*, one body from two—that's how intimate Adam and Eve, husband and wife, are to be. Their souls are wrapped up in each other, so intertwined, so tightly bound that where the world sees two, God sees one. That doesn't erase their distinctness. But it does put their distinctness in a single circle. From now on, there is no longer such a thing as *just Adam* or *just Eve*. There's no defining a husband or a wife in solitude. These are persons defined in relation to each other. They are joined. That's why preachers echo the words of Jesus in modern-day wedding ceremonies: "What therefore God has joined together, let not man separate" (Mark 10:9). God is the unifier, the joiner. *God* is responsible for the unity of a marriage.

One Flesh with Anxiety

Now, how does this play into our anxiety? Start by focusing on the intimate union of husband and wife, and then ask yourself a question that might seem to have an obvious answer: *what can one spouse hide from another?* The answer, of course, is "Nothing!" Sure, you can *attempt* to hide things, and people do this all the time. But it's corrosive to the relationship. Besides, the context of marriage won't allow such hiding to succeed. We're talking about *one flesh*, remember? Hiding something from your husband or wife is, in a sense, trying to hide something from *yourself*, from your true identity. You can't have full identity in isolation from your spouse. Your struggles are not your own. Your joys are not your own. Your hopes and dreams are not your own. They *belong* to you both. I know that flies in the face of a Western American culture that prizes individualism and personal freedom above all else, but what can I say? Western American culture and the Bible are worlds apart. If you're used to defining yourself in isolation, frankly, that's simply foreign to the Great Story. We have our distinctness, our uniqueness as creatures of God, certainly. But that uniqueness *never* eclipses or overrides our joint identity as one flesh. *There's distinctness in unity.* In marriage, there's no such thing as distinctness outside of unity. If your view of marriage suggests that there is such a thing, then you have a patently different view of marital union from that of the Bible.

This intimate union between husband and wife means many things. For starters, it means you can't shield your spouse from your anxiety. We may have noble reasons for wanting to do this. "I don't want to hurt my spouse." "I don't want my spouse to have to deal with this, too." "I just need to figure this out on my own." "My spouse doesn't really understand what I'm going through. Why drag him/her into it?" I'm sorry—none of those reasons trumps the biblical view of marriage. If you're married, whatever you experience, your spouse is going to experience alongside you, and vice versa. And if that's not the case, you'll experience a rift in the relationship—a disconcerting sense of distance. Why? Because you're one flesh, and yet you're trying to act as if you're still two, as if you're separate! If you're married, God has ordained for you to walk through your battle with anxiety as one flesh. It's not a matter of whether or not you *could* deal with anxiety on your own; it's a matter of whether or not you *should*. And the Great Story is very clear about this: you shouldn't.

We've seen throughout this book that God has an amazing way of drawing strength out of weakness. We've seen this in looking at Paul's journey as a Christian. It's a journey that ultimately belongs to Christ, whose painful weakness paved the way to glorious strength. Christ set the path. Paul walked on it. You will walk on it. I will walk on it. We can't be tempted to start with strength and move to more strength. That's a modern Western way to think. In fact, that's the world's way of thinking. "Stronger! Stronger! Stronger!" The Great Story has the opposite and paradoxical chant: "Weaker! Weaker! Weaker!" Why?! Because God's power is made perfect in weakness (2 Cor. 12:9).

You need to walk through the weakness with your spouse. Grip hands, squeeze your eyes closed in faith, and ask God to show his strength in you. It's not going to be a glorious path. It *shouldn't* be a glorious path. It'll be a cruciform path, a trail of precious tears that sometimes soak into the dry soil of daily despondence. But don't be fooled. God is a tear-gatherer. He knows your passions and your pains, and they're forever etched in his memory. He knows. And your spouse should know, too. Your spouse's sympathy and empathy for you is a complement to the H of our CHRIST acronym. Christ knows exactly what you're going through already. Do your very best to let your spouse know. It will take constant upkeep, steady work, and intentionality. But it's worth it because you're one flesh.

My Experience

Let me set out some of my own experience with this. God has blessed me with a wife who is patient, long-suffering, genuine, sympathetic, and self-sacrificing. From the very moment I entered my battle with anxiety, she's been next to me, watching me, studying the history of my responses to panic and pressure, to the harrowing symptoms of anxiety, to the feelings I hate and the thoughts I shudder at. She's listened as I rehearsed struggle after struggle, fear after fear. She's studied me. That's what great spouses do: they study each other. She might not think of it this way, but I can tell she's been doing it faithfully. How? Because of what she says to me.

Here are some of the things she's said to open conversations about my struggles with anxiety. Notice how each of them reveals her involvement with me, her one-flesh commitment.

"In the throes of anxiety, we don't want to be fixed right away; we want to be heard. We want to be seen."

I'm so sorry you're dealing with this. We often rush to offer solutions to problems. I'm guilty of this all the time. I want to fix things as fast as possible. But in the throes of anxiety, we don't want to be fixed right away; we want to be *heard*. We want to be *seen*. We want someone to look at us where we are and call out the location. "I see you! I see! And I don't like it any more than you do!" We yearn for someone to sympathize with us in our anxiety, and Christ does this. But that sympathy begins by a recognition of where we are, not a directive for where we *should* be or where we *could* be if only we did X. My wife begins many conversations about my anxiety simply by saying, "Hey, I see you." You wouldn't believe the comfort that brings me. It's the comfort of being located, of being *found*.

I'm going to pray for you right now. It's embarrassing how quickly we dismiss the effectiveness of prayer. Prayer isn't *wishful thinking*, but we tend to treat it that way, and then (surprise, surprise) we stop doing it.[2] We learned to stop wishing for things a long time ago. But prayer is not divine *wish granting*. It's not a matter of asking God for something really, really intensely. That can certainly be part of prayer, and God tells us to ask him for whatever we need as we seek his will (Matt. 18:19; 21:22; Mark 11:24; John 14:13; 15:7, 16; 16:23–24; James 1:5–6; 4:2–3; 1 John 3:22; 5:14–15). Prayer is personal dialogue with God that matters. It's "a means of fellowship with our heavenly Father."[3] It's an act of communion, an act of relationship, with the one who is in control of everything. And it *matters* because "God ordains prayer as a means to change history. There are things that happen because of prayer, and things

---

2   For a short take on the difference between praying and wishing, see "The Difference between Wishing and Praying," http://piercetaylorhibbs.com/the-difference-between-wishing-and-praying/.

3   John M. Frame, *Systematic Theology: An Introduction to Christian Belief* (Phillipsburg, NJ: P&R, 2013), 1054.

that do not happen because of no prayer."[4] That doesn't mean we control history. It means that God controls history, and in his sovereignty, he's given us a place in it. That's what Frame means when he says that God "ordains prayer as a means to change history."

"Demons are going to be dispelled. Satan is going to be silenced."

Taking that into consideration, when my wife tells me she's going to pray for me, I'm confident in the *action* that God is going to take. My wife's prayer isn't going to change the mind or will of God. But it is going to find a place in the course that God has ordained for history. In that sense, there will be repercussions for her prayer. Things will happen because of her prayer, because God ordained it to be that way. When she prays for me, I have faith in God's action. I have faith in God's hearing of her voice on my behalf. I have faith that something is going to happen. Demons are going to be dispelled. Satan is going to be silenced. Bodily sensations are going to be interpreted with spiritual purpose. God is going to work. To put it in terms of C. S. Lewis's *Chronicles of Narnia, Aslan is going to move.*

Having my wife tell me that she's praying for me when I'm battling anxiety is like providing a rung on a ladder. I'm trying to climb out of chaos. I'm halfway up the ladder, but I can't see the next rung. I'm grasping at air. I'm reaching for what I can't see. My wife's prayer tells me, "Don't stop reaching. It's right there; just keep your hand up. The next rung is just ahead of your hand." God, how I need that when I'm crippled by the feelings of anxiety! And I'm sure you need it, too.

I know it's really tough, but try to focus on X. This comment points to the I and S of the CHRIST acronym. My wife is reminding me of what I've learned. She's telling me to identify a focus and stay engaged. That focus is something in the environment around me. If this seems foreign to Scripture, just remember that God often tells us to look at parts of creation in order to learn something about him or about ourselves. "Look at the ants," God told Solomon (Prov. 6:6). "Look at the birds," Jesus told his followers (Matt. 6:26). Look at the world around you to learn about yourself

---

4   Frame, *Systematic Theology*, 1054.

and about the God who cares for you. There's so much to learn![5] And as you focus, stay engaged by speaking to God. This is a continuation of prayer. Don't think of prayer as momentary speech. Think of it as *continuous* dialogue, because even if you're not speaking to God, he's speaking to you. Why do we restrict ourselves to praying only with our eyes closed and our hands folded? There's nothing keeping us from praying with eyes wide open, talking with God in the public air. Will you look like a crazy person? Probably, but that's not surprising. You *should* look like a crazy person. What's wise in the eyes of God is foolishness to the world (1 Cor. 1:20–21; 3:19; 2 Cor. 1:12). What's crazy in the eyes of the world is sane in the eyes of your heavenly Father. Don't let stares of strangers dampen your dialogue with God.

Tell me what's going on. This is the T from our CHRIST acronym. Because God has designed us for communion, for dialogue with him, there is great power in speech. Vibrating our vocal chords does something to calm and settle us. It also gives us the ability to do what Bavinck said we so desperately long to do. Remember what he said about Adam? "He must be able to express himself, reveal himself, and give himself. He must be able to pour out his heart, to give form to his feelings. He must share his awareness with a being who can understand him and can feel and live along with him." When I'm anxious, I want to pour out my heart; I want to give form to my feelings. When my wife asks me to tell her what's going on, she's providing a door for me. I walk through it with words. I vibrate my vocal chords and start painting a portrait of myself for her. And she listens. She watches as I paint. And once again, her action in doing this says, "I see you."

I know you can do this, and I know that you know it too. My wife is an expert when it comes to reminding me of what I promised myself I'd never forget. I've come through many battles and wars with anxiety. I've come *through* them. That means I've lived to tell the tale. I've seen God's faithfulness take shape on the road of weakness and suffering. I've seen how close to him anxiety will bring me. I've seen and felt the relief of knowing something is behind me. My wife calls history to my attention, and she affirms her confidence in God's work. Note that, as well. It's not confidence in what *I've* been able to do. It's confidence in what she's seen *God* do in me.

There are other things she's said to me, but these examples illustrate just how helpful and encouraging it can be to walk through anxiety with your spouse, to take a one-flesh approach to the suffering you're facing. In a marriage, there's no solitary experience. While we're distinct, and we walk through things that our spouse

---

5   I've begun providing examples in *Finding God in the Ordinary* (Eugene, OR: Wipf & Stock, 2018).

may not be able to sympathize with directly, we're one flesh. We are *with* each other—till death do we part. And even then, we don't part in the Lord.

I don't know what my road of anxiety has for me in the future. But I know two things, and I'll hold onto them with every ounce of prayer I can muster: (1) God is *with* me and will be using anxiety to do things in me that I can't even imagine; and (2) my wife is *with* me. There's great power in *with*. Don't pass that preposition by.

Theology: Marriage and the Trinity?

One of the things I've become more aware of as I grow in my relationship with God is how *everything* good in the world, and everything good inside us, is reflective of him. That shouldn't be too surprising. An artist's hands are responsible for the colors on the canvas, so when we look at a canvas, there's a sense in which we can see his hands—the turning of his wrists, the pressure he's applied with the brush, the soft touches of relaxed fingers that led to detail. The artist is tied to his work. It's similar with creation. God has made all things to "speak" of him, to reveal him.[6]

Does this apply to marriage? Certainly! John Frame writes, "love between husband and wife pictures God's love for his people (Ezek. 16; Hos. 1–3; Eph. 5:25–33), which begins with a love within the Trinity itself (John 17:26)."[7] Love has an ancient home. That home is not in you or in me; it's not in the collective human race; it's in God. In the beginning, there was love because in the beginning there was God.

I like how Dumitru Stăniloae, a Romanian theologian, once put it. He wrote a book entitled *The Holy Trinity: In the Beginning There Was Love*. In the beginning, before time and space were spoken into being, before the stars were burning, before the earth was turning, there was love. "God is love," he writes, "and therefore life and light in themselves, because he is the supreme unity of three individual persons in communion with one another."[8] God, the Bible tells us, does not just *love* others; he *is* love (1 John 4:8). The God who *is* love is the God who *gives* love and the one in whose image *we* love. Love in the Trinity—which we can say takes the form of eternal and mutual expressions of glory among the Father, Son, and Spirit—is the origin, the hearth, of the love we express to each other.[9]

---

6   See chapter 3 in *The Speaking Trinity & His Worded World: Why Language Is at the Center of Everything* (Eugene, OR: Wipf & Stock, 2018).

7   John M. Frame, *Systematic Theology: An Introduction to Christian Belief* (Phillipsburg, NJ: P&R, 2013), 794.

8   Dumitru Stăniloae, *The Holy Trinity: In the Beginning There Was Love*, trans. Roland Clark (Brookline, MA: Holy Cross Orthodox Press, 2012), 14.

9   On the mutual love and glorification among the Father, Son, and Spirit, see Frame, *Systematic Theology*, 480–81.

In this sense, the love we express to our spouse is not original, really. It's imitative. At our best, we love according to an eternal pattern of love. We fall embarrassingly short, of course, and we can't love one another in the same way that the Father loves the Son and Spirit. God is God, and we are not. But God has made us image-bearers, so we *must* love in a way that images the eternal love of God. And we *must* love in a way that images God's own love for us. What does that look like, exactly?

It looks like *self-lessness*. If we want to image God's love, we can't be self-centered, for the persons of the Godhead love and glorify the other persons, not themselves. The Son glorifies the Father, and the Father glorifies the Son (John 17:1–5). And in Jesus Christ, God actually gives himself *for us*! Christ's crucifixion is the ultimate act of self-sacrifice. Loving like the Trinity means we have to be both *others-centered* and *self-sacrificial*. True love is never primarily concerned with the self or the advantages and benefits *we* can get from it. In fact, it's quite the opposite. True love for your spouse involves actions that bless that person *regardless* of your benefit. Even more than that, it involves actions that bless that person when you may even take a hit for it. Christ, remember, didn't love us because we were lovely; he loved us when we were hideous and hateful; he loved us to make us lovely. "God shows his love for us in that while we were still sinners, Christ died for us" (Rom. 5:8).

"Anxiety curves us in on ourselves. It bends our necks downward so that we're always checking how we feel, what we fear, where we'll go next."

This has many implications for marriage in the context of anxiety, but I'll just leave you with one: *take time every day to show genuine interest in your spouse, and make a habit of sacrificing your own wishes for his or hers.* Anxiety curves us in on ourselves. It bends our necks downward so that we're always checking how we feel, what we fear, where we'll go next. That curving makes it very hard to show genuine interest in someone else. If you want to do that, you have to bend your neck the other way. You have to look at your spouse in the eyes and say, "How can I be helpful to you today?" Or, "How have you been doing with the kids lately? Can I get you some special one-on-one time with them?" Or, "Can I make dinner one night so you can take an hour or two off?" These are the sorts of questions I *should* be asking my spouse regularly, but my anxiety can make me look away from her and towards myself. Try to do one thing today that requires you to bend your neck in another direction.

If we're going to love after the pattern of God, we have to make continual and conscious efforts to pull our minds away from anxiety-steeped self-focus and put it on someone else. Intensely focusing your attention and energy on someone else is one way you can combat your anxiety and bless others at the same time. This is another reminder that our anxiety is a tool in the hands of God, if we're willing to be shaped by him through it, and to respond to others with our new shape.

Reflection Questions and Prayer

1. If you're married, how has your spouse been involved in your struggles with anxiety?

2. What do you think the role of a spouse is for someone dealing with anxiety? What biblical support can you find for your thoughts?

3. If you're not married and don't plan to be, how does this chapter encourage you? Think about God's ordained plan for human relationships in the context of suffering.

4. What are some things your spouse has said to you that help you to manage your anxiety? Why do those things seem to help you?

5. If you don't speak with your spouse much about your anxiety, can you set up a plan to do so? You might be able to do momentary check-ins where you simply say, "Hey, this is how I *feel*. And this is what I *need*." Having a plan in place for communication will make things much easier.

6. How does anxiety make you feel curved in on yourself? Name a person and an action that you can take up today as a focus that might divert your attention away from yourself.

Prayer (for married readers)

My God—Father, Son, and Spirit,
You made us for relationships.
You are a relationship that transcends our imagination.
And you've made marriage to reflect the mystery

Of personal union.

Help me to take a one-flesh approach to anxiety.

Help me to talk through my anxiety *with* my spouse,

To lean on my other half,

To know that I'm loved and prayed for,

And that it matters.

Help me to communicate clearly,

Consistently,

To be found by my spouse in every anxious trial.

Help us both to pray through anxiety,

To watch you shape us to your Son's image.

Keep our feet steady on the path of weakness,

And when we fall down,

Let us fall into your grace and mercy

With confidence.

Prayer (for unmarried readers)

God, I do not have a spouse right now,

And I do not know what your plans are for me here.

But thank you for creating us for relationship.

If I am to be a spouse one day,

Help me to find ways to practice listening,

The art of putting someone else ahead of myself,

The art of communing with another.

Teach me to pray with resolve,

To know that you are acting.

Build me into someone who is ready

To be one flesh with another.

And if marriage isn't what you have for me,

Then keep my heart focused on the sympathy of Christ.

Let me know more about his love for me,

His self-sacrifice and endless compassion.

Help me to learn, little by little,

How great a love you have for me,

And how you walk alongside me

Through every swell of anxiety.

Show me the heart of communion with you.

Draw me near.

Give me patience unending and hope unyielding.

CHAPTER 13

Parenting with Anxiety

KEY IDEA: We can show our children what it's like to work out our anxiety in relationship with God.

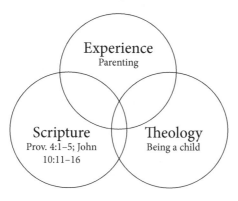

In this chapter, I want to talk about dealing with anxiety in the context of family life. Again, I realize this won't apply to everyone, but I do believe there's something for you in this chapter even if you don't have children. After all, every one of us is a child in the most important sense (John 1:12; Rom. 8:14; Gal. 4:7; 2 Cor. 6:18). We'll get to that soon enough.

Anxiety before Kids

I dealt with anxiety long before I had kids. And it was very different then. At that point, I wasn't thinking about *influencing* someone else in addressing the spiritual troubles we encounter. That doesn't mean I wasn't influencing others; it just means I wasn't aware of it. Back then, I was very *self*-focused. I was constantly thinking about my own feelings and experiences, which were always followed by a train of questions so loud that it seemed to block out almost everyone and everything else: How anxious had I been today? Was I too aware of my breathing? Were my meds going to stop working? What do I have to do in the next few days that's outside of my comfort zone? When can I read my Bible next?

In the previous chapter I noted that anxiety makes us curved in on ourselves. There's a phrase for that. John Calvin used this phrase to refer to sin in general: *curvetus in se*. It means "curved in on oneself." Follow the image from the previous chapter. Think of your whole body being shaped like a "C." The top of the C is where your head is, and it's bent so far around towards your middle that you can only see yourself. That's it. No family. No friends. No needs of others. To see those things, you would need to strain your neck quite a bit, and that'd be uncomfortable. We don't want to be uncomfortable, so we just stay curved in on ourselves. That's a trademark of anxiety (and it's a trademark of sin as well).

Before I had kids, that inward curving would certainly have the potential to hurt my wife, family, and friends. Self-centeredness always hurts someone. But these people were gracious and patient, and they did whatever they could to help and comfort me during those years. They showed a thousand kindnesses that probably went unnoticed. They helped me along, if I let them. And slowly . . . *very* slowly, I grew. Old habits were deconstructed. New ones were built up block by block. Then torn down. Then built up again. I learned much about the process of building and how quickly our confidence can hit ground zero with one bad experience, one panic attack, one rough week.

Anxiety after Kids

When you have kids, something happens. Whether you like it or not, an invisible mirror follows you around everywhere. And that mirror is perfectly angled to take whatever image you're portraying, whatever light or darkness you're giving off, and direct it towards *your* little image-bearer (Gen. 5:3). The mirror never goes away. It's always somewhere close to you, always catching things you think no one is watching, always sending whatever it finds to your children. Now, my friends, we're in a whole different arena with anxiety. Now everything we do is *influencing* someone else.

There are a number of different approaches to this new challenge, some healthy and others not so healthy. Let me go over the unhealthy ones first.

Unhealthy Approaches to Anxiety with Children

The first approach might be called *shield-and-deny*. If you're taking this approach, then you do whatever you can to keep your kids from seeing your anxiety. This is very tempting for us as parents because we want our children to be confident and secure in the family. We want them to feel safe and protected, hedged in by unwavering strength and fearlessness. Then, if the hedge seems to break down one day, when our efforts to shield them from our anxiety fail, we *deny*. We blame our feelings and behavior on something else. We offer cursory explanations, or we just avoid the topic of discussion altogether. We push it down inside ourselves, as far as it can go. And we play pretend. We're pretty skilled at this because we've play pretend with our kids many times. Is playing pretend with anxiety all that different?

It is. When we shield and deny our kids from what we're dealing with, we both suffer. On the one side, our anxiety isn't being addressed, so it festers inside of us, like a disease that goes unchecked. Sure, we might protect our kids from the anxiety in the moment, but we can't protect ourselves. On the outside we're calm; on the inside, our feet are churning water like a duck on a pond. And that churning is going to hurt us. It's an act of suppression, and suppressed emotions and messages only grow more potent when we push them away. On the other side, children are extremely perceptive (remember the mirror illustration). That means they see not only your anxiety but your every effort to cover and conceal it. They know when you're hiding something, and that sends a very dangerous message to them: closing off your soul to those whom you love is OK. That's not a message you want to send—not when your kids are 4 or 14 or 24 or 40. We're creatures made for communion with God and others. Creating disunion, even with the noble aspiration of protecting your kids, is harmful to the core of who we are, and to who they are. The *shield and deny* approach leads to a host of spiritual and relational problems. It looks appealing for protective parents, but it ends up hurting both sides in the end.

Now, does that mean you should pour yourself out in front of your kids? Should you come home from work and uncoil the massive and ugly snake of anxiety in the living room? "Kids, I had a lot of anxiety and trouble breathing this morning on my commute to work. I had several different fears, but let me paint a picture of each one for you. First, I thought . . ." Bad idea. First of all, you probably won't get very far because you'll have to explain a string of terms and concepts that are foreign to them, especially if they're under the age of 10. What is anxiety? What do you mean by "trouble breathing"? The more you say, the more you'll have to stop and explain. Second of all, you'll make them panicked to walk out the door in the morning. Unloading all the specifics of your spiritual and psychological struggles on your children isn't going to empower them; it's going to terrify them. You are a key figure of strength and stability for your kids. If you repeatedly shatter yourself in front of them, then they assume that they're shattered too (or they're about to be if it hasn't happened yet). This is what makes the *shield and deny* approach so appealing to us: it offers the illusion of protection, but it's just that, an illusion. So, we don't want to confuse our kids; neither do we want to terrify them. What is it that we want to do?

Difficult problems have complex solutions. The key in this case is *moderation* and *contextualization*. It terms of moderation, you want to be open and honest with your kids when you're struggling, but you don't want to give them so many details that they become confused or terrified. What does this look like specifically? Well, it depends on the age and maturity of your children. With a five- and three-year-old, it might just take the form of, "Daddy had a rough time today. Some days we have a rough time. But God's still with us." With older kids who understand what anxiety is, the wording can be more specific. If your kids are adults, then giving even more specifics might be appropriate. You'll need to judge that as best as you can. The point is to reveal yourself to them in words. Relate to them. Commune with them. Show your humanity. And point to the God of hope. Remember, the Christian life does not revel in strength; it revels in weakness. Don't be afraid to be weak in front of your children. In doing so, you're giving them the perfect opportunity to see *God's* strength at work in you. They'll see that something beyond you is responsible for your hope and healing. Regarding contextualization, try to put the problem in terms and situations that are more familiar to them. They might not know what you mean by "anxiety," but they know what you mean by "afraid" or even "sick." For young kids, you might even just say that you don't "feel good," and then pray with your kids. Model prayer for them. Show them what you do when you need help in the Great Story. You ask for help from the Helper. You pray out loud. And then you look for God's response. You can also contextualize your expressions by relating to situations that they have been in. "Remember when you were really nervous to go into your kindergarten class? Sometimes daddy feels like that. So, I have to pray and ask God to help me learn. He teaches me when I pray to him."

"Show them what you do when you need help in the Great Story. You ask for help from the Helper."

One day I was dealing with swells of panic at work. I couldn't focus because currents of adrenaline kept coursing through my veins. I texted my wife. "Would you pray for me? I'm having a really hard time with my nerves today?" My wife responded by doing a video call with my son, Isaac, who was only three at the time. She prayed for me with him in her arms. I hung my soul on every word of that prayer. I stared and smiled at my son, thinking, "God, I hope he doesn't have to deal with this." But I could see from his face that he didn't know something terrible was going on. He was just saying hi to daddy and talking to God as we'd shown him. He got to see his daddy pause from the routine of daily work and ask for prayer. He got to see his daddy weak. I want him to remember that. I want him to remember that his daddy is weak, but his daddy's God is strong.

There are countless ways to moderate and contextualize your communication with your kids. You'll have to try it out, prayerfully and in conjunction with your spouse. You might even get the input of a Christian counselor or pastor. The more wisdom you can implement in this situation, the better. Just don't *shield and deny*.

The second approach is what you might call the *parent-friend* approach. On the opposite side of the shielder and denier is the parent who treats his or her child as a friend. Don't get me wrong, I want my children to know that I love and care for them, but there's a big difference between a friend and a parent. There's a hierarchical relationship for the latter. And when that hierarchy is breached, problems result. For instance, if you share your experience with anxiety and tell your children that you decided to skip out on work for the day, they might take your communication as permission to do the same whenever they feel like not being in school (which could be quite often!). That's not to say that you should lie about what you did, but there's a difference between lying and not outlining every detail. If my son asks if I went to work one day, and I didn't go, then I'm obligated to tell the truth. But if I'm in the position of explaining how I'm feeling and what I've been struggling with, I'm not compelled to outline every decision I made in light of my anxiety. Some of those decisions (many of them, in fact) may not serve as good examples for how to deal with anxiety. But if I have a parent-friend approach, I might just share everything. That's what friends do, right? We open ourselves to one another. We share the disappointments and fears and failures and regrets. Your friends understand that when you do this, you're not trying to direct them in any way; you're just trying to lay your heart out so that they can offer sympathy, and perhaps some godly counsel. It's not the same with your children. Regardless of whether or not you wanted it to be this way, you have a position above your child, to care for and direct him or her in the ways of God. You are a parent first and foremost. Trying to be a friend to your kids all the time ends up undercutting your God-given authority as a parent. It weakens, or perhaps even eliminates, your ability to govern and shepherd your child. Once you've put yourself on the same level as your child, it's very hard to get back into a place of authority. And it's confusing to kids because you're acting inconsistently.

You don't want to be a *shielder and denier*, and you don't want to be a *parent-friend* either. Neither of those approaches is biblical.

A Biblical Approach to Anxiety with Children

A biblical approach to anxiety takes into account your identity as a creature of God, Christ-follower, and shepherd.

First, as creatures of God, we're limited. We're finite. We don't *make* our identity; we *take* it from the God who gives. We've already discussed our identity as creatures made for communion in the Great Story of Scripture. Here I want to focus on the union of being *limited* and being bound for *communion* (with God and others).

Our limitation is a sore subject, I know. Contemporary Western culture acts as if that limitation is an obstacle to our true identity. We have to ignore or bypass limitation in order to be who we really want to be. But that's a fantasy. No one has ever surpassed creaturely limitations. We can *act* as if we're self-sufficient, but there's no ultimate use in doing so. As one of my favorite theologians put it,

> Man can make himself believe, if he wants to, that he has done everything himself and that he is bound by nothing. But in every respect he remains a dependent creature. He cannot do as he pleases. In his physical existence, he remains bound to the laws laid down for respiration, the circulation of the blood, digestion, and procreation. And if he runs counter to these laws and pays no attention to them, he injures his health and undermines his own life. The same is true of the life of his soul and spirit.[1]

We like to think of ourselves as *purely original*. While it's true that each of us is unique, that doesn't mean we're original. Uniqueness is related to comparison; originality is related to source. In comparison to others, there is no one exactly like us. But in terms of origin, we're not the source of ourselves. We're *derivative*. Our life has been derived from the life of the Father, Son, and Spirit. Even if people reject

---

1   Herman Bavinck, *The Wonderful Works of God: Instruction in the Christian Religion according to the Reformed Confession* (Glenside, PA: Westminster Seminary Press, 2019), 180.

this idea, they have to at least say that our life is derived from the life of our parents, and their parents' life from their parents', and so on and so forth, all the way back to the beginning. But where did the first humans derive their life from? From the life-giving breath of God himself. *God* breathed life into us (Gen. 2:7; Job 33:4). So, we are derivatives. We have limits. We are not governors of ourselves. Practically speaking, this simply means that we have *needs* that can't be satisfied in isolation. We have needs that only God and others can satisfy.

This is problematic only if we're unaware of the primary *purpose* for which we've been created. We were created with needs, but that isn't a weakness. It's not an obstacle to be overcome. It pairs perfectly with our divinely given purpose: *communion*. We were not made for solitude. We were not made to be complete in isolation. Finitude is built into the fabric of our being, but that's not a curse; it's an intentional creation by the God who dwells in self-communion. As creatures of this God, we yearn for communication, for connection, for relational synapses to fire throughout the day. Finitude and communion combine to make us long for speech.

That's critical to remember when it comes to our identity and our role as parents. We were made by God to commune with him and with our children. While we moderate and contextualize our communication with our kids, we still *communicate* with them. We still need to express the negative side of humanity: the sadness, the anger, the frustration—and yes, the anxiety! If we can communicate openly with our children about what we're experiencing, they won't be blindsided later in life when they come up against the same issues, and they probably will. Genetics creates the same door for multiple generations. You can do all you want to deny the doorway, to shield your children from it, and maybe they *won't* have to walk through it. But if they do, their anxiety will be compounded by a sense of foreignness, and a lack of skills for dealing with the situation. I don't want that for my kids, and I'm assuming you don't either. Our identity as creatures made *for* communion with the God *of* communion requires communication from parent to child. It requires openness, a healthy degree of transparency. It requires the conveyance of *wisdom*.

Just look at the focus on conveying wisdom in Proverbs 4:1–5.

[1] Hear, O sons, a father's instruction,

and be attentive, that you may gain insight,

[2] for I give you good precepts;

do not forsake my teaching.

³ When I was a son with my father,

tender, the only one in the sight of my mother,

⁴ he taught me and said to me,

"Let your heart hold fast my words;

keep my commandments, and live.

⁵ Get wisdom; get insight;

do not forget, and do not turn away from the words of my mouth.

Instruction, precepts, teaching, words, wisdom, insight—these are the gifts of a father to a son or daughter. They are the gifts of language, the gifts of communion. We need to give these gifts to our children.

"Our identity as creatures made for communion with the God of communion requires communication from parent to child."

Second, a biblical approach to anxiety and children focuses on our identity as Christ-followers. What does that mean here? A few things are worth mentioning. Such gifts are part of who we are—passing away, but bound for communion.

For starters, it means that we realize our own adoption *in Christ* and let that manifest our childlike status before God. That sounds horribly stiff, doesn't it? Is this just a Christian platitude, something we have to say because we know it's biblical, and yet we're clueless when it comes to application? No! Our childlike status comes from constant references to God as *our* Father. Our kids know that *they* are children, but do they know that *we* are, too? Do they see us constantly accepting parental rebukes from God's word? Do they see us asking for things from our heavenly Father in prayer? Do they see us longing to draw nearer to God as our divine parent? Or have most of our interactions with our children been sapped of this loving, parental relationship? When our kids think about the interaction between us and God, does God seem more like an idea than a reality, more like a principle than a person? If so, that isn't the mark of a Christ-follower. Christ's followers know they've been adopted in him. They know that God is Christ's Father, and so he's our Father as well. Our children need to see that we're children too—always reliant on the most generous, patient, self-giving parent there ever was.

There are several more specific implications of this, but let me give you just two. First, showcasing our childlike status before God helps them see *both* what to expect in the world *and* how God is related to it. Anxiety happens. It's part of the world we live in. We can debate about the cause and treatment—physiological, spiritual, or both (I argue for the latter), but that debate won't change the fact that it's here. It's with us. As I said earlier, we don't want our kids to be blindsided. Yet, more important than the presence of anxiety is the presence of *God* and his knowledge of the world. He knows about anxiety. Recall the H of our CHRIST acronym. God's own Son suffered the ravages of a world ripped apart by sin and corruption. He knows what we're experiencing, and he cares deeply about it. What's more, he has the power to change, shape, and direct us in the process. He even has the power to remove our anxiety, our thorn in the flesh, if he so chooses.

Now, my children have responded naturally to this truth with an ancient human question: *why do we still have to deal with this if God can take it away?* This is a tough one for parents, since much of our experience (at least with young children) tells us that we should end pain and suffering for them as soon as possible. The word I go back to in these contexts is *relationship*. In a previous chapter, we talked about how God wants a relationship with us. He wants us to know him on a deeper level, to trust him, to hope in him. In the context of a broken world, that means knowing, trusting, and hoping *in the midst* of pain and suffering. Spiritually speaking, pain and suffering are just steps on a staircase. We set our feet on them so that we can go higher, closer to the counsel of God. As we set out feet down, we look up. We keep our eyes fixed on Christ. And in that constant gazing, a relationship slowly begins to blossom. That's some poetic imagery for something that oftentimes feels anything but poetic. Anxiety is a horrific form of suffering. I don't like it any more than anyone else. But we have to keep bringing ourselves and our children back to the context and the God-ordained purpose for it: *relationship*. Nothing we can experience in this life goes beyond that word.

The second spiritual benefit of showcasing our childlike status before God in the presence of our children is that they get to see that *we are not the strong ones*. I know, I know—we have so much enthusiasm for strength. My kids think I'm as strong as Hercules right now because I can lift two pillows above my head. They sincerely believe that daddy is "so strong!" In comparison to them, of course, I am. But in reality, I want them to associate strength with God. In fact, eventually I want them to associate strength with *weakness* because that's exactly what Christ did, and that's what Paul wrote down for us. "When I am weak, then I am strong" (2 Cor. 12:10). Strength lives in God. And how do we get that strength? (No one likes this answer, but it's the only true one.) Through weakness! Our kids need to see that, especially because of how paradoxical it is. Daddy is not the strong one; God is. Mommy is not the strong one; God is. And that's okay. In fact, that's a *good* thing, because even if we feel strong right now, weakness is coming. It's always creeping up behind us—through age and sickness. As with pain and suffering, weakness is part of our world. We can't run *from* it; we have to run *into* it! Why? Because that's what our Savior did and that's what he's told us to do. I've said it before, and I'll say it again: Weakness is the way. *Weakness* is the way. Say it over and over until it becomes a mantra for your daily life. And let your kids hear you. Everyone else around them is going to sing the opposite message. They need to hear the truth from you. You are not the strong one.

So, we are creatures, Christ followers, and also shepherds of our children. But what do shepherds do? Well, for starters, shepherds are simply *present*. They don't let their sheep wander aimlessly on the world's hillsides. They stay with them. And when they're with their sheep, they aren't cognitively removed—daydreaming or distracted by their smart phone. Tim Witmer discusses what he calls *the principle of presence* with our children.[2] It's a simple principle, but we still find it so difficult to implement. We need to be *with* them if we're going to shepherd them. That requires intentionality and concrete planning, on a daily and weekly basis. This can be very hard for some of us to implement.

Most of the time, I feel as if the technology in my life has given me great new opportunities and some novel ambitions, but it hasn't given me more *time*. When I'm at home, in fact, it's had the opposite effect: I feel as if I never have enough time to do what I feel needs to get done. Or is it what I feel I *want* to get done? It's hard to tell the difference sometimes. But in the midst of the mental chaos, I forget one thing, the most important thing: to be *present* with my kids. Put the phone down. Stay away from the computer. Sit on the carpet and do a mermaid puzzle. Grab a colored pencil and sketch a dinosaur with your five-year-old. Ask your child a question, and maintain eye-contact for more than 10 seconds. Be present. The more I parent, the more I see how important it is to just be present and engaged with your children.

---

2   Timothy Witmer, *The Shepherd Leader at Home: Knowing, Leading, Protecting, and Providing for Your Family* (Wheaton, IL: Crossway, 2012), 47–59.

It doesn't stop with presence. Presence puts us in the perfect position to guide, to lead. That's what shepherds do—with a staff and sincerity. They don't always lead well, but they lead. And that's critical, because children, like sheep, are also looking to be led. Witmer writes,

> Children desperately need direction in life. They want to know what they should do. They will look to their parents to find answers in these matters. If the answers are not clear, they will find them elsewhere: from their peers, media, or culture at large. . . . We must reiterate that the goal toward which we lead our children is that they come to know the Lord and follow him. Your goal should be the same as that of the Lord our shepherd, who "leads [us] in paths of righteousness for his name's sake."[3]

Notice that we're simultaneously sheep and shepherds, leading and following. We're called to a life of trust, trust in the divine voice of the Good Shepherd. And we turn the shoulders of our children to the same voice. Recall Jesus's words to his disciples:

> [11] I am the good shepherd. The good shepherd lays down his life for the sheep. [12] He who is a hired hand and not a shepherd, who does not own the sheep, sees the wolf coming and leaves the sheep and flees, and the wolf snatches them and scatters them. [13] He flees because he is a hired hand and cares nothing for the sheep. [14] I am the good shepherd. I know my own and my own know me, [15] just as the Father knows me and I know the Father; and I lay down my life for the sheep. [16] And I have other sheep that are not of this fold. I must bring them also, and they will listen to my voice. So there will be one flock, one shepherd. (John 10:11–16)

We lead our children by teaching them to listen—to hear and to heed. This is what it means for Christian parents to lead by principle but also by example.[4] Our children should see us chasing after the speech of God, hanging on every word, called to attention at the mention of it. But they also need to see how we put that speech to use in our daily life. The combination of seeking God's word and living it out provides the best guidance for our children.

---

3   Witmer, *The Shepherd Leader*, 87.

4   Ibid., 88–89.

"We lead our children by teaching them to listen—to hear and to heed."

I'll end with an example. I grew up with three brothers, so teasing was part and parcel of daily interaction. Early on, I developed a twisted joy in teasing my brothers, in finding subtle ways to get them aggravated or on edge. Family always knows what buttons to push, and I was happy to push them. But as I took on the role of fatherhood, I realized that this tendency for teasing was going to be much more destructive than I thought. My wife was kind enough to point out whenever she saw me doing this with one of our kids, and shortly after she began doing so, I came across Ephesians 6:4, "Fathers, do not provoke your children to anger, but bring them up in the discipline and instruction of the Lord." I was a provoker. It seemed harmless most of the time, but little acts of disobedience—moments of ignoring the speech of God—are never little. I had to work on shutting my mouth when I really wanted to tease one of our kids, even jokingly. I can't be a provoker of my children and at the same time tell them to follow the speech of God, to listen to the divine voice. That's hypocrisy. Of course, we're all hypocrites at times, and sometimes we aren't even aware of it. But when the Spirit makes us aware of it, we need to act in faith. We need to turn into sheep before our children, show them the Shepherd, and lead them to him. In those moments, we are the best shepherds to our own little sheep.

Your children, in the end, are really not so different from you. They are called to a life of trust. *You* are called to a life of trust. They are called to follow the divine voice. *You* are called to follow the divine voice. As you parent your kids and suffer from anxiety, they need to see this connection. They need to see you modeling the habit that you hope and pray they will take up. And they need to see you communicate with them so they aren't blindsided when they start facing adversity in a thousand ways.

As a parent, you're a shepherd. With anxiety, you're a weak shepherd, but a shepherd nonetheless. Follow. Lead. Speak. Listen.

Theology: You Are a Child

We've already alluded to this earlier, but take a moment now to remember who you are: *you're a child*. That's no insult. In fact, it should bring a smile to your face. You'll never, ever be an orphan. In the presence of God, there are no orphans, neither is there anyone who has transcended his childhood. We're all playing around the feet of God and will be for eternity. Let's draw this out a bit and then gather some implications for our struggles with anxiety.

All of the relationships we have in life, and all of the roles we play in relation to others, are relative to someone else. In relation to my mother, I'm a son. In relation to my brothers, I'm a brother. In relation to my wife, I'm a husband. In relation to my kids, I'm a father. The same truth holds when we look to God. In relation to God, I'm a child. You're a child. We always will be. This is part of what it means not only to be a creature of our heavenly Father, but also to be *adopted* by him.

Remember when Jesus was badgered by a swarm of children? Their parents brought them to him in hopes that he might lay his hands on them and pray for them. As Jesus's followers attempted to deal with these knee-high nuisances to the "serious" ministry of Christ, he said something quite profound: "Let the little children come to me and do not hinder them, for to such belongs the kingdom of heaven" (Matt. 19:14). Just before this, he had told his disciples, "unless you turn and become like children, you will never enter the kingdom of heaven" (Matt. 18:3). And in John's Gospel, he glorifies our identity as children: "But to all who did receive him, who believed in his name, he gave the right to become children of God, who were born, not of blood nor of the will of the flesh nor of the will of man, but of God" (John 1:12–13). *Children of God*—there's something very special about that expression, and each of these passages reminds us of this.

First, God's kingdom—his rule and reign that covers every corner of the cosmos—is not open to anyone who's too proud to be a child. The kingdom of heaven *belongs* to children. They *possess* it in their open, trusting embrace of Christ. Second, if you can't lower yourself to find wide-eyed joy in child-like faith, you can't enter that kingdom. You'll remain an outsider. Because the kingdom of God is reserved for child-like faith, you can't get in if you don't bend down. Third, being a child of God means that you were born "not of blood nor of the will of the flesh nor of the will of man, but of God" (John 1:13). God is the one who makes you his child. There's nothing you can do to force his hand, just as there's nothing your children can do to earn or disavow your parenthood. The child who rages, "You're not my daddy anymore!" is comical because he's shouting something with boldness that can't ever be true. He's not in control of whether or not he's your son. Neither are we in control of being God's children. He's chosen us in Christ before the foundation of the world (Eph. 1:4). How do these things help us in our anxiety? Here are three ways.

1. *Your anxiety is a constant reminder of your helplessness.* That doesn't really sound like a good thing, does it? That's because, as adults, we believe that self-sufficiency is a watermark of maturity. If we're helpless, if we're in need of someone else, we're deeply embarrassed or distressed. We feel as if we've fallen short. But in light of the fact that you and I are children before God, helplessness is no more of a vice than it is for our toddler who can't drive. Think about it. You don't fault a four-year-old for not being able to drive to the grocery store and pick up what she needs for lunch. She's helpless in that respect, but the helplessness is worked into the fabric of your *relationship.* As a parent, *you* are there to drive to the store and get the groceries. Her "helplessness" is really just a contour in the parent-child relationship. It's not a *bad* thing; it's just part of the relationship. That's the way we should be looking at our ultimate helplessness before God. The fact that we need God isn't something to be embarrassed about. The fact that we're helpless without him is a contour in the divine-human relationship. It's a marker of love, in fact! When anxiety strikes us, we should be proud of our helplessness because it showcases the relationship we have with the God who has promised to care for us. We throw ourselves on him as a child throws herself on her father. Think of it in the context of 1 Peter 5:6–7, "Humble yourselves, therefore, under the mighty hand of God so that at the proper time he may exalt you, casting all your anxieties on him, because he cares for you." Children love skipping stones on the water. Skip the stones of your anxiety on the ocean of God. They're not going to hurt him. In fact, through them, he's going to show you just how much he cares for you. In your anxiety, glory in helplessness, for doing so is really glorying in the relationship God has with you.

2. *It's not more noble to be self-sufficient in your anxiety.* This is the opposite of the previous point, and I press it home here because it takes a lot for us to let this go. "Glorying in our helplessness before our heavenly Father is already a stretch; can't we at least hold on to some dignity?" My friends, our dignity blossoms when we find solace in our savior, and in him alone. We're most dignified before the children of men when we're most dependent on the Son of man. But even more important than the dignity is our ability to get inside the kingdom of God. Jesus didn't say that

if you lacked childlike faith, then it would be *hard* for you to enter the kingdom of heaven. He didn't say that you could hold on to your dignity and still squeeze through the kingdom door. No—he said if you lack childlike faith, you *will never enter* (Matt. 18:3). Don't be deceived by the world: it's not more noble to walk through your anxiety with dignity and a sense of self-sufficiency. In fact, those very things are what keep the kingdom door closed to you. Fall apart like a child before your heavenly Father. Front your need for him in every hour. That's the most noble thing you can do with your anxiety, because it places all of the nobility where it should be: with God himself.

"There's no such thing as a sheep who "made it" by wandering off into the wild, trying to take control of his pastured life."

---

3. *God is stewarding you in your anxiety.* That's basically another way to restate the thesis of this book. God is in control of your experiences, and he's using them with a purpose. By now, you know what that purpose is: Christ-conformity. And the more you look like Christ in his suffering and death, the more you will shine like Christ in his resurrection (Rom. 8:17). The more you struggle to catch your breath, to swallow, to step back from the cliff of panic, the more you are being prepared for glorious strength in Christ. So, though a thousand self-help books will tell you that you need to take control of your anxiety, don't buy into it. You'll never be fully in control of it, and that's a very good thing. God is your shepherd. There's no such thing as a sheep who "made it" by wandering off on his own into the wild, trying to take control of his pastured life.

Reflection Questions and Prayer

1. If you have children, what are some of the fears you have in dealing with anxiety in their presence?

2. If you don't have children but believe you might someday, how would you hope to encourage them in the midst of your anxiety?

3. What are some concrete things you could communicate to your children

about your anxiety (remember to be moderate and contextual)?

4. Think of one time when your child observed your behavior and acted similarly. Were you happy with the action? If not, what do you wish you would have done differently?

5. What are the benefits and drawbacks or sharing your experience of anxiety with your children?

6. Taking what you have learned about anxiety so far, what are some practical ways in which you could shepherd your children through their own experiences with anxiety? Try to think of basic principles that God has revealed to you in Scripture and find a way to implement them in a concrete way for your children. Having them memorize a Bible passage such as Philippians 4:6–7 is a great start!

7. Discuss the truth that you and your children are all children of God, who is our Good shepherd. What are some ways you have been shepherded by Christ? How can you communicate that to your children?

8. How do you struggle to see yourself as a child before God? What do you think that might be keeping you from doing? In what ways could you better serve God if you *did* see yourself more consistently as his child?

Prayer

Father of all, Good shepherd, Holy Comforter,

You have always shepherded us

With words from your mouth.

You spoke. We heard.

But we did not listen.

We still have trouble listening.

But you have no trouble speaking.

As we parent our children,

Please help us to listen to your voice,

To *know* you through your voice (John 10:14).

Help us to follow,

So that we might turn

And help our children follow.

Teach us to speak with them
And to hear them.
Teach us to be *with* them.
And help us to model
Sheep-like reliance
On your words.

Reader Resource: A Prayer To Teach Children

Children need simple, direct prayers to pray when they face anxiety. Because I deal with anxiety so much, I'm constantly thinking about what I could do to help my kids with this when they encounter it. One of the things I can do is teach them to pray. The prayer below is something children (and adults) can memorize easily and put into practice the moment anxiety strikes.

God, you are big, and I am little.
There is no place where you are not.
My fear is strong, but I feel brittle.
Help me remember what I forgot:

There's nothing that can take my life
Because you bought it long ago.
I squeeze my troubles, toil, and strife,
Then stretch my fingers and let go.

You're making me like Jesus now.
So even though I long for peace,
I'll ask for patience to somehow
Stand firm until the torrents cease.

CHAPTER 14

How It Will Be

KEY IDEA: Uninterrupted communion and peace with God will be ours. Until then, keep speaking.

W e're nearing the end of the book now, and there's something that I know has been on your mind, because it's always on our minds: peace. Will I ever have it? When will I feel it? How long will I have to walk through anxiety before I find some? There will be moments of peace that come more frequently as you learn more about your anxiety and how God is using it, I promise. But the light of hope we keep our eyes fixed on is also in the future. After the long and harrowing battle with anxiety in this life, after every arrow has been fired and every sword put back in its sheath, there are two things that await us for eternity: communion and peace. We experience them sometimes now, but later we'll have them in a way we can't imagine. In other words, these are already-but-not-yet gifts from the God of peace.

Let's start by looking at communion once more, and then we'll focus on peace. The two are deeply related for creatures made in the image of God.

What We've Always Wanted

Think back as long as you can, to your earliest memory, when life was a hint of a whisper of promise, like the sun just beginning to crest on a dark landscape. What do you remember wanting?

One of my earliest memories was about wanting restoration, wanting everything to be okay. I was five, standing on top of a septic mound behind our house as the sun was going down. I had asked my mom to make me a paper airplane. She didn't know how, but she didn't tell me. She did her best to fold the paper so that it resembled a plane. Then she handed it to me and quickly walked back into the house. I watched her walk away. And as I held the paper airplane in my hands and watched her open the screen door, I could see that she was looking down. I knew . . . I had some visceral sense that she was embarrassed or disappointed and that she didn't want me to know about it. I never said anything. I just remember—and can still feel today—having this deep rift open in my heart. I hated that she felt embarrassed, that the world was somehow broken, fractured. And now I had to walk through this fractured world somehow. The image and the feeling were carved into me like words in tree bark. They won't ever leave.

In that memory, I wanted restoration. I wanted things to be fixed. Yet, the more I think about it, the more I realize that this restoration would have taken the form of *communion*. It would have been the restoration of a *relationship*. No embarrassment. No remorse. No covering things up with a sheet of shame. There would only be union of persons—speech and listening, "yes's" and "amens."

"What we've always wanted is shaped by who we've been made to be."

You see, what we've always wanted is shaped by who we've been made to be. Remember when we talked about who God is and who we are? I gave you a quote from a theologian named Geerhardus Vos. As he wrote about what it means to be God's image bearers, these are the words he offered. Read them with me once more: "That man bears God's image means much more than that he is spirit and possesses understanding, will, etc. It means above all that he is disposed for communion with God, that all the capacities of his soul can act in a way that corresponds to their destiny only if they rest in God."[1] We're bent on communion. It's what we were made for. It's what we were crafted to crave.

This is such a great hope to keep before us as people who struggle with anxiety. Do you know why? Because one of our greatest underlying fears is *isolation*. Isolation is the opposite of communion. It's the opposite of what we were made for. That's why it's so potent and threatening!

I remember early in my battle with anxiety having to leave my wife (who was then my fiancée). She had to go back home for a college break, and I had to go back to our college town where I was living, and back to my old job. As I left the restaurant where we had lunch and climbed into my car, I had a sinking feeling in my chest, as if I had swallowed a bowling ball. The weight of being alone, of being without this woman I loved so much, was heavy. I hated it. It made me feel so low and weak. But as I drove back to my apartment, the feeling started to lift as I focused on the landscape. "God was with me," I reminded myself. There's no where I can go where he is not. He's right next to me now. I had to rehearse the promises of God's presence all the way back to my apartment as I drove past the farm fields and rural homes of Lancaster, Pennsylvania. The threat of isolation, of being alone, is potent precisely because we were made for communion with God and others.

Some of my favorite theologians have spent much time and energy trying to drive home this point. Here are some of the words they've put together. Read them slowly. This is theology for the heart, not just the head. The first should be familiar to you.

> **John Owen:** Communion is the mutual communication of such good things as wherein the persons holding that communion are delighted, bottomed upon some union between them. . . . Our communion, then, with God consists in his communication of himself to us, with our return unto him of that which he requires and accepts, flowing from that union which in Jesus Christ we have with him.[2]

> **Herman Bavinck:** Religion is communion with God. Without it humans cannot be truly and completely human. The image of God is not a superadded gift but belongs to human nature. That communion with God is a mystical union. It far

---

1 Geerhardus Vos, *Anthropology*, vol. 2 of *Reformed Dogmatics*, ed. and trans. Richard B. Gaffin Jr. (Bellingham, WA: Lexham, 2014), 13.

2 John Owen, *Communion with the Triune God*, ed. Kelly M. Kapic and Justin Tayler (Wheaton, IL: Crossway, 2007), 93–94.

exceeds our understanding. It is the most intimate union with God by the Holy Spirit, a union of persons, an unbreakable and eternal covenant between God and ourselves.[3]

John Murray: Here indeed is mysticism on the highest plane. It is not the mysticism of vague unintelligible feeling or rapture. It is the mysticism of communion with the one true and living God, and it is communion with the one true and living God because and only because it is communion with the three distinct persons of the Godhead in the strict particularity which belongs to each person in that grand economy of saving relationship to us.[4]

There's too much here to unpack completely, but we have to at least pause and stare for a few moments. Stare with me.

First, notice that we can't have communion with God apart from Christ. John Owen says that God communicates to us, and we communicate with God, but that communication flows *from our union with Christ*. We must be united with a divine person to have communion with the personal God. Or, if you want to think of it in terms of the Son as the Word of the Father, we have to be united with the Word if we want to have words with God. Union with Christ comes before communion with the Trinity.

Second, Bavinck points out that we will *never* find fulfillment, satisfaction, or peace apart from communion with God. No such thing exists. We long for "that most intimate union" with everything in us. It's the cup of water in the desert of spiritual warfare. We long for it; we need it; without it, we fall and fade and perish.

Third, our communion with God is *distinct* communion with each person of the Godhead—Father, Son, and Spirit. Isn't that easier to embrace than a vague sense of communion with "the divine"? We commune with our heavenly *Father*, who adopted us in Christ (Gal. 4:4–7). We commune with the *Son*, who poured out his own lifeblood not just for those around him, but for those buried in the past and those hidden behind the curtain of the future. We commune with the *Spirit*, who comforts, guides, and teaches us at this very moment. Our communion is with divine *persons*.

---

3   Herman Bavinck, *Sin and Salvation in Christ*, vol. 3 of *Reformed Dogmatics*, ed. John Bolt, trans. John Vriend (Grand Rapids, MI: Baker Academic), 304.

4   John Murray, *Redemption Accomplished and Applied* (1955; repr. Grand Rapids, MI: Eerdmans, 2015), 183.

That last point stands out to me: we are headed for *personal intimacy*. Our destination is relationship without end. That's what we've always wanted. In fact, it's what we've always needed.

What We've Always Needed

Right now, you might be dealing with a rough patch of anxiety. Or maybe you aren't and you feel just fine. But either way, there is something you and I *need* at every moment, in every hour of every day. It's the thing that gives us purpose and meaning and vigor: *communion with God.*

It's true that communion with God is our eternal destination, but it's also the road we travel. It's beneath our feet—right now. We walk on communion with God. What do I mean?

God is our *environment*. Do you know that? Meditate on that word for a moment. In Acts 17:28 Paul affirms that *in God* we live and move and have our being. We walk around in a God-saturated environment—every landscape, every roadway, every city, every block of suburbia. There is no place where God is not.

Now, you might think, "Of course, but what does that have to do with my *need* for communion with God?" Think of it this way: you can't live when you're out of touch with your environment. Physically, we all live in an environment that requires our constant engagement. We breathe the air. We move our bodies. We eat. We drink water. We sleep. We navigate through a thousand dangers a day. We do this without thinking because it's a natural habit.

Yet spiritually, if God is our ultimate environment—if it's *in him* that we live and move and breathe—then we have a *need* for engagement with him. It's true, we don't stop breathing if we don't engage with God through prayer and worship. But what about your soul? We're so bent on materialism that we don't tend to monitor our spiritual well-being. And that's precisely what Paul is talking about in Acts 17:28! Our physical world is everywhere supported by God and reveals much about him (Ps. 19:1–4; Rom. 1:20; Col. 1:17; Heb. 1:3). The world in which we walk is soaked in the presence of God, which means our spirits, our souls, confront God everywhere. We can't live without God's presence, because it's simply impossible. That's not the way the world has been made. And if that's true, then every soul is being shaped and molded each day in a way that mirrors the shaping and molding of our bodies. Our bodies need the physical world to function. Our souls need a God-saturated environment to live and move and grow. We were created with a soul-based *need* for a God-environment.

"We were created with a soul-based need for a God-environment."

Communion with God, then, isn't just a want; it's a need. It's a spiritual staple. Without communion with the God who is all around us, our souls shrivel up and become sickly. They wither and fade, like a flower parched in the sun. And in eternity, there will be no want of spiritual water. The river of God will flow in the midst of us (Rev. 22:1). We'll commune with God without interruption. We'll be more spiritually alive than we can imagine. We'll have a divinely measured pulse, a heartbeat that goes beyond time.

In eternity, we'll have what we've always wanted, but we'll also have what we've always needed. We'll have communion with the Father, Son, and Spirit.

Communing through Speech

Still, we have a hard time wrapping our minds around what this means. And we should! It's hard for us to imagine unending communion with God in a world that seems to press down on us with anxiety all the time. But I have a biblical response to one concrete sense of *how* we'll commune with God: speech.

Recall from the Great Story that God is a speaking God who communes with himself, and we are speaking creatures made in his image. We were made for communion, for discourse with divine persons. And in eternity, that's exactly what we'll get.

We'll speak with the Father and his every providential detail, the depth of his love, the mysteries of his kindness. We'll talk of sanctity and sacrifice, of the measure of might, of gratitude and giving. From our side, there will be a whole lot more listening than speaking, but there will be conversation. There will be communion. That's what we were made for.

We'll speak with the Son and his constant, ever-present communication with God's people. We'll talk of blood and burdens, of the weight of obedience, of grace and the greenery of faith. He will have more words for us than there are drops of water in the seven seas, and we'll hang on every one of them, absorbing every syllable with serenity.

We'll speak with the Spirit and how his mere presence *is* peace. We'll talk of silence and seasons, of the power of patience, of comfort and control. There will be pauses between the discourse, too—time for us to just process the depth and delirious joy we have in very Spirit of God!

Right now, on this side of eternity, our communion with God comes through speech, too. But it's intermittent. We're too easily distracted. We don't hear God's voice because we don't read his word, and when we do read it, we don't meditate on it; we don't rest our souls on it for long enough. We don't speak back because we don't pray, especially in busy seasons. And the older we get, the more we realize that there are no busy *seasons*. Life in general is just busy. In the chapter on prayer, I noted that Martin Luther is said to have told others that he was so busy at one point in his life that he had to pray for three hours a day instead of one. Oh how I wish that were our habit! My prayer right now is that you and I would pray *more* as times seem tighter, that we'd long for God so badly in the midst of our turmoil that we'd seek out his wings (Ps. 17:8) and pull them down in front of us, and just stay in his shadows.

Peace

Communion with God is bound up with the notion of peace, which we so long for in our anxiety! As anxiety coils around our necks like a 50-pound boa, we scream for peace. But peace, my dear reader, is not the absence of anxiety. We think that it is, that peace is some psychological state of wanting nothing, a strangely Christian sense of nirvana. We think that peace is the absence of any harmful feelings. But that's a shallow and worldly view of peace. Real, lasting peace is not the absence of anxiety; it's our closeness to the Lord. Peace, in other words, is God's presence.

It was Augustine, in his *Confessions*, who famously wrote that our hearts are restless until they rest in God. We tend to focus on the word "rest," but why not on the phrase "in God"? I believe that was Augustine's real concern. There are many places where we can rest our hearts, but none of them will satisfy. None of them is strong, sturdy, and eternal. The only place we can set our hearts is on the table of God's personal presence.

Peace as Personal Presence

One of my favorite books is *Pilgrim's Progress*. Towards the end of the first part, Christian crosses the river of death and stands before the gates of paradise. Two "shining ones" explain what awaits him on the other side. "There your eyes shall be delighted with seeing, and your ears with hearing the pleasant Voice of the *Mighty One*. There you shall enjoy your Friends again, that are gone thither before you; and there you shall with joy receive even every one that follows into the Holy Place after you."5 Do you see the focus on *personal presence*? Eternity is a place of peace not because it's the absence of pain and suffering. Sure, those things will be distant memories, and that's no small encouragement! But it's the personal presence—of Father, Son, and Spirit; of our brothers and sisters in Christ—that marks paradise.

I've repeated many times that God is one who communes with himself, and we were made for communion with him and with each other. We are what I like to call *with-creatures*. We were made to be *with* God, who has unparalleled satisfaction in being *with* himself, but who, as one theologian put it, had so much *with* that it spilled over into creation. "The fountain of love brimmed over."6 That fountain is God himself, the God who is *with* himself and yet is so full that he chose to let that fullness brim over into creation so that he could be *with* us. The whole story of Scripture is about the God who aims to be *with* his people. That's where the story starts, and that's where it ends. And because we're creatures who reflect God, we're also made to be *with* others.

For *with-creatures*, the greatest peace is having *with* in all of its divine and human fullness. *With* God. *With* others. *With*. *With*. *With*. Peace is the unending personal presence of *with*.

Looking towards the Peace of With

Of course, right now that *with* is always interrupted. It's broken and battered . . . but resilient. We look in hope towards the peace of *with*. We get shimmers of it here and there. When I watched my wife walk down the aisle, I was filled by the ecstasy of *with*. Joy and passion coursed through my veins and set my feet tapping. When I hugged my three brothers the moment after we watched our father pass away in our living room, I was filled with the longing of *with*. When I welcomed each of our

---

5   John Bunyan, *Pilgrim's Progress: From This World to That Which Is To Come* (1895; repr., Carlisle, PA: Banner of Truth, 2009), 185.

6   Michael Reeves, *Delighting in the Trinity: An Introduction to the Christian Faith* (Downers Grove, IL: InterVarsity, 2012), 43.

children into the world, I was enraptured by the newness of *with*. Ecstasy, longing, newness—these elements of *with* in the present point us to the unimaginable finality of *with* in eternity.

So, in the present, we do all we can to cling to the *with* of God and to the *with* of others. How do we do that? You know my answer by this point: language. We commune with God in prayer, worship, and Scripture reading. We commune with others in the church by speaking with them and praying for them. And we can even notice a sort of "speech" in the natural world—a revelation of God in every created thing—that helps us to commune with him.

It's in using speech, in using language, that we constantly face our anxiety and watch how God is shaping us to Christ through it. Recall once more the CHRIST acronym. Notice how language is tied to each element, and how peace lies in the background.

C - consider the feelings. We looked at how the feelings we experience with anxiety can serve as spiritual medicine, purging and refining our thoughts, pushing us to rely on Christ in our weakness so that the power of *his* resurrection might be made known through our bodies. One of the ways we consider the feelings as spiritual medicine is to remind ourselves by reciting that very truth: "God, I hate these feelings, but I know that you use them to make my soul stronger. Their bitterness is leading to my spiritual bravery. Help me swallow this medicine in the moment—with faith and trust." We use *language* to help us remember and trust in God's providential use of our anxiety. And the longing behind the words we utter is peace. In fact, this is when we desire peace the most, and God knows that. He reads our hearts with second-by-second precision, and as we rely on him more and more, peace comes to the surface—not necessarily because the feelings have disappeared, but because every other false hope and distracting desire has been removed from our line of sight. It's just him. And that's exactly what we want. Remember: peace is the personal *presence* of God. The more we focus our attention on him and his presence with us, the nearer peace will be to us.

H - he knows. Again, we use language and prayer to remember the concrete truth that—no matter what we're going through—Christ knows. He knows how we feel. He knows the sensations: the throat tightness, the withdrawal from reality, the tingling of our limbs, shortness of breath, the thudding heart. He knows. But because that truth is so beyond us, we need to remind ourselves of it constantly. We need continual convincing (which the Spirit works in us) that this is, in fact, the truth.

We're not alone. Someone else *knows*. In fact, the one who loves us *most* knows. And peace comes in communion through that knowledge, through knowing that we *share* our experience with the God who bears our burdens. And one day, we'll know the peace of his presence without interruption. Until then, we have the peace of knowing there's a perfect sympathizer who's always interceding for us with our heavenly Father, and who has sent the Comforter to us as a lordly companion.

R - *remember the promise*. To remember the promise, we use words. We recall the passages of Scripture that draw us into the promise. We recite Exodus 14:14, or Psalm 9:9–10, or Psalm 23, or Matthew 28:20. There are so many options! And the Spirit of peace comes to us as we recite with patience. The word of God burns as a lamp to our feet (Ps. 119:105). And with the light, darkness and dread have no choice but to flee. They scatter before the sovereignty of our risen Savior. We have peace, once again, in the personal presence of God—which is with us through his written word.

I - *identify a focus*. When we identify a focus, that may not seem to involve language, but we live in a worded world.7 The world, in a sense, "speaks" of God because it always has something to say about him. It is always revealing the character and nature of God—because that's the way he made it. When we identify a focus in the world, we can start by asking the Spirit to help us see how God is reflected there.8 And I cannot tell you how peaceful it can be to finally understand in those moments that you are *surrounded* by God. Identifying a focus and seeing how it reveals God draws us into seeing his personal presence in the world around us. It's a beautiful gift, and there's no end to the things he will teach us about himself through this.

I'll give you another example. I was once walking into the nursery school to pick up my son and daughter one morning. I was anxious because it was a slight break in my routine (that's one of my triggers for anxiety). It was a beautiful morning. The sun was high in the blue sky, and the air was clear and brisk. I looked at the shadow of my body on the sidewalk, and I thought of how the sun was causing that shadow. The light was not passing through my body, so the outline of that impediment had created the shadow. The shadow was evidence of light. However, the real source of light is not the sun; it's God himself, who was a light even before the sun and stars were made (note that there was morning and evening even before

---

7   See *The Speaking Trinity & His Worded World: Why Language Is at the Center of Everything* (Eugene, OR: Wipf & Stock, 2018).

8   For examples, see *Finding God in the Ordinary* (Eugene, OR: Wipf & Stock, 2018).

God made the sun and stars in Gen. 1:14). The sun was shining on me because God is always shining. My shadow was not just evidence of the sun; it was evidence of God's presence behind the sun! I looked down at my shadow and smiled because it was a little reminder of God—not a distant deity who had set the world in motion like a clock, but a God who was always and everywhere revealing his presence to his people, even in shadows on the sidewalk!

S - stay engaged. In the midst of anxiety, we fight to focus. The devil loves distraction. He loves pulling our eyes away from God's vision and pulling our ears away from God's words. We have to claw our way back into the focus at every moment. I do this by speaking—either out loud or in my head—and asking God questions about the focus I've identified. Prayers that God would show you his character in the world around you *never* go unanswered (no prayers, really, go unanswered). Use words to draw yourself back to the focus. And once more, peace is waiting for you in the realization that the presence of God isn't something you go searching for; it's something that already surrounds you. You're not asking God to help you find something; you're asking God to help you see something that's already there.

T - talk. Lastly, we use language explicitly to connect with others and pull the focus off of ourselves. Anxiety is a black hole: it draws everything to itself and keeps us from noticing the needs and passions of others around us. It keeps us curved in on ourselves. When we talk to others, we stiff-arm anxiety and engage with another creature of God in a way that is truly selfless. It's hard to explain the feeling, but whenever I do this, there's a freeing emptiness of self-concern that lies in the background of my conversation. I'm truly fixated on the cares and concerns of someone else. It's a beautiful thing, and the feeling itself strikes me by revealing how often I'm still concerned about myself when I'm asking how someone else is doing! And let me tell you: peace is certainly here, as we give ourselves wholly to another, as we resign our attention to self and give all of it to others. Peace lies in self-less passion and concern for another.

In short, the CHRIST acronym makes use of language and draws us to peace at every step. But the final and lasting peace that we long for is yet to come. That peace is the unending personal presence of God. That's not a hope or a dream or a delusion. It's a reality we're drawing closer to with every passing second.

Theology: Already and Not Yet

At the start of the chapter, I mentioned that we have communion and peace with

God now, but we'll have it without interruption in the future. The peace and communion we so desperately long for is an already-but-not-yet gift of God. And this already-but-not-yet gift is actually rooted in our resurrection and the remaking of all things by the Word of the Father.

Think about resurrection first. Do you feel resurrected right now? Probably not. I don't either. It's the early morning right now, and I've had a bit too much coffee (surprise, surprise), so I feel awake and jittery, but I don't feel resurrected. Yet, Paul tells us something that pushes against our feelings: we've already been raised from the dead with Christ in one sense. He reasons with the Colossians, "If then you have been raised with Christ, seek the things that are above, where Christ is, seated at the right hand of God" (Col. 3:1). It's not "when you are raised with Christ in the future"; it's "if you *have been raised* with Christ." There's a sense in which we were buried with Christ in baptism (Col. 2:11–12), and we have already been raised with him. We are *already* new creatures, new selves. In 2 Corinthians 5:17, Paul says, "Therefore, if anyone is in Christ, he is a new creation. The old has passed away; behold, the new has come." We're already new in spirit; we have tasted resurrection. We've already been raised from spiritual death.

But we haven't been raised physically, with a new resurrection body. And that body will be *very* different from the anxiety-wracked frame we carry around right now. Paul outlines the differences between our old and new bodies in 1 Corinthians 15:35–49. Note the stark contrast between these bodies!

> [35] But someone will ask, "How are the dead raised? With what kind of body do they come?" [36] You foolish person! What you sow does not come to life unless it dies. [37] And what you sow is not the body that is to be, but a bare kernel, perhaps of wheat or of some other grain. [38] But God gives it a body as he has chosen, and to each kind of seed its own body.[39] For not all flesh is the same, but there is one kind for humans, another for animals, another for birds, and another for fish. [40] There are heavenly bodies and earthly bodies, but the glory of the heavenly is of one kind, and the glory of the earthly is of another. [41] There is one glory of the sun, and another glory of the moon, and another glory of the stars; for star differs from star in glory. [42] So is it with the resurrection of the dead. What is sown is perishable; what is raised is imperishable. [43] It is sown in dishonor; it is raised in glory. It is sown in weakness; it is raised in power. [44] It is sown a natural body; it is raised a spiritual body. If there is a natural body, there is also a spiritual body. [45] Thus it is written,

"The first man Adam became a living being"; the last Adam became a life-giving spirit. [46] But it is not the spiritual that is first but the natural, and then the spiritual. [47] The first man was from the earth, a man of dust; the second man is from heaven. [48] As was the man of dust, so also are those who are of the dust, and as is the man of heaven, so also are those who are of heaven.[49] Just as we have borne the image of the man of dust, we shall also bear the image of the man of heaven.

We'll have a resurrection body that makes our current body seem dead by comparison. It's coming, my friends. It's coming. I can't wait for that body!

But through Christ God has also already begun to remake the world. All the things that cause us distress and anxiety, the threat of isolation, the murmurings of constant doubt and dread, the broken relationships, the callousness of a world full of people who are focused on other things besides God—it's all going to change. The tide has already begun turning. Redemption is coming, and there's nothing anyone can do to stop it. This redemption is holistic, for Christ himself said he will make "all things" new (Rev. 21:5).

What bearing does this already-but-not-yet redemption have on our anxiety? For starters, we can be encouraged to know that the healing has already begun. Our anxiety might feel ravenous and unstoppable, but it's already hemmed in by the brick wall of God's sovereignty. It has limits. It can't go wherever it wants. In moments of great turmoil and stress, we can close our eyes in prayer and address the long-term guest of anxiety with sobering truth and confidence: "You don't have free reign. God has already begun to end you. I can be patient. I'll wait on the Lord. You're going to have to leave soon."

Second, we can prayerfully search for the newness of resurrection that's already bound to our souls. Remember, you have already been raised with Christ. There's new, immortal, unstoppable resurrection life inside your heart. It's not a wish; it's already a reality. We don't tap into this very often, do we? We don't look for the divine, resurrection life that's already in us. But that's probably another marker of our lack of belief. I know that in my own life, I often doubt the basic truth that resurrection is already in me. Why? Probably because I'm so prone to trust my *feelings*, even though I know they're often unreliable. I don't *feel* resurrected, so I think that I mustn't be yet. But that's the lie of the world, a lie developed over millennia, a lie that says what you can't see and feel and experience must not be real. That runs in direct contrast to the kingdom of God that's going to outlast all of the things we see and feel and experience right now. Remember, the kingdom of heaven is not visible because it's not an earthly kingdom. It's a heavenly kingdom. Its glory is on the inside right now, but soon the inside will be on the outside. Soon what we grasp with the eyes of faith will be gripped with the bare feet of finality (1 Cor. 13:12).

The already-but-not-yet of our faith is something we need to constantly draw on for both support (already) and hope (not yet). But both the support and hope need to be grounded in constant rehearsals of God's promises, of the work that Christ has already done on our behalf, of the ways in which the Spirit of God has already been shaping us to the image of Christ. Take a few moments now to write down some of the ways that the Spirit has already been shaping you to Christ. Then list some ways in which you long to be shaped in the future.

Reflection Questions and Prayer

1. How do you see a need or desire for communion with God in your own life? In other words, when do you most *need* or *desire* communion with him?

2. What sorts of activities or things get in the way of your communion with God right now? Discuss with others how you might set up a regiment for communing with God daily.

3. What do you most look forward to in speaking with God for eternity? What do you want to know about? What do you want to hear? What do you want to say?

4. Communion with God naturally leads to communion with others. Choose someone in your life and discuss your communion with God on a regular basis (weekly, perhaps). Checking in with a brother or sister in Christ is a great way to lean on the temple of Christ, of which you are just a stone.

5. What moments in your past evoke a sense of peace? Describe what made you feel peaceful in that moment. Was it related to the personal presence of God?

6. We have looked at peace as the personal presence of God. How does that view of peace differ from other common definitions of peace?

7. If we are *with creatures*, then we find our peace in being with God and with others. Who in your life brings you peace simply by their presence? Tell that person this truth—if not in person, then in a letter.

8. The CHRIST acronym draws us to use language and experience peace in the midst of anxiety. Which of the steps in this process is most difficult

for you? Talk with someone else about the difficulties you face, and ask that person to pray for you in a specific way. Keep a record or journal concerning how God is working to help you overcome the difficulty and draw closer to him.

9.   Think of someone else in your life that battles anxiety. Write out a prayer for that person regarding present and eternal peace. After you've written the prayer, consider either giving it to that person or praying the prayer daily for a period of time. Check in with the person regularly to see how God might be working and how you can keep praying for them more specifically.

10. What are some of the already-but-not-yet dimensions of your own anxiety? What signs of resurrection life do you see in your own life as you continue to wage war with anxiety? What are the things you long for most when you think of the future?

Prayer

Father, Son, and Holy Ghost,
You are the one we want the most.
You are the one we need the most.
We long for you.
We are parched for your presence,
Even though you offer it to us
Around every corner.
Help us to prioritize *you.*
Help us to order our life around *you.*
Give us the fortitude to seek you
Amidst every little distraction,
To choose you amidst a thousand choices,
To push away all that competes for our hearts
And offer ourselves up
In the particular moments and choices and times
That you give to us each day.
Help us to live for communion with you.
Give us the grace to spread that joy of communion

With others in the body of Christ.
And let the warmth that you breathe on us
Be felt by a watching world.

My Maker, Savior, and Comforter,
Your personal presence is my peace.
I am a *with* creature. And you are a *with* God.
I long for uninterrupted peace in your presence.
I don't know when that will come.
But I know it *will* come.
Help me to look forward to it with passion.
Help me to strive towards it with courage.
Help me to seek it with all I have
And to not be distracted by lesser promises of peace.
I know I will struggle and fail.
I know I will trip and tumble.
But help me trust that your hands
Are ever open before me,
Ready to receive,
Ready to embrace,
Ready to be *with* me.

CHAPTER 15

Struck Down but Not Destroyed

W ell, friends, I've given you a lot of myself in these pages. We've gone all the way from being crushed to seeing how we're already resurrected in the power of Christ. The central message of this book is that God can and will use your anxiety to do things you can never imagine. Anxiety, in that sense, isn't something to run from; it's something to *learn* from. And God is a masterful teacher through it. He brings us to weakness in order to build up his strength in us. He calls us to bow down in order to lift up our heads. He asks us to trust him in order to draw us nearer to himself. To use the image of John Chrysostom, an early church father, anxiety will end up being nothing but a cause for a crown—a means of building and shaping us to the glorious, royal image of God's own Son.

As you continue to face your anxiety, I encourage you to return to this book to relearn the lessons here. That's what I've been doing for twelve years, and that's what I plan on doing for the rest of my life. We need repeated instruction. We need constant reminders. We need to jump off the same truths multiple times before our spirit trusts the foundation. That's just a reality of being a slow learner—and all of us are slow learners in some way.

But as you turn your attention back to the concrete circumstances of your daily life, remember this: those of us who battle anxiety are truly struck down, but not destroyed (2 Cor. 4:9). Anxiety takes the wind out of our sails. In fact, sometimes it feels more like having the wind knocked out of our chests! We bend down to the earth in weakness. Others will see it. And that is okay. Why? Because the linchpin of the Christian faith is having our weakness reveal God's strength. As J. I. Packer put it in one of his book titles: *weakness is the way*. We're going to be pushed down repeatedly. We'll battle swells of anxiety throughout our days. Life is not about avoiding and eliminating our anxiety. It's about conforming to Christ through it. Because of who God is and what he has done for us in Christ, being struck down is a blessing, not a curse. It puts us in the perfect place to be made strong *in our weakness*. It's a blessing to be struck down but not destroyed, for that puts us on our knees, where we should live until God lifts us up to walk through the gates of paradise into his perfect and unending presence. You can say with every rough patch of anxiety, "I'm struck down but not destroyed." And that little truth isn't just a fact; it's an encouragement. Once we're struck down, we're in the perfect position to hear God's voice, to trust in his words, and to walk in the newness of life he's set aside for us (Rom. 6:4).

But Why Me?

If you find yourself asking *why* in this process (and all of us do at times), I offer the words of a wise sage who is now with the Lord. We all will run into moments where we cry out, "Why me? Why do *I* have to deal with this?" It's at this point that we can turn the question around.

> If in some way, your faith might serve as a three-watt night light in a very dark world, why not me? If your suffering shows forth the Savior of the world, why not me? If you have the privilege of filling up the sufferings of Christ? If he sanctifies to you your deepest distress? If you fear no evil? If he bears you in his arms? If your weakness demonstrates the power of God to save us from all that is wrong? If your honest struggle shows other struggler how to land on their feet? If your life becomes a source of hope for others? Why not me?
>
> Of course, you don't want to suffer, but you've become willing—like your Savior, who said, "If it is possible, let this cup pass from Me; yet not as I will, but as You will" (Matt. 26:39 NASB). Like him, your loud cries and tears will in fact be heard by the One who saves from death. Like him, you will learn obedience through what you suffer. Like him, you will sympathize with the weaknesses of others. Like him, you will deal gently with the ignorant and wayward. Like him, you will display faith to a faithless world, hope to a hopeless world, love to a loveless world, life to a dying world. If all that God promises only comes true, then why not me?[9]

Why not you? Why not me? Each morning—and each moment throughout the day—is another opportunity to bow our heads in weakness, open our palms to receive God's strength, and testify to a watching world. God is shaping you to Christ through your anxiety. Let him work. Let him impress that image on you. Let him then use you to show others that the God who suffers *with* us is the God who is always

---

9   David Powlison, *God's Grace in Your Suffering* (Wheaton, IL: Crossway, 2018), 116–17.

for us.

My dear reader, anxiety will not win the day. Christ already has.

Keep Learning!

We all need to keep learning throughout our journey with anxiety, so I invite you do so by having a look at the extra resources for this book. Just visit http://piercetaylorhibbs.com/struck-down-but-not-destroyed/. I've also created a Facebook group ("Christians Battling Anxiety") where we can continue to grow with and pray for one another as we combat the anxiety in our lives. Join a community of Christians who are watching God work amazing things through our anxiety!

Appendices

The following appendices offer additional thoughts and Scripture references that may help you as you continue to walk faithfully with your anxiety. For those who are interested in learning more about the naming and labeling of anxiety, "The Names We Use" presents some discussion. The other appendix offers words from Scripture and from other sources that may help you when you recite them in the midst of a swell of anxiety. I hope they are a blessing to you.

The Names We Use

When I began writing this book, I was hesitant to use the term "anxiety disorder." Christians respond to that label in different ways, and I want to be careful about how we name things, because naming says a lot about how we perceive the world.

In this appendix, I'll be engaging with a book by Michael Emlet, *Descriptions and Prescriptions: A Biblical Perspective on Psychiatric Diagnoses and Medications* (2017). This book is a welcome resource for Christians, since its author was a practicing family physician, received extensive training in biblical counseling, and has been engaged in the latter for years. In other words, he has experience with both the medical and spiritual sides of things such as anxiety disorders.

Before we get into discussing the term and its usefulness, we need to remind ourselves of the purpose and power of naming.

The Purpose and Power of Naming

As with language in general (which I call *communion behavior*), naming has its roots in God himself. God was the first one to name parts of the world. He named the day and the night after speaking light (Gen. 1:5). He named the heavens, the earth, and the seas (Gen. 1:8, 10). He also gave Adam his name (the same Hebrew word for "earth").[1]

We don't often stop to think about *why* God named parts of creation. Why did God use names? (Answering this question will help us begin thinking about why *we* use names.) We find a suggestion in Genesis 1:3–4. "And God said, 'Let there be light,' and there was light. And God saw that the light was good. And God separated the light from the darkness." What does naming do? First, naming *identifies* and *distinguishes* one thing from another.[2] Second, it situates the elements of the world in a *context*. In other words, we know what one thing is called in relation to what other things are called. "Day" and "night" are not just two distinct labels. They also have

---

1   I have a lengthier discussion of language and the importance of naming in *The Speaking Trinity & His Worded World: Why Language Is at the Center of Everything* (Eugene, OR: Wipf & Stock, 2018). I also commend Vern Poythress's discussion in his book *In the Beginning Was the Word: Language—A God-Centered Approach* (Wheaton, IL: Crossway, 2009), 23–33.

2   My language here (and the thought behind it) comes from Kenneth L. Pike's teaching on the *contrastive-identificational* features of every unit of language. See Pike, *Linguistic Concepts*. Also see my discussion of this in *The Trinity, Language, and Human Behavior: A Reformed Exposition of the Language Theory of Kenneth L. Pike*, Reformed Academic Dissertations (Phillipsburg, NJ: P&R, 2018), 35–47.

meaning in relation to one another and in relation to the rest of the world. Lastly, naming includes *variation*. Each time we use a name in a new context, there are slight variations in terms of meaning and articulation. This variation doesn't threaten the identity or context of names; it just shows that there can be difference amidst overall sameness.

These features of names have their roots in the nature of God. God is the Trinity: Father, Son, and Holy Spirit. Ultimately, names reveal identity because the Father distinctly identifies himself as Lord and Creator. He is separate from what he has made, even though he is revealed in it (Rom. 1). He is "like no other" (Isa. 45:5). Names have a context because context is rooted in God's character. The Spirit is the personal context for the love between the Father and the Son (and the love of the Father and the Son for the Spirit). Because there is context in God, there can be context in the world he has created, which reflects and reveals him. Lastly, names have variation because the Son is a "variation" or "manifestation" of the one divine essence. He is a distinct person of the Godhead, and yet bears the same essence as the Father and the Spirit. Much more could be said, but this is not the place to develop this.[3]

Here's the point I'm trying to make: names reflect the character of the triune God. They function according to his purposes because they reflect who he is. By extension, they *have* power because he *is* power.

"Names reflect the character of the triune God."

In addition to revealing God's character or nature, names also reflect God's Lordship, his sovereignty over his creation. And, in his grace, God has given us the ability to name elements of the world. This is part of what it means for us to be made in the image of God. God's Lordship and sovereignty are *not* ours, but we do rule over the world as stewards, pointing others to God's ultimate dominion (Gen. 1:26, 28). What's more, because we're creatures disposed for communion with the Trinity (recall Geerhardus Vos's understanding of the image of God), there is a communal benefit to naming. Naming allows multiple people to refer to the same thing. When we talk about the same object or phenomenon, there is a sense in which we are communing with one another. We are gathering around something in order

---

3   See Hibbs, *The Trinity, Language, and Human Behavior*, 97–125.

to better understand it.

I know—all of that might seem a bit heavy, but we need to lay the ground-work here so that we can discuss the name "anxiety disorder" in the rest of this appendix. In sum, naming is a divine ability that has been passed on to us as God's image bearers. Naming reflects God's trinitarian character and Lordship. In light of this, we need to be very careful about how we use names and what they might suggest to others. In particular, we need to incorporate God's divine *purposes* into our naming.

The Name "Anxiety Disorder"

Let's now consider some of this in relation to the name "anxiety disorder," touching on how the use of this label has been received by Christians.

First, the label "anxiety disorder" is meant to have a distinct identity, a distinct meaning. It is not the same thing as what we might call "common anxiety," that is, the sorts of anxiety that many of us experience in predictable situations: being overwhelmed by work, struggling with a particular fear (for example, the fear of flying), worrying about finances. These are important experiences, and God uses them for the good of his people (Rom. 8:28), but they are not the same as an anxiety disorder. The latter is on a different level, severely crippling people and threatening their execution of the most basic daily tasks.

Second, this label has variation, especially in terms of its referent—that is, a specific person's anxiety disorder. No two people are the same. Everyone is unique, and so every person's anxiety disorder is unique. In that sense, the label "anxiety disorder" cannot lump all people into a single category that is void of variation. There must be variation in the application of the label because there is variation in people.

Third, this label fits into a context, the context of psychiatric diagnoses. It is a label that has been given to people who share a set of symptoms (even though these symptoms manifest themselves with slight variation).

Let's try to keep these things in mind when we think about how Christians have responded to the label, something that Emlet has discussed in *Descriptions and Prescriptions*. He advocates for what he calls "the Goldilocks principle."[4]

The Goldilocks Principle

The name probably gives away the meaning. Essentially, some Christians are too cold toward psychiatric diagnoses, considering them unbiblical and perhaps speculative.

---

4   Emlet, *Descriptions and Prescriptions*, 1–3.

Others are too hot toward them, believing that psychology is an almost inerrant approach to many of humanity's problems. The Goldilocks principle puts us squarely in the middle, allowing us to "take seriously what help psychiatric categories and medications provide but also recognize their limitations."[5]

I find the Goldilocks principle helpful for at least three reasons. First of all, we can't avoid diagnosing what we see in the world. "Interpreting—or diagnosing—our experiences is unavoidable. Part of being human is classifying, organizing, and interpreting our world."[6] Emlet goes on to note something that we discussed earlier: naming (diagnosing) is a God-given, image bearing ability. We were endowed with this ability as God's creatures. God named parts of the world, so we name parts of the world, including sets of common human experiences. My question for those who balk at the label "anxiety disorder" is this: If it's not an anxiety disorder, what's *your* diagnosis? You do have one, whether you're conscious of it or not.

A psychiatric diagnosis, after all, is not a mysterious label that conceals the hidden intentions of those who are out to get you. It's just a name that we have given to a common set of symptoms and experiences, as reported by people. The benefit (and also the danger) of a diagnosis is that it gives us "a particular view of the person and possible responses to that person."[7] Remember that: a *view* of the person, along with possible *responses*.

That leads to the second reason I have for embracing the Goldilocks principle: It reminds us that diagnosis (which is unavoidable) is bound up with treatment. Whatever your diagnosis is, that determines the response. A patient who is diagnosed with a head cold will be treated very differently from someone diagnosed with a brain tumor.

Now, we can debate about which view of the person and which response is biblically, physically, and psychologically accurate. In fact, that seems to be where all of the trouble comes in. How do we solve the problem? How do we alleviate the symptoms? How do we find a cure? Those are basic questions in the medical and psychiatric fields. But they are also basic questions in the field of Christian belief. What spiritual evil is at work here? How does God provide hope and healing? How do we cope with the problem in the long run?

That leads to my third reason: the Goldilocks principle gives us room to

---

5   Emlet, *Descriptions and Prescriptions*, 2.

6   Emlet, *Descriptions and Prescriptions*, 10–12.

7   Emlet, *Descriptions and Prescriptions*, 7.

explore the spiritual roots and implications of an anxiety disorder. The diagnoses and treatments of the medical and psychological fields are not the end-all. They recognize important facets of our world and our experience, but not *all* facets. Sometimes they can misjudge the most important elements of life, such as the *purpose* we have for living in the first place.

This is critical for Christians because we must *sift* what we gather in our interactions with medical professionals, psychologists, and counselors who do not share our faith. When I was little, we had an older metal sifter for baking. It was a tin cylinder with a handle on one side and a wooden crank on the other, which spun a thick wire. Inside was a thin, metal net. You poured flour in, turned the crank, and the wire pushed the flour against the net, forcing it through tiny squares. The flour came out the bottom of the sifter, free of lumps. In a similar way, we get suggestions and analyses from others, pour them into the sifter of our biblical faith, and then start cranking. What we have at the end is a refined understanding of the problem and its potential solutions. We don't ignore what we hear from others who don't share our faith, for God has given grace and truth even to those who are at enmity with him (Matt. 5:45; Eph. 2:3–4). But neither do we accept wholesale whatever we're told.

Identity, Variation, and Context

It's at this point that I want to get further into the language theory of a Christian linguist named Kenneth Pike, whose work I have studied in depth and who, I believe, offers very helpful insights through some of his language theory. Remember that language is central to who God is, who we are, and what the world is like, so it matters how we think of it! To that end, try to stay with me for the next several paragraphs.

We can take the Goldilocks principle and the sifter of biblical faith and apply them to the discussion of identity, variation, and context for the label "anxiety disorder." I will use my own experience in what follows.

In terms of identity, I have been given the label "anxiety disorder" by a medical professional. That label accounts for my symptoms and experiences and sets me apart. It contrasts my symptoms and experiences with those of others. My struggle with anxiety is different from more common struggles with intermittent situational anxiety. My physical symptoms are more severe, and the way in which I process events is different. However, my biblical faith also tells me that anxiety is shared to some degree by all of God's people (Matt. 6:25–34; Phil. 4:6–7). So I should not let my label isolate me from brothers and sisters in Christ who can pray for me and offer biblical encouragement. My faith also tells me—and this is crucial—that Christ is the ultimate solution *to* human suffering and that God has specific purposes *for* my suffering. My faith tells me that God has perfect control of all things, and is using every trial and discomfort I come across to shape me to the image of his Son (Rom. 8:29) and to draw me closer to himself. God, in short, has great plans and purposes for my anxiety. So, as we discussed earlier in the book, I don't just want to eliminate it; I want to *learn* from it. I want God to use it so that I might grow. I want God to govern my identity.

In terms of variation, while I share my label with many others who have been diagnosed with an anxiety disorder, I know that my struggle is unique. My experiences are both shared and unique. God recognizes and values that uniqueness because it reflects his unique relationship with *me*. There is and always will be only one Pierce Taylor Hibbs. My doctor and counselor help me consider ways to address my anxiety as a unique person. For example, I went through a time when it was extremely difficult for me to drive anywhere at night. My counselor tried to help me find ways to avoid driving at night, and also gave me suggestions of what I might do when this was unavoidable. However, my biblical faith tells me that the suffering I faced when driving at night had a divine purpose. I quickly realized that when I drove at night, I was ten times more likely to pray fervently. Because I felt scared and hypervigilant, I recognized my own frailty and almost effortlessly turned to God for strength and encouragement. God uses my unique label to lead me in a unique relationship with himself. I want God to govern my variation.

In terms of context, I've received the label "anxiety disorder" in a particular era of human history. Ours is a time when medical and scientific discovery is impressively advanced. Doctors, psychologists, and counselors are able to see and understand things about the human body and mind that were previously unknown. My label fits within this context as a diagnosis, and that diagnosis comes with explanations, responses, and treatments. These include psychiatric medications, counseling, mental exercises, and so forth. However, my biblical faith tells me that my historical context has both new challenges (unknown side-effects of medications or results of psychological therapies, for example) and yet is governed by the same old truths. The answer to my suffering is still a Spirit-driven relationship with Jesus Christ, one that brings us to worship and glorify God. My faith also tells me that there is an ultimately *personal* context for my anxiety, and this may not be accepted by the medical professionals or counselors I encounter. That personal context is first and foremost the context of the living personal God. "In him we live and move and have our being" (Acts 17:28). I don't experience anxiety in a cold and purposeless universe. Secondly, the personal context includes my relationships with others in the body of Christ, and those outside the church as well. Inside the church, I'll have opportunities to build others up with what God is teaching me through anxiety (this book is a good example). I will also have opportunities to be blessed and encouraged by them. Outside the church, I'll have opportunities to talk about my anxiety in a way that draws people to God. The personal context of my anxiety is paramount. If I forget it, I run the risk of growing distant from God and simultaneously hurting other image bearers whom I might help.

The Label and God's Purposes

The identity, variation, and context of my label, along with the Goldilocks principle and my biblical faith, helps me to see how I can benefit from the grace God has shown to those in the medical and psychological fields and yet still give God the authority and control in my life. I want to end this appendix by reminding us that the labels we have are not outside of God's purposeful plan for our lives. I know that seems obvious, but I have found that people who struggle with an anxiety disorder need constant reminders of this.

The name "anxiety disorder" cannot be seen as isolated from God's purposes in our lives. It cannot be segregated from God's Lordship and sovereignty. He is *using* something for his greater purposes. In this sense, "anxiety disorder" is not an abstract term that marks us as somehow "flawed" in the world's eyes. That label is an instrument, a part of our world that God is using to help us better understand him and ourselves. One thing I have found to be helpful in this sense is to *define* what we mean by "anxiety disorder."

Here's a common definition by the American Psychiatric Association:

Anxiety disorders differ from normal feelings of nervousness or anxiousness, and involve excessive fear or anxiety. . . . Anxiety refers to anticipation of a future concern and is more associated with muscle tension and avoidance behavior. Fear is an emotional response to an immediate threat and is more associated with a fight or flight reaction – either staying to fight or leaving to escape danger. Anxiety disorders can cause people to try to avoid situations that trigger or worsen their symptoms. Job performance, school work and personal relationships can be affected. In general, for a person to be diagnosed with an anxiety disorder, the fear or anxiety must (1) be out of proportion to the situation or age inappropriate; and (2) hinder your ability to function normally.[8]

Here's my definition (notice how I try to account for God's purposes):

An anxiety disorder is a God-governed struggle that many people encounter and through which God draws us to trust in him for salvation and peace. While people with anxiety disorders have extreme difficulty carrying out basic daily tasks, they can also grow exponentially in their relationship with God and with others as God continually reveals to them his good purposes for every instance of suffering and fear. The oppressive physical symptoms of an anxiety disorder are often used by God as instruments for spiritually instructing and strengthening his people in Christ, by the power of the Spirit, for the praise of his glorious grace.

Let us continue to pray and think about how God can and has used the name "anxiety disorder" for our spiritual good, trusting that his good purposes will *always* triumph, because Christ has unquestionable victory over every threat to our peace and communion with the Father, Son, and Spirit.

Reflection Questions and Prayer

1. What do you think of the label "anxiety disorder"? Is it helpful? Harmful? Both?
2. What are the benefits and dangers of using this label?
3. How has the church, in your experience, misunderstood the use of this label in the past? In other words, how has your church and the church at large treated people who bear this label?
4. Are there other labels that you might give to someone who struggles with acute anxiety?

---

8   "What Are Anxiety Disorders?" American Psychiatric Association, accessed April 21, 2018, https://www.psychi-atry.org/patients-families/anxiety-disorders/what-are-anxiety-disorders.

Prayer

My God, I know that labels can be helpful and harmful.

I know that they reveal something of your character

And that they direct us toward certain responses.

But I also know that you are Lord of labels and names,

And *your* response to us in Christ is what matters most.

Thank you for already responding to my anxiety,

For already taking on flesh in the person of Jesus

And for suffering the labels of men.

Christ is my label now; he is my identity.

Let my heart, mind, and body,

Clenched tightly as a fist in the face of fear,

Unfold before the simple and pure truth

That you are using *everything* to draw me to yourself.

Words Worth Uttering

There are thousands of words worth uttering. In this appendix, I'm offering you some of the ones that have helped me the most. In the storms of anxiety, they have been my lifeboats. I hope they carry you to where you're going.

- Roll into your anxiety, as if it were a wave. It may roll you, but you'll roll back stronger.

- "The earth is the Lord's and the fulness thereof; the whole world and all those who dwell therein" (Ps 24:1). I belong to God. I am his possession. He is *always* watching over me.

- "You prepare a table before me in the presence of my enemies; you anoint my head with oil; my cup overflows" (Ps. 23:5). Anxiety might be my enemy right now, but God is anointing me and *will* provide all I need.

- "Blessed be the God and Father of our Lord Jesus Christ, the Father of mercies and God of all comfort, 4 who comforts us in all our affliction, so that we may be able to comfort those who are in any affliction, with the comfort with which we ourselves are comforted by God. 5 For as we share abundantly in Christ's sufferings, so through Christ we share abundantly in comfort too" (2 Cor. 1:3–5).

- "The Lord is a stronghold for the oppressed, a stronghold in times of trouble. 10 And those who know your name put their trust in you, for you, O Lord, have not forsaken those who seek you" (Ps. 9:9–10).

- "O Lord, my heart is not lifted up; my eyes are not raised too high; I do not occupy myself with things too great and too marvelous for me. 2 But I have calmed and quieted my soul, like a weaned child with its mother; like a weaned child is my soul within me. 3 O Israel, hope in the Lord from this time forth and forevermore" (Ps. 131).

- "Look at the birds of the air: they neither sow nor reap nor gather into barns, and yet your heavenly Father feeds them. Are you not of more value than they?" (Matt. 6:25)

- "But they who wait for the LORD shall renew their strength; they shall mount up with wings like eagles; they shall run and not be weary; they shall walk and not faint" (Isa. 40:31).

- "So do not fear, for I am with you; do not be dismayed, for I am your

God. I will strengthen you and help you; I will uphold you with my righteous right hand" (Isa. 41:10).

- "I sought the LORD, and he answered me; he delivered me from all my fears" (Ps. 34:4).

- "For I am convinced that neither death nor life, neither angels nor demons, neither the present nor the future, nor any powers, neither height nor depth, nor anything else in all creation, will be able to separate us from the love of God that is in Christ Jesus our Lord" (Rom. 8:38–39).

- "Trust in the LORD with all your heart and lean not on your own understanding; in all your ways submit to him, and he will make your paths straight" (Prov. 3:5–6).

- "Do not be anxious about anything, but in every situation, by prayer and petition, with thanksgiving, present your requests to God. And the peace of God, which transcends all understanding, will guard your hearts and your minds in Christ Jesus" (Phil. 4:6–7).

- "Come to me, all you who are weary and burdened, and I will give you rest. Take my yoke upon you and learn from me, for I am gentle and humble in heart, and you will find rest for your souls. For my yoke is easy and my burden is light" (Matt. 11:28–30).

- "And let the peace of Christ rule in your hearts, to which indeed you were called in one body. And be thankful" (Col. 3:15).

- "Our anxiety does not come from thinking about the future, but from wanting to control it." – Kahlil Gibran

- "Present fears are less than horrible imaginings." – William Shakespeare

Feedback

I want to hear from you! Was this book helpful? Did it provide what you were hoping you'd find? Would you recommend it to a friend? The best way you can express your thoughts on the book and let others know about it is to leave a review on Amazon. This helps other strugglers get a sense of what they can expect from the book. It's also a huge help to writers! Would you do that for me? Just follow the instructions below.

1. Go to my Amazon author page (amazon.com/author/piercetaylorhibbs) and click on this book.
2. Click next to the Amazon rating, which will show you the current reviews.
3. Click the button that says "Write a customer review."
4. Follow the steps to leave your review.

I'm legitimately interested in what you think. Be honest. I promise I won't be offended. Thank you for reading the book! That in itself is a huge blessing to me.

Connect and Grow

Want to connect with me and grow in your spiritual development? You can join my email list to get free downloads that will help, and maybe you'll pick up some inspiration on the way. I'll keep you posted about new publications and give you exclusive content, too! There aren't any strings attached. To join, visit http://pierce-taylorhibbs.com/subscribe-and-connect/. Right away, you get a free download of my ebook *In Divine Company: Growing Closer to the God Who Speaks*.